CHICAN@ ARTIVISTAS

CHICAN@ ARTIVISTAS

Music, Community, and Transborder Tactics in East Los Angeles

MARTHA GONZALEZ

University of Texas Press ✦ Austin

Copyright © 2020 by the University of Texas Press
All rights reserved
First edition, 2020

Requests for permission to reproduce material from this work should be sent to:
Permissions
University of Texas Press
P.O. Box 7819
Austin, TX 78713–7819
utpress.utexas.edu/rp-form

♾ The paper used in this book meets the minimum requirements of ANSI/NISO Z39.48–1992 (R1997) (Permanence of Paper).

Library of Congress Cataloging-in-Publication Data

Names: Gonzalez, Martha, author.
Title: Chican@ artivistas : music, community, and transborder tactics in East Los Angeles / Martha Gonzalez.
Description: First edition. | Austin : University of Texas Press, 2020. | Includes bibliographical references and index.
Identifiers: LCCN 2019052089
    ISBN 978-1-4773-2112-6 (cloth)
    ISBN 978-1-4773-2113-3 (paperback)
    ISBN 978-1-4773-2138-6 (ebook)
    ISBN 978-1-4773-2139-3 (ebook other)
Subjects: LCSH: Music—Political aspects—California—Los Angeles. | Mexican American women—Political activity—California—Los Angeles. | Gonzalez, Martha.
Classification: LCC ML3917.U6 G69 2020 | DDC 306.4/8420979494—dc23
LC record available at https://lccn.loc.gov/2019052089

doi:10.7560/321126

This work is dedicated to all of the Eastlos Chican@ artivistas, especially my partner, Quetzal Flores. Although this book bears my name, it was a collaborative effort. We struggled, thrived, and theorized these moments together and alongside our community.

CONTENTS

ACKNOWLEDGMENTS

I am indebted to many people for the completion of this project. No one can do it alone. My deepest gratitude goes to my academic advisors, Michelle Habell-Pallán, Angela B. Ginorio, María Elena García, Shannon Dudley, and Marisol Berríos-Miranda, for their invaluable advice and commitment to my work. Thank you to the Department of Gender, Women, and Sexuality Studies and to Priti Ramamurthy at the University of Washington for introducing me to feminist development thought. I extend my immense gratitude to mentors across the country who have advised and encouraged me throughout, including Olga Nájera-Ramírez, Antonia Castañeda, Russell Rodriguez, George Lipsitz, Josh Kun, Richard Mora, Steven Loza, Angela Ginorio, Deborah Vargas, Luis Alvarez, Daniel Sheehy, and Ruben Hernandez-De Leon.

I walked alongside many Eastlos artivistas and other local and translocal community members throughout the years. The people who were most instrumental in shaping the energy and discourse of this project were Rudy Ramírez, Felicia "La Fe" Montes, Marisol Torres and all of Mujeres de Maiz, Jo Anna Mixpe Ley, Laura Palomares, Suyapa Portillo, Aztlan Underground, the Blues Experiment, Miguel Rodriguez, Gabriel Tenorio, Omar Ramirez, Jose Ramirez, Jacob Hernandez, Juan Perez, Tylana Enomoto, Rocio Marron, Rosa Marta Zarate, Sarah Rosencrantz, Shirley Alvarado del Aguila, Marco Loera, Aloe Blacc, César Castro, Xochi Flores, Roberto "Tata" Flores, Carolina Sarmiento, Luis Sarmiento, and the Sarmiento family. In Mexico: El Maestro Gilberto Gutiérrez, Ramón Gutiérrez, Wendy Cao Romero, Tacho Utrera, Patricio Hidalgo, Zenen Zeferino, Annahi Hernandez, Rubí Oseguera Rueda, Laura Rebolloso, Kali Niño, and the rest of the Entre Mujeres familia.

Thank you to my colleagues and intellectual comadres Micaela Díaz-Sánchez, Sara P. Díaz, Mónica de la Torre, Manoucheka Celeste, and the rest of the WOCC sisters for the unwavering support. Women Who Rock graduate seminar feedback sessions under the direction of Michelle Habell-Pallán also provided professional guidance over the years; thank you especially to Tiffany Lopez, Sherrie Tucker, Daphne Brooks, Sonnet Retman, Miriam Bartha, and

Maylei Blackwell. Beyond the academy I am grateful to the Pacific Northwest community of fandangueros from the Seattle Fandango Project.

My gratitude also extends to the University of Texas Press team, including Kerry Webb, Lynne Ferguson, Andrew Hnatow, and freelance editor Abby Webber, for their guidance and patience.

I have received generous institutional funding over the years from the University of Washington Graduate Opportunities and Minority Achievement Program (GOMAP), the Ford Foundation Dissertation Fellowship (2012), the Fulbright–García Robles Fellowship (2008), the Woodrow Wilson Career Enhancement Fellowship (2016), and the Faculty Success Program (2019). I could not have finished this book without the support of Scripps College, Dean Amy Marcus-Newhall, and all of my colegas in the Intercollegiate Department of Chicana/o Latina/o Studies, especially Tomás Summers Sandoval and Rita Cano Alcala.

Most of all I am indebted to my family, who have seen me through it all, especially my brother, Gabriel Gonzalez. My sisters, Claudia Miranda and Karla Benavidez, helped our families stay together, and my nieces and nephews continue the legacy of music and art in our family. Thank you to my mother-in-law, Consuelo Valdez. A special thank you to my mother, Martha Romero Hernandez, who has advised me throughout my life but mostly demonstrated to me the power of hope and perseverance through her own skill set, survival strategies, and general life outlook.

Y por fin, gracias a mi niño hermoso, Sandino Gonzalez-Flores, who has trekked the many roads with us and who will no doubt continue the legacy of music and social justice in our family. Lastly, thank you to my partner and my love, Quetzal Flores, who encouraged my venture into academia but continues to remind me that my first home will always be in music.

CHICAN@ ARTIVISTAS

Introduction

We need *teorías* that will enable us to interpret what happens in the world, that will explain how and why we relate to certain people in specific ways. . . . We need theories that will point out ways to maneuver between our particular experiences and the necessity of forming our own categories and theoretical models for the patterns we uncover. We need theories that examine the implications of situations and look at what's behind them.

GLORIA ANZALDÚA, *Borderlands/La Frontera*

So the circumstances of our lives and our labor enable what we can know.

PRITI RAMAMURTHY, lecture at the University of Washington, 2011

I have traveled the world as a professional musician. Experiencing music in many fronts, sites, and social locations has demonstrated to me that music is understood and engaged in a number of ways. I have had music experiences that as a performer were oppressive and have left imprints of shame and trauma in my memory. But there have also been moments of hope. Music in this sense was inspiring, a conduit of freedom and a malleable tool for those who envision social change. These moments, in particular, have allowed me to see how music could be a liberatory process, a deliberate act of love, and a source of empowerment for self and community.

My labor as a musician over the years enables what I "know" and thus what I recount and theorize in this book. It is an autoethnographic account of varied music moments experienced on a professional stage, panhandling on street corners, and in the throes of community organizing amid the many struggles and deep trenches of social movement. Importantly, the varied experiences I recount and theorize in this book altered how I conceive and practice the craft at present. Most of all, it demonstrates how over time a music practitioner like me experienced a fundamental change in philosophy.

Theorizing music through an autoethnographic lens, beginning with early childhood memories, will elucidate a range of methods, social theories, and transformations that happen along the way in various social settings. Drawing from postcolonial, Chicana, black feminist, and performance theory, *Chican@ Artivistas: Music, Community, and Transborder Tactics in East Los Angeles* maps an intimate individual and community process. To this end, *Chican@ Artivistas* is my *testimonio*, from the musician my father raised me to be, to what I have become for myself and alongside my community—an "artivista," or artist-activist.

My political and social coming-of-age in the early 1990s was shaped alongside and in conversation with other Chican@ artists from East LA.[1] Our collective experiences and dialogue prompted us to identify with *artivista* as more than a political identity but as the way in which we relate to our craft and, more specifically, how we apply our skill set in the context of a dominant capital market system.

I respectfully acknowledge the extensive legacy of Chican@ artists who generated art and music before the 1990s, especially those who have dedicated their work to elevating the culture, visibility, and beauty of Mexican and Latin@ communities and have been engaged in social movement efforts. Indeed, Chican@ art, in theory, could be deemed "political" by virtue of identifying with Chican@ identities, ethics, or the history of the Chicano movement. Early Chican@ artist-activist efforts executed by prominent collectives, such as Asco and the Royal Chicano Air Force,[2] for example, were instrumental in building a canon, a repertoire, and a trajectory that we now celebrate, reference, and critique. Indeed, collectives such as these, as well as the individual artist careers that spun off from these efforts, were in part an inspiration to the 1990s generation of East LA artists. Their visual, music, and performance art had an impact within our community as well as in the mainstream art and music industry worlds. Although such activities were important interventions, market systems nevertheless have ways of extracting and appropriating these efforts from communities. This in turn isolates the products from the roots of their inception. As a result, the deep-rooted message or process-based community effort is lost in the purview of the art itself. Indeed, market systems accept and proliferate any message or artifact so long as it is a thriving commodity. Becoming a part of or appealing to an industry thus often signifies a watered-down message fit for sales, or a commodity so far removed from its reality that the consumer is unaware of its radical origins. A political message, no matter how radical, is thus absorbed into a system that essentially mutes its roaring potential.

So what happens to Chican@ art generations after the establishment of a canon? What happens when our artists become so busy that they are unable to remain connected to the next generation of artist-activists? How are we to uphold such emancipatory labor for the next generation? How can we sustain such momentum, and with what social resources?

The 1990s Chican@ art community that I owe my experience to takes its cues from its radical predecessors and yet is precisely distinct by the ways in which members have utilized their artistic and creative abilities to develop participatory, process-based community art practices—that is to say, approaches to art and music practice that focus on relationships and process rather than outcomes and products. In studying, organizing, and engaging with Zapatista communities and philosophy, 1990s Chican@ artivistas became increasingly aware of the neoliberal agenda and how the political economy affected more than our pocketbooks and economic survival. There began a focus and a greater awareness that revolved around the approach to our creative expression and how capital market logic had a bearing on individual and collective creativity—specifically, and for the purpose of this study, the "social relations of music." I refer here to the social relations of music as the value systems concerning music knowledge, reception, and practices upheld by social institutions. In this way, my study focuses on *convivencia* as an aesthetic and moral philosophy in and around artivista organizing approaches and art practice. *Convivencia*, stemming from the Spanish words *con* and *vivir*, or "to live with," is the mindfulness of presence with others. Being present and engaging together in mind, body, and spirit via participatory music and art practice, convivencia has become an invaluable code of ethics in artivista philosophy.

Style and Approach

This book will oscillate between personal narrative, or testimonio, and academic theory. It will delve into deep descriptive moments of being in the trenches of social movement in East Los Angeles, Chiapas, and Seattle and then shift into a theoretical matrix reading of the moment. With the passing of time and with further academic training and inquiry, I came to realize these moments were informed by various intersections and systems of power that can be examined for the greater good. The narratives throughout will make visible the intersections of race, class, gender, and sexuality embedded in the push and pull of an all-encompassing globalized political economy. It is the proliferation of this system and its respective xenophobic US nationalist agenda that builds a war on migrants and on difference in all of its manifestations. Its social logic isolates us from each other through its commodity culture that is inherently competitive and transactional. These lived realities and the respective resistances are corroborated, augmented, and upheld by Chicana and black feminist theoretical frameworks, postcolonial theory, US third world economic development theory, ethnomusicology, and performance studies. In this way, this study is an academic theorization of a music practitioner's memories and how transformative lived experience changes one's conceptions of music over time.

Beginning this book with an intimate look at music's function in my early childhood, chapter 1, "Music Misunderstood," considers first my father's understanding of music, which I believe was shaped by Mexican nationalism of his time. My early experience in music and brief life background is relevant to my Chican@ artivista formation and praxis, for I examine early subjective ideas of music practice in the home, informed by my father's beliefs on the value and meaning of "success" in music. I demonstrate how his views were shaped by ideas of "progress" and "modernity" instilled by the thriving Mexican national cultural production and rhetoric of his time. The work of Mexican cultural theorists such as Andrea Noble and Juan Pablo Silva Escobar are important touchstones concerning early Mexican cinema as postrevolutionary nation-building tools.[3] In addition, Guillermo Bonfil Batalla's concept of México Profundo and the "imaginary Mexico" is an important point of departure for my study, for Batalla articulates an ideological formation concerning the indigenous subject as "extinct" and the mestizo as the dominant Mexican identity.[4] Although Batalla arguably idealizes the *indígena*, both ideological constructions have undoubtedly shaped early Chican@ social movement identity formation in the United States and are therefore important in examining present Chican@ artivista ideology and artivistas' departure from or reinforcement of the social construction and idealism of the *indígena* as a racialized backward subject.

Drawing on the work of Thomas Lemke and Wendy Larner, I impart their analytics of the neoliberal subject, self-discipline, and governmentality and how the latter has played a part in the social relations of music.[5] By theorizing and recounting these personal and community practices, I will begin to demonstrate how capital markets have been instrumental in the most intimate arrangements of music and art practices, including one's own capacity and creative autoperception. Finally, my father's untimely death did not undo his life's work but rather solidified his hauntings. Much as our present society and the postmodern narratives of modernity are the hauntings of colonization, my father's teachings and overall specter continued to loom over my understanding of music.

Chapter 2, "Chican@ Artivistas: Resistance to Capital Market Systems and the Mind/Body Split," examines early scholarship that questioned Western society's relationship to music. I center political economy and its social bearing on Western music practice and conception. Building on the work of musicologists, ethnomusicologists, and music theorists, such as John Blacking, Christopher Small, Thomas Turino, Marisol Berríos-Miranda, and Susan McClary, I demonstrate how these notable authors have made similar claims regarding the social relations of music.[6] I build on their scholarship by further delving into capitalism as a social force. I also examine the literature on colonialism, postcolonial studies, and feminist development theory in order to trace how social and cultural tools have been used for the consolidation of nation-state, social, and ideological power, which is ultimately how the social relations of music are constructed and maintained.

It is important in the work of US third world feminists, and by extension a Chicana feminist analysis, to trace material practices in colonial history in order to understand the legacy of mind/body split, allowing one to better deconstruct ideologies concerning the body that ultimately give currency to systemic structures. I begin this exploration by examining the scholarship that looks at imperial social and political tools stemming from colonization, specifically the tools of torture and terror during slavery. I am concerned with how these techniques continue to thrive and shape our perceptions in relation to our creative labors. The black feminist scholars Bibi Bakare-Yusuf and bell hooks argue that colonization conceived and thrived on the extraction of capital from black bodies and the "flesh."[7] I argue that although Chican@s do not have a history rooted in American slavery, the economic venture to extract labor from bodies is a multisited practice. Early colonial cultures in the Americas and elsewhere also used the tools of torture and terror to shape racialized and gendered mind-sets and perceptions for social, economic, and political control.[8] By understanding and relating this systematic body/mind logic to creative expression, one can better understand the current social relations of music.

Feminist development literature has been a useful tool in understanding the social relations of any given society, from the most intimate aspects to the global-systemic. One of the most important interventions in the field of development studies is *Reversed Realities: Gender Hierarchies in Development Thought* by Naila Kabeer. Kabeer maps a history and intellectual discourse concerning women in development. A "structuralist perspective" to development practices urges a social relations analysis that extends an interconnected understanding of a subject's position in society. Social relations, as Kabeer articulates, are important to a complete understanding of the "concrete conditions" in both women's and men's lives.[9] In relation to gender, for example, social institutions can inform the extent of one's access, mobility, and opportunities in society. Kabeer identifies social institutions as markets, states, religion, and kinship/family, concluding that these social institutions intersect and inform societies to affect varying subjects. They lead to the organization of social and political life by "creating and regulating ideologies," which lead to specific social practices that have concrete effects.[10]

Conceiving capital markets as *social* institutions gives currency to my study on Chican@ artivistas. I argue that participatory music and dance practices are rare in capitalist societies due to the fact that capital markets as *social* institutions have arranged the way we think, interact, and therefore engage with music more generally. Importantly, and as a beginning road to unpacking this dilemma, I revisit embodied music experience via my introduction into the community of Chican@ artivistas and my early years in the East LA–based Chican@ rock band Quetzal.

Chapter 3, "The Popular Resource Center and Centro Regeneración in Highland Park," is an autoethnographic account of my first interactions with the Popular Resource Center, or Centro Regeneración. The Popular Resource Center was a nonprofit organization that worked out of an old warehouse in the Highland Park neighborhood of northeast Los Angeles. I recount how the humble warehouse became an important site for artists to gather and have important dialogues and how a small, interdisciplinary Chican@ artivista collective eventually co-organized the most innovative cultural *encuentro*, or encounter, of its time, the Encuentro Cultural Chicano/Indígena por la Humanidad y contra el Neoliberalismo (Chicano/Indigenous Cultural Encounter for Humanity and against Neoliberalism).

Chapter 4, "The Big Frente Zapatista: Using Art as a Tool of Critical Dialogue," continues the discussion of the important work generated out of the Popular Resource Center and specifically the organizing in and around the Encuentro Cultural Chicano/Indígena por la Humanidad y contra el Neoliberalismo. The Ejército Zapatista de Liberación Nacional (EZLN), their philosophy, and pedagogy had a profound impact on Chican@ artivista methods and epistemologies, which laid the groundwork for visions that shaped and continue to inspire projects within East Los Angeles communities. By examining this important encuentro between seventy East LA artivistas and the indigenous Zapatista Mayan community of Oventic, I demonstrate how music and art served as dialectic tools and how the process of collective communal engagement drew out multiple subjectivities between Chican@ and Mayan participants. Through communal artistic processes, varying subjectivities, although existing in multiple and intersectional ways in our daily lives, were highlighted and deconstructed in the artistic processes. As a result of the encuentro, Chican@ artivistas began to generate collective and creative work utilizing the social techniques learned in translocal dialogue with Mayan communities.

An examination of the literature in performance studies, particularly the work of the performance theorist Diana Taylor, summons the important performative work being enacted by Mayan and Chican@ artists. In *The Archive and the Repertoire*, Taylor beckons a reorientation of the ways social memory and cultural identity in the Americas have traditionally been studied. In her view, writing has come to stand in for, and against, embodiment.[11] As Taylor urges, a great deal of significance and insight into stories, struggles, and memories can reside in performance practice.

In keeping with the community-building methods that were generated at the 1997 encuentro, chapter 5, "Fandango Jarocho as a Decolonial Tool," is an exploration of the translocal dialogues and community networks that developed through the praxis of *fandango jarocho*, the participatory music and dance of Veracruz, Mexico. Importantly, this chapter tracks the liberatory exercise fandango has served for various communities in Veracruz, California, and Seattle. I provide a brief historical overview of fandango, giving meaning to the importance of the early 1980s resurgence instigated by the *movimiento jaranero*, or *jaranero* movement (itself a pushback on Mexican nation-state modernist rhetoric), in Mexican communities and how the dialogue with Chican@ and Latin@ communities eventually manifested as the translocal dialogue I will refer to as *fandango sin fronteras*, or fandango without borders.

I observe this translocal movement, and the urgent need to initiate an engagement of participatory music and dance practices by Chican@ artivistas, as a reflection of indigenous pedagogies that stem from Zapatista philosophy and approach to community building through the encuentro. Although fandango can be regarded as an ephemeral practice, it nonetheless adheres to the politics of space and identity in Chican@ "Eastlos," or East Los Angeles, life, where disenfranchisement and globalization has had an effect on local economies and social services. In a city like Los Angeles, where space is scarce and under-siege land becomes "extinct," space becomes one of the many issues of power and access when attempting to build community.[12] Thus this chapter marks how Chican@ artivistas come to understand that fandango is a community practice and phenomenon that can manifest and disappear. Even with its ephemeral quality, fandango nonetheless instills in participants the sociality of community. In this sense, Chican@ artivistas and *fandangueros* are always "in situ: intelligible in the framework of the immediate environment and issues surrounding them."[13] As I demonstrate, fandango becomes the perfect tool to form and maintain community that can adapt to the volatile issues of space in Eastlos life.[14] Furthermore, fandango "stretches the spatial and temporal framework" of performance to interconnect what may seem like "separate geographical and political areas."[15] Taylor's "hemispheric perspective" adheres to Chican@ artivistas' translocal dialogues with both Mayan communities in Chiapas and *jarocho* communities in Veracruz.[16] In this sense, embodied practices like fandango are "an episteme and a praxis, a way of knowing as well as a way of storing and transmitting cultural knowledge and identity, that is not adherent to political or nation-state boundaries."[17]

Chapter 6, "Los Guardianes de la Convivencia," is an autoethnographic account and analysis of various projects that resulted from the efforts generated by *fandango sin fronteras* ethics. I discuss the project Entre Mujeres, which was undertaken in Veracruz from fall 2007 to June 2009, as well as the origins and rise of the Seattle Fandango Project. Both community-based projects are examples of how artivista praxis, via translocal dialogue and experience, has been implemented in communities to produce a substantial body of work that is collective, liberatory, and, most important, self-sustaining.

The Entre Mujeres project made visible the ways in which recording traditions exclude women from recording and music composition participation by the way in which recording facilities are situated and implemented. I recount how low-cost portable recording options, such as Digi 001 interface and Pro Tools, facilitate transnational musical dialogues between US-based Chicana and Latina musicians in Los Angeles and *jarocha* musicians in Veracruz. Ultimately, new recording technologies utilized by women across borders compel one to rethink the "who, what, and where" of musical production, specifically the pedagogical shifts that occur when one recontextualizes the sound booth with the kitchen space.

Although I had previously experienced the collective songwriting process in the 1997 encuentro, it was during the Entre Mujeres project that principle epistemologies of convivencia, testimonio, trust, healing, and knowledge production became visible to me as a participant. Through the encuentro as well as Entre Mujeres, I have witnessed time and again how the collective songwriting method in process creates space, builds community, challenges multiple patriarchal systems, and produces knowledge that is accessible beyond the academy. Songs as texts, or what I call "sung theories," are accessible archives that can communicate important embodied knowledge theory across time, disciplines, borders, generations, and other ways of knowing. I end this chapter with a brief account of the FandangObon, a multiracial and multicultural yearly event in Los Angeles that fuses *bon odori* Buddhist music and dance tradition with the fandango. The legendary singer, dancer, and cultural activist Nobuko Miyamoto and the LA-based nonprofit Great Leap have led FandangObon programming. Through Great Leap, a multicultural arts organization founded by Miyamoto, the yearly event has embodied the ethics of convivencia as seen through the union of two different participatory practices. Recognized by the Smithsonian Folklife Festival in 2016, it was one of many model participatory, intergenerational, and interracial community music and dance practices chosen to represent the state of California for the festival's *Sounds of California* series curated by the Alliance for California Traditional Arts.

The conclusion, "Imaginaries: The Grammy and the Graduate Student," begins with a lyrical analysis of the title track of Quetzal's Grammy Award–winning 2011 album, *Imaginaries*. The song and album were inspired by *The Decolonial Imaginary: Writing Chicanas into History*, by Emma Pérez, and the conclusion is a consolidation of the varied methodologies discussed throughout this book. I utilize the "Imaginaries" lyrics as a point of departure in order to demonstrate how the efforts of Chican@ artivistas, however flawed, continue to challenge ideas of space, community building, knowledge production, and mentorship. Although many have stayed rooted to the practices centered around relationality and participatory music and art practices, challenges persist, especially with a new generation. In this sense, this chapter is an epilogue to the activities and ways in which Chican@ artivista momentum continues to thrive, but also a window into how the varying social techniques are being challenged, distorted, or improved by a younger generation of Chican@ artivistas.

CHAPTER 1

Music Misunderstood

As I rummaged through an old cardboard box of photographs, I found my father's red 1970s scrapbook. It is wire bound, with brown, sticky surfaces, and each page is covered by yellowed cellophane. Acidity has eaten some of the pictures, and time spent abandoned in boxes amid dozens of moves has blurred others. It is an important piece of my family history, and so I have kept it. I don't know why I ended up with it. My older brother, Gabriel, is in most of these pictures. The photo album is filled with newspaper clippings, promo film shots, Polaroid pictures, concert flyers, and tickets. My father used to save just about everything that had my brother's name or image on it. I faintly remember how he would set up on the kitchen table and spend hours putting albums like these together. He meticulously numbered the pages and labeled the photographs. And although the pages are filled with my brother's successes, the album mostly reminds me of my father's perpetual sadness and discontent. Nevertheless, there is a profound collective meaning to my family's history in music directly related to this photo album. It is a material trace of my father's longing—his longing for respect, fame, and fortune as a result of a music career he never acquired but, rather, vicariously lived through my brother's successes. It is also a historical account of my family history amid a unique moment in the Mexican music scene in the late 1970s.

My father adored music, and he always dreamt of becoming a professional *ranchera* singer. I imagine that as a newly arrived immigrant from Mexico in the late 1960s, becoming a singer could be a worthwhile venture. In his mind's eye, a professional singer undoubtedly secured respect, wealth, and prestige, or at the very least it was some way out of poverty. But my father's dreams of living a professional music life died with the birth of his family. He married my mother when they found out she was with child. As far as he was concerned, this greatly hindered his prospects. His dream life in music involved no familial responsibilities. No *chamacos mocosos* running about, no early bedtimes, sick children, or wife to consider. Yet despite fatherhood and the pressures of immigrant life, he nonetheless continued to strive to acquire a musical career for some time.

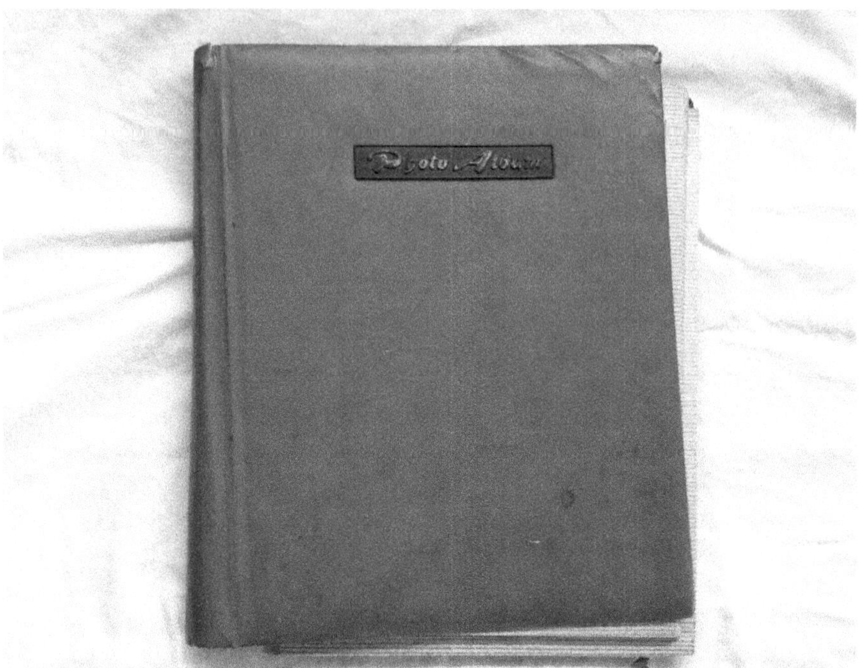

My father's red wire-bound photo album.

In one of multiple efforts, my father entered an amateur singing contest in hopes of being "discovered." This particular contest was being broadcast from the now historic "El Mercadito" commercial center in Boyle Heights, Los Angeles, via the popular Mexican FM radio station KWKW Radio 13. The day of the competition my mother searched for the station on an old portable transistor radio. When the show started, we all leaned in to listen to the program. We sat through various singers before my father had his turn. The announcer finally introduced him, and as the mariachi kicked in, we held our breaths.

We had listened to my father sing plenty of times in the shower, at family gatherings, or in our living room. He had a wonderful Javier Solís–like voice. It was an intentional inflection, as we were aware that he modeled his timbre and delivery after the famous 1950s Mexican crooner Javier Solís. On this day his nervousness got the better of him. As my father began to sing, his voice quivered and he stumbled through lyrics. He managed to get through the song, and the announcer interviewed him after, as he had the other artists. Again, we could hear the fear in his voice as he politely answered the announcer's questions. My father had studied and learned the great etiquette and elegance by which all the artists of his time would

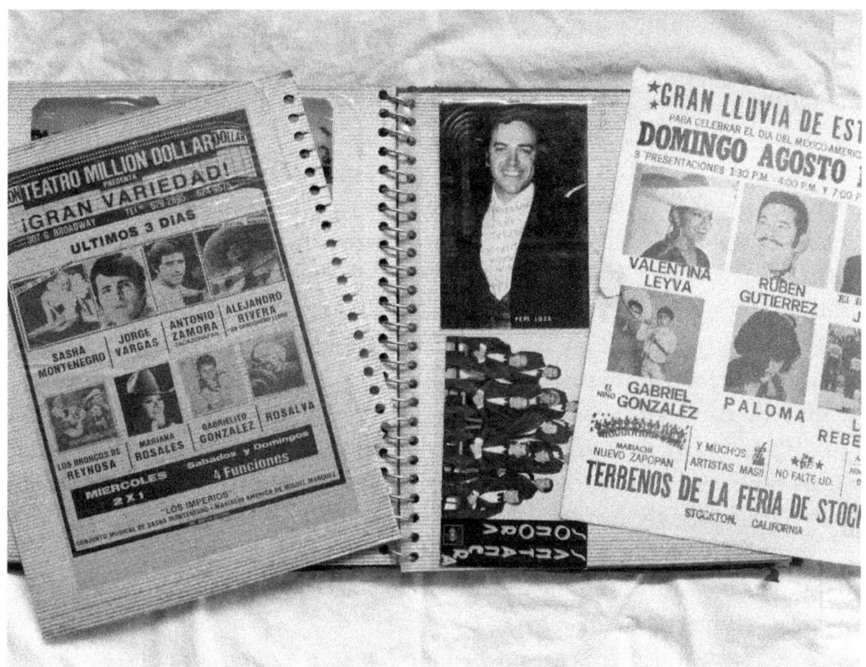

Inside cover of my father's wire-bound photo album.

express themselves. After all, La Época de Oro, the golden age of Mexican cinema, still resonated in the hearts and minds of Mexican popular culture in the late 1970s, and my father prided himself on being a *profesional*. He was meticulous about his overall presentation and image, paying special attention to his outfits and stage presence, as well as the language he utilized in addressing an audience. He had a way with words, and his interview went well.

My father received second place for the KWKW Radio 13 contest. Although this would have been considered a significant accomplishment for most, we knew it was not enough. As we waited for him to come home, we created a "¡Felicidades!" sign. When he walked through the door we ran to congratulate him. Huddled in our embrace he fought back tears. It's hard to say what he got choked up about. I think we all felt sad for him, for we knew the extent of his longing. In retrospect this was the first time I began to feel we were "in the way" and that he was not happy with his life and current situation. My father held on to his dreams and sanity a few years before he spun into his deepest, darkest moments. But his longing for music slowly made him distant from us. Nothing and no one could take the place of his dreams.

My Father's Dreams and Hauntings

My father was born Carlos Xavier González in 1946 in Guadalajara, Mexico. He immigrated to the United States in about 1962. He followed his mother, who had immigrated some years earlier in order to seek work. My grandfather left my grandmother with four children. Catalina Perez Sanchez saw immigration to the United States as the only way to provide for her children.[1] My father and his brothers and sisters were left in the care of my great-grandparents, who weren't the most nurturing couple.

Once living in Los Angeles, my father attended Belmont High School at the age of seventeen but never earned his high school diploma. A year later he met my mother in downtown LA at the Alexandria Ballroom. Downtown Los Angeles was a thriving site for immigrant youth at the time. My mother recalls that my father asked her to dance and then never left her side. Like many marriages, theirs was a "shotgun" wedding. When my mother found out she was pregnant, they went back to Guadalajara, married, and returned to LA to have my brother, Gabriel. Soon thereafter, I came along and then my sisters, Claudia and Karla Maria.

When he wasn't working, my father's life revolved around music. He listened, he sang, and he spoke of music constantly. He owned a shiny black wall piano and a guitar, both of which he did not know how to play. He used to lay *partituras*, or sheet music, open on the piano as if he or someone in the house had just played. I think the very presence of these instruments made him feel close to music, and he strongly believed that at some point in his life he would take the time to learn. My mother was also creative. She had a wonderful voice and was a great mambo dancer. My mother instilled music in us by way of lullabies. The lullabies of Francisco Gabilondo Soler ("Cri-Cri") and Libertad Lamarque were a constant in our home. Lullabies accompanied by her funny hand gestures and dances were the most memorable and peaceful times for me.

One weekend my father's family met at a yearly carnival in Whittier Narrows Park. We often gathered at this park some twenty miles east of downtown LA. There was mariachi entertainment, and my father decided to enter my brother, Gabriel, into an amateur singing contest that was being held. My father instructed the mariachi to play a famous ranchera standard titled "El Rey" by José Alfredo Jiménez. It was a fall afternoon and the sun was setting as the mariachi completed the intro to the song. My seven-year-old brother opened his mouth and sang. Although he was a child he delivered the song as if he were the most seasoned performer. The audience cheered in astonishment to witness a seven-year-old deliver with such passion. Along with the cheers, *gritos*, and encouragement, the audience began to toss coins and dollar bills onto the stage. Men and women threw quarters, dimes, and nickels as my

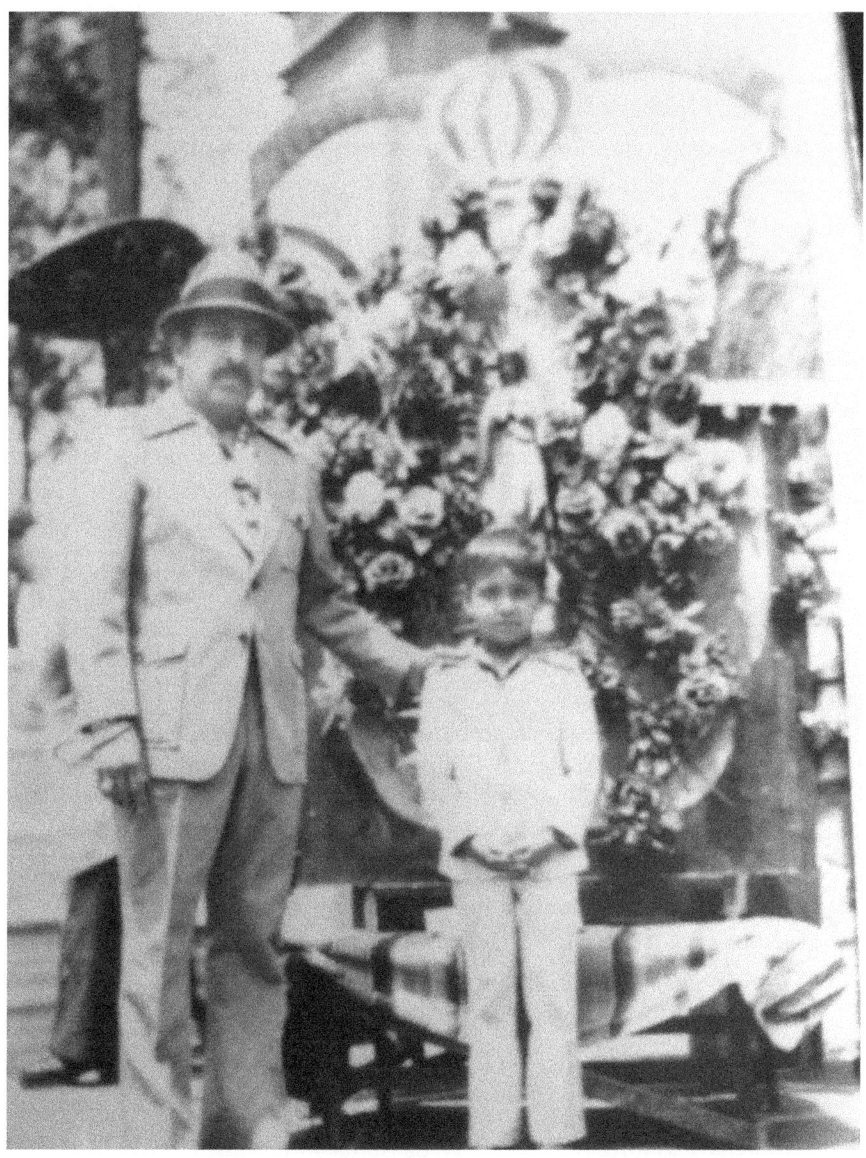

My uncle, Fernando Hernández, and my brother, Gabriel Gonzalez, in Mexico City.

brother smiled and looked over at my father, who urged him to bow and pick up the money. My brother went home with a first-place trophy that afternoon. In an instant, my father redirected *his* dreams of being a professional musician toward molding his eldest son, my brother, Gabriel Gonzalez.

Fernando Hernández and My Brother's Career

Fernando Hernández was my *tío* by marriage. He was a flashy, confident man who loved to hang out with Mexican artists who made their way through California on Variedades, or variety show circuits.[2] He soon became a music promoter and booking agent in Los Angeles. It was a thriving Mexican immigrant economy. Touring the Mexican Variedad circuit was a good way for singers to share travel and food expenses. Multiple artists toured together with one mariachi that accompanied them all. Singers such as a young Vicente Fernández, Lucha Villa, Aida Cuevas, Mercedes Castro, and Juan Gabriel were some of the most notable figures that came through the Variedad circuit, which gave them significant exposure to the Mexican community in the United States. My *tío* helped promote the events as well as hosted after-parties for the artists in his home.

Tío Fernando was a hypermasculine figure. He was a flashy dresser who wore polyester shirts that exposed gold chains on his hairy chest. He carried wads of cash and was always cracking jokes. Tío Fernando had taken interest in my brother after hearing him sing at a family party. Despite my mother's reluctance, my father agreed to have my uncle jump-start Gabriel's career. Tío Fernando soon ushered him in to contests and singing engagements all over California through the Variedad circuit.[3]

After rigorous coaching in oral music tradition by my father, Gabriel was soon appearing on bills with some of the most respected Mexican artists of the times. The Variedades often stopped off at the historic Million Dollar Theater in downtown LA. My sister Claudia and I were later encouraged to join my brother by singing harmony, or *segunda*, with him. Our act became known as "Gabrielito González, 'La Actuación Infantil'" (The children's act). We had the privilege of opening for Lucha Villa, Mercedes Castro, Aida Cuevas, Vicente Fernández, Federico Villa, and Yolanda Del Rió, to name a few artists. I still remember exploring the Million Dollar Theater in downtown LA, running on sticky floors through backstage wings while dodging rattraps. The smell of stale popcorn and nachos lingered in the air as we listened to the mariachis warm up in the basement. The house mariachi at the Million Dollar Theater was Mariachi América de Miguel Márquez, and in my brother's best interest, my father would bring the mariachis a bottle of tequila to rehearsals. My father believed that this was a necessary gesture of appreciation and respect for the mariachis, who worked all night long accompanying the singers. He found that the artists who respected and treated mariachis well would receive the most enthusiastic accompaniment.

Having been born in Los Angeles, my brother's place of birth was concealed at first. The record company that soon signed him felt that his birthplace would turn off Mexican patrons who were ranchera fans. With no child labor protection acts in Mexico and my father's drunken permission, Tío Fernando worked my brother nonstop from the time he was nine to eleven years old; he was frequently missing school, traveling, doing late-night gigs, and filming. Gabrielito González was soon known as "La Sensación Infantil, con el Auténtico Sentimiento Mexicano" (The child sensation, with the authentic Mexican sentiment).[4] Despite my mother's protests, my father's word was always final. Although she worried tremendously about my brother, she had three other children to tend to. My mother mostly dealt with her daughters, combing our hair, applying our makeup, and sewing our skirts for performances.

It is saddening to think of these times, for although these experiences were rich in music and culture, I knew that my family was falling apart. My father's drinking worsened, and he became extremely abusive to us all. After many years of a turbulent homelife, homelessness, and living in and out of our relatives' garages and trailers, my mother finally left him when I was eleven years old. After their divorce, my father tried to keep in touch with us, but he soon lost his battle with alcoholism and disappeared into the streets of East Los Angeles. It was up to my mother to raise four children, alone.

El Artista Vagabundo

Despite years of imploring my father to quit his drinking, visits in and out of rehabilitation, and troubles with the law, my father eventually became a homeless vagrant. He would occasionally come by to see us. During some of his visits, he would show up visibly intoxicated and dirty. Alcoholism had made him delusional, and he would go on rants, describing some big plans he had with some famous Mexican composer. Other times he would disappear for long periods of time. When this happened my brother would take to the streets to look for him. His transient name was El Artista, the artist. My brother would eventually track him down under this name, with the help of other homeless folks. This was the only way we knew that our father, El Artista, was still alive. These were especially difficult times as we saw his health and appearance deteriorate with each visit. Slowly he began to lose all his teeth and became increasingly thin and frail. Despite his situation, my father never abandoned the idea that he would one day "make it" in music.

In retrospect, his longing for music was always somewhat distorted. Some of my first childhood memories are of my father sitting on the floor, intoxicated, gazing at the record player and conducting to imaginary musicians and singers. Sometimes he would force us to sit with him and learn his favorite classic Mexican *rancheras* or *baladas*. Although my father was absent for the rest of our lives, I inherited most of my musical influence from him. After he disappeared for good, his ideologies, beliefs, and teachings in music continued to haunt me. His ghost lingered for some time. As the sociologist Avery Gordon recollects, "To write ghost stories implies that ghosts are real, that is to say, that they produce material effects."[5] In this way, it is indeed a ghost story. My father's beliefs had material effects on his children, and his reality was a "systematic haunting" of "modernity's violence." Everything I was destined to learn anew in a new community would slowly exorcise his teaching from my psyche. As Gordon recognizes, "Only the conscious horror of destruction creates the correct relationship with the dead: unity with them because we, like them, are the victims of the same condition and the same disappointed hope."[6]

The Social Relations of Music

Our thinking has now been overdetermined by commoditization.

> PRITI RAMAMURTHY, course lecture for Women and International
> Economic Development, University of Washington, winter 2010

When I reflect on the sociocultural impacts capital markets have had in all areas of human life and interaction, the "social relations of music," to me, are the most profound. I refer to the social relations of music as the value systems concerning music knowledge, reception, and practices upheld by social institutions. Social institutions, such as nations, states, family, and kinship, regulate culture and human interaction in the most intimate ways. Post-Enlightenment Western culture, and particularly the industrialization of music under capitalism, has had the greatest and most significant impact on all music practices. When considering the social relations of music in my family, I can better understand my father's hauntings—his inner struggles and the value system he imposed on our family. As the feminist economic development theorist Priti Ramamurthy states, capitalist logic dictates much of what we live. The very nature of how we tend to function in US society revolves around economic capital and its constant proliferation of commodities. My father, like many, carried this belief into music and music practice. I make the distinction here between the avid listener and those who seek to take up music in a more intimate way. At present, to be "discovered" by a record company, agent, or manager, and to make a living in the professional music world, is the quintessential and naturalized progression of what it means to be a "success" in Western societies' understanding of music. Western perspectives on music practice are inextricably infused with ideas of professionalization and upward economic and social mobility. I can see how the power and prestige of being a "professional singer" was the only way my father could visualize participation in a music world.

I don't assume that my father's longing to live a life of a professional musician was what drove him toward becoming an alcoholic. I cite my father as an example of what I believe is a common ideology in Western music practice. Unpacking and identifying the complicity of nations, states, family, and other social institutions as important factors in securing market capitalism's arrangement of the most intimate social constructs and behaviors is important in understanding one's lived experience. Globalization and neoliberalism are significant social forces not strictly relegated solely to an economic realm. Regardless of the terms we use to signify capital economic order on a global or local scale, feminist development theorists refuse to uproot economic logic from its social underpinnings. Wendy Larner has examined the popularity of "neoliberalism" and the ways in which scholars in varied disciplines articulate this social force.[7] Larner contends that neoliberalism has "usurped" globalization as the concept used to describe contemporary forms of global economic restructuring.[8] Larner states, "Although neoliberalism may have a clear intellectual genesis, it arrives in different places in different ways, articulates with other political projects, takes multiple forms, and can give rise to unexpected outcomes."[9] Neoliberalism indeed operates at multiple scales.[10] That is to say, "not only is it a supranational project (neoliberal globalization), it involves nation-state and local (particularly urban) political projects."[11] Larner encourages one to gain the details and complexities of the processes involved, particularly the "new domains of analysis"—that of bodies, households, families, sexualities, and communities—and, as I see it, the social relations of music.[12] Neoliberal economic forces affect how we relate to music, the role it plays in our lives, and our ultimate relationship with it, be it transactional or otherwise. Similarly, Michel Foucault addresses the important ways "governmentality" makes visible the "governing of others," but most importantly, a "governing of the self."[13]

Governing of the self, or of technologies of the self, resonate in my attempt to understand my father's value systems, desires, and actions concerning music in his life. When I consider the degree to which capitalism has arranged individual subjects' interaction and relationship to music, I can better understand my father's value system. One cannot negate self-discipline as central to the social domination of capital markets' arrangement of the social relations of music and communities. As Foucault has stated, "I think that if one wants to analyze the genealogy of the subject in Western civilization, he has to take into account not only techniques of general domination but also techniques of the self."[14] Indeed, my father disciplined himself and by extension his household and children to identify and to seek music via the pursuit of a professional career in it. The nuances of this power constituted themselves through various means. I consider the visible, versatile equilibrium of power, with its complicities and conflicts, coercions and processes, and the ways in which we construct ourselves in the process.

La Época de Oro del Cine Mexicano: Modernity and Professionalization as Tools of Self-Discipline

There is a circumstantial pride in a past that is somehow assumed to be glorious, but that is experienced as something dead, a matter for specialists and an irresistible attraction for tourists. Above all, it is assumed to be something apart from ourselves, something that happened long ago in the same place where we, the Mexicans, live today.

GUILLERMO BONFIL BATALLA, *México Profundo*

Considering the theoretical models of the neoliberal subject, self-discipline, and governmentality as the fundamental catalysts of change from a community music perspective to a neoliberal sense, I can see how my father was a product of his time. It is important to situate my father's social formation, however, within the historical period in which he grew up, which had an impact on the value system he enacted as an adult. My father, after all, grew up at the height of La Época de Oro del Cine Mexicano (the golden age of Mexican cinema). Through the medium of film, La Época de Oro was a key tool in the creation and maintenance of modern Mexican national identity. From 1939 to 1969, the films of this golden era often portrayed varying topics concerning Mexican life and the history of Mexico through tales of valor, love, and war. Directors such as Fernando de Fuentes and Emilio Fernández were key figures during this important and prosperous time for Mexican cinema and the arts in general. These films romanticized a Mexican past that typically portrayed indigenous ways and people as historically significant yet "extinct" in order to justify a modernist project. The national project also perpetuated a masculinist discourse.

As the Mexican social scientist Guillermo Bonfil Batalla argues in *México Profundo: Reclaiming a Civilization*, the romanticizing of a "Mexican past" usually involved a construction of the indigenous subject as extinct. Referencing Mexican intellectuals from José Vasconcelos to the anthropologist Manuel Gamio, Bonfil Batalla demonstrates the social, political, and ideological groundwork, from the early conquest to the present, to describe the ways in which those in power have dealt with the "Indian problem" in Mexico. The ideology of the *indio* as extinct was being articulated through various mediums. The Mexican film theorist Andrea Noble notes the importance of filmmakers in postrevolutionary Mexico, specifically the work of the Soviet filmmaker Sergei Eisenstein, who is most notably known for his work in *¡Que Viva México!* Although *¡Que Viva México!* was not finished in Eisenstein's lifetime, it nonetheless imparted an ideology and techniques of visual representation, most notably the montage, that changed the face of cinematography. As Noble states, "Eisenstein enjoyed the support and friendship of some of the country's leading artists and intellectuals of the time, including Diego Rivera, David Alfaro Siqueiros, Adolfo Best Maugard, Jean Charlot, and Gabriel Fernández Ledesma," to name a few.[15] As a result, Eisenstein's film *¡Que Viva México!* left an enduring yet controversial legacy, as Eisenstein's visual treatment of indigenous subjects, landscapes, and daily living through the montage has been seen by some as a voyeuristic look at the "other." Through *¡Que Viva México!* came the birth of "Eisensteinian excesses" of representation, which although exalted in his time have since been critiqued for their essentialism.[16] Noble reminds us that Eisenstein's visual representation of indigenous people and their cultures, however unsettling at present, was in accordance with the *indigenista* discourse of its time. Rather, "as an avant-garde auteur of international standing," his vision "converged conveniently" with official government policy.[17] As Noble elaborates, "The paradox turns on the fact that while indigenismo emerged from the Revolution as a crucial and nation-defining cultural concept, the Revolution itself was not fought in the name of race. Instead the conflict was couched in terms of class."[18]

Indigenismo was, therefore, as it had been in the preceding centuries, an "elite discourse deployed in the name of a nation-state struggling to consolidate and legitimate its identity."[19] To date, "Eisenstein is frequently invoked as an enduring influence—for better or for worse—on Mexican visual culture more generally."[20] Most recently, the anthropologist Alex E. Chávez introduces the concept of the "ranchero chrono-trope." The ranchero chrono-trope, as a racist and necessary depiction, has been exercised by both the Mexican nation-state as well as the US empire in their respective interests of dominance and labor exploitation of Mexican subjects on both sides of the Mexico-US border.[21] Chávez recounts a subject that dwells "at the spatial periphery of modernity and always in a temporal past tense."[22] The ranchero, his rancho, his customs, and his ways are romantic and quaint but nevertheless expendable. The ranchero chrono-trope was invoked then and continues to hold meaning and value to this day.

Thus, popular culture or art supported by the Mexican government from

1920 to 1940 had a nationalistic character that centered on indigenous artifacts, ways of being, and dress codes. As a social construction, the *mestizo* was needed to bring order to the chaos brought about by the Mexican Revolution that began in 1910. For all intents and purposes, it was an imagined identity in relation to the reality and true plural nature of the country.[23] That is, despite the reality that Mexico has a multitude of indigenous populations and cultures, the indigenous subject was conceived as "extinct" in nation-state narratives. The construction of the *mestizo* served as a way to consolidate power and gather the public's imagination under one identity. This was an easier task than to assess the material reality and existing indigenous populations within Mexico. Nonetheless, "the Revolution of 1910 has accorded to the image of the Indian a special privilege, that of serving as one of the major, official symbols of nationalism."[24] Bonfil Batalla affirms that it has been an "*ideological* exaltation of the Indian, which has made his presence visible in the public sphere under State control."[25] Furthermore, it is in music, dance, literature, and other arts that the theme of the Indian provided the basic elements for shaping a vast nationalist current under government patronage.[26]

State powers take ideological control in a multitude of ways. Under capitalism, states construct commodities that are beneficial to their cause. One can say that the greatest commodity during La Época de Oro was nostalgia. The emotional currency of the *indio*, or Indian, was based on nostalgia, which intrinsically implied a "moving forward."[27] As Bonfil Batalla powerfully states, "Through an adroit ideological alchemy, that past became our past, that of the Mexicans who are not Indians. However, it is an inert past, a simple reference to what existed as a kind of premonition of what Mexico is today and will be in the future. It has no real connection with our contemporary reality and our collective future."[28]

Film, music, and cultural artifacts succeeded in articulating *indigenismo* as a commodity in order to assert a cultural *mestizaje*. In this way, the extraction of the *indígena* image, artifacts, and clothing was a disembodiment from the source—the *indígena* people. The modernist project of *indigenismo* was a "lifting" of cultural artifacts while shedding the multitude of history, practices, belief systems, and ways of life that gave birth to them. The ethnomusicologist Thomas Turino has also explained the myriad ways that nation-states and competing minority social groups utilize music and emotion for the consolidation of power, noting that "nationalism is basically emotional, and has to be succeeded."[29] In this sense modernity always implies a replacement of the "old" with the "new." Turino states, "As a key symbol in this ideology, the term *modern* is used unreflexively to assert an all-pervasive 'present,' whereas the 'traditional' is relegated to an inferior historical past."[30] Naila Kabeer articulates similar ideologies from a feminist development theory standpoint: "While modernization theorists used different combinations of social and economic factors to explain the process of change, they generally shared a common emphasis on changes in values and attitudes as a critical prerequisite for the transition to the modern society."[31]

As Kabeer indicates, there must be "changes in values and attitudes as a critical prerequisite for the transition to the modern society."[32] The norms and customs of the so-called third world stand against the rational self-interest toward the goal of achieving modern status.[33] Such was the case in postrevolutionary Mexico. The use of the Indian as a "cipher for a proto-national identity" was important to the overall formation of a Creole self, distinct from the "Spanish peninsular identity" of the *mestizo*.[34] The collective identity of the *mestizo*, however, significantly embraced the conceptual death of the Indian by conceiving the *indio* as extinct in order to successfully embrace the premises of modernity.[35]

My point is that nation, modernity, and gender have all been naturalized in such a way that we overlook how they have impacted both public and private social behavior. Modernity as an ideology can be used by those in power under any economic institution—be that capitalism or socialism. Modernity as a condition and an ideology always implies a linear progression that nations must aspire to. Seldom understood is that modernity, as an idea set forth by the West, has no real end. That is to say, there is no determinant, no endgame, no way of assessing if a country has reached "modern" status. Most significantly, the modernist project implies an "us" and a "them." Western ideology sets the standard and the rest of the world must follow or be considered "un-modern" and in need of "development."

La Época de Oro—its music, film projects, and ideologies—was a powerful tool in maintaining Mexican rhetoric of the *mestizo* as the prime citizens of the Mexican nation, and all at once succeeded in communicating ideas of progress and modernity. The construction of Mexico as a homogenous society, particularly after the revolution, was attractive to markets, tourists, and investors. As Noble states, "In the final analysis, *indigenismo* was not really about incorporating a complex, pluralistic notion of the multiple indigenous ethnicities within national culture."[36] Rather, "the ultimate and paradoxical aim of official *indigenismo* in Mexico was thus to liberate the country from the deadweight of its native past or, to put the case more clearly, finally to destroy the native culture that had emerged during the colonial period. *Indigenismo* was therefore a means to an end. That end was cultural *mestizaje*."[37]

To be sure, La Época de Oro del Cine Mexicano succeeded in both instilling the value of modernity and progress while simultaneously instilling the value of the professionalization of the Mexican musician. The films and the ideology embedded in them were significant in defining my father's conception of music. Stories of meritocracy and individual triumph fueled the ideological economy of the *mestizo* in films.

The How and the Why

These memories lie silent on my lap. The dilapidated red photo album reminds me of how I used to understand music. Like my father, I too began to pursue a professional life in music in my late teens. I joined groups whose sole purpose was to acquire music stardom. For some projects, my brother, sister, and I worked together like my father taught us. These were long days and nights of dealing with crooked managers and producers who exploited our labors. As a young female singer I was often pressured and expected to wear very little clothing for performances or told to show "more skin." On other occasions, I was fired for not "dressing the part." I left many more projects for being sexually harassed. At some point in my late teens, I retreated from music practice altogether.

For a time, I hated ranchera music because it reminded me of my father. When you grow up believing that music only exists one way in society, and social and commercial markets reinforce these ideas, it is difficult to break from or imagine other models for how music can function in the life of a lover of music. I would face many more challenges in music as a young woman before I had a change of heart. The change in perspective for me has been mostly in the *how* and the *why*. Despite my father instilling his belief system in regard to music, fate or destiny had a different path for me.

I now understand that my father's concept of music was directly related to the "cultural milieu" of the age in which he lived. When an ideology is being espoused through multiple cultural and social currents, there is an inevitable reduction of possibilities and other ways of being. This can be said for any country that is driving an ideological sentiment for nation-state control. I believe that my father's material possibilities were limited. His entire formation in music revolved around professionalization. Never mind that the country he was born in had many other conceptions of music practice via the multitude of living indigenous cultures within its borders. These examples were not conducive to the moral order or political/economic project of the day. The times had spoken. His world had been shut down of alternative possibilities. After many years and with this new understanding, I have been able to forgive him—and myself. For despite the anger and contempt I had toward my father, and for all the abuse he inflicted on our family, I understand the bigger economic and governmental order that prompted and shaped his belief system and by default my turbulent childhood.

CHAPTER 2

Chican@ Artivistas

RESISTANCE TO CAPITAL MARKET SYSTEMS AND THE MIND/BODY SPLIT

I was twenty years old and meeting Professor Steven Loza about the possibility of joining the ethnomusicology department at the University of California, Los Angeles (UCLA). It was 1993 and I was excited at the prospect of being a student at UCLA but also nervous and in disbelief that there could even be a place for me in the department. For starters, I did not have what I considered to be "musical abilities." I understood "real" music as the Western classical experience and, like many, had been instilled with an understanding that the structures, epistemologies, and overall aesthetics of Western music were superior to any other forms of music. Furthermore, I had never considered my experience to be of interest to anyone, least of all a college or university.

To my surprise, Professor Loza assured me that my father's informal yet rigorous training in Mexican popular music was more than valid. He said that my presence, ideas, and experience as a woman of color were strongly needed on campus, and he encouraged me to audition. Walking through Schoenberg Hall the day of my audition was terrifying. Despite my nervousness, in the audition I spoke of my extensive "informal" music training and experience with authority. I performed two ranchera songs a cappella. Two weeks later, I received word that I had been accepted into the program. I could not believe it! I was thrilled but wondered what was to come. I initiated my studies in the ethnomusicology department in the fall of 1993. In retrospect, the courses, curriculum, and reading material my first year in the program were all a blur, with the exception of John Blacking's *How Musical Is Man?*

How Musical Is Man? is a classic 1973 text in the field of ethnomusicology and is a result of Blacking's two-year stay among the Venda people in South Africa from 1956 to 1958. A classical pianist trained in the rigors and repertoire of Bach, Chopin, and Mozart, Blacking understood that music was a system of order with a set of rules and patterns invented and developed by exceptional European musicians. But his fieldwork in Africa, in particular his study of music practice in Venda culture, gave him new insight into how other cultures *conceived* of music, musical ability, musical practice, and music's function in society. In the course of his research, Blacking deconstructs not only his elite gaze but also his *own* (Western) culture's relationship to music. That is, he awakened to a "deeper understanding" of his own relationship to music in conversation with the Venda.[1]

Early on in his study, Blacking concludes that his relationship to music was a result of "selective reinforcement."[2] In contrast, experiences with the Venda taught Blacking that music "can never be a thing in itself, and that *all* music is folk music, in the sense that music cannot be transmitted or have meaning without associations between people."[3] Blacking realizes that "the functions of music in society may be the decisive factors promoting or inhibiting latent musical ability, as well as affecting the choice of cultural concepts and materials with which to compose music."[4] Blacking humbles himself to the possibility that all music has essential processes that can be found in the constitution of the human body, particularly "in patterns of interaction of human bodies in society."[5] His understanding that music can never be a thing in itself stressed the importance of how a culture positions music, music practice, and interaction with music. Indeed, his understanding of music is a consequence of his social and cultural environment.[6]

A key passage that is reiterated throughout Blacking's book exemplifies what interested me most about his project: "We must ask why apparently general musical abilities should be restricted to a chosen few in societies supposed to be culturally more advanced. Does cultural development represent a real advance in human sensitivity and technical ability, or is it chiefly a diversion for elites and a weapon of class exploitation? Must the majority be made 'unmusical' so that a few may become more 'musical'?"[7] Blacking places our Western understanding of musical "abilities" under question. He recognizes the "social relations of music" by expressing a desire to engage in an analysis of the cultural, historical, and political dynamics that have shaped music affect, understanding, practice, and production in Western society.

Blacking's personal discovery and new understanding of music underscored something I had felt all my life. My experience in music, however consciously informal, erratic, and far removed from an elite upbringing, was nonetheless the result of my Mexican immigrant experience. My experience had been one that did not judge me on the grounds of being "unmusical." In fact, because my siblings and I had been told we had "musical abilities," we were pushed into a life of professionalization. As discussed earlier, my father's ideas of music and musical success were strongly tied to Mexican nationalism. Despite Mexico's diverse participatory music culture, there was no alternative in the mainstream to the ideological music order of the country at the time. The national rhetoric in Mexico, like many other places in Latin America, privileged progress and modernity, and the professionalization of the Mexican musician was the call to order through both film and other cultural production.[8] Blacking's suggestion that social and cultural dynamics are important influences in one's understanding of music and music practice validated my own experience. But whereas Blacking draws attention to the social differences between Western and Venda musical practice, I have come to see the differences more specifically in terms of how the political economy has structured and naturalized these values.[9]

In what follows, I map my own change in understanding of music and art, based on my introduction into the world of Chican@ artivistas in East LA. My coming of age in this community marks the ways in which I began to experience another way of engaging with music and creative expression.

Quetzal from East LA

After my father's untimely death, my relationship to music was correlated with his lost dreams, pain, and suffering. Despite my early childhood experience, I continued to engage in recording studio work and music projects with my brother and sister. I experienced major legal turmoil as well as harsh gender dynamics and outright sexual harassment during varying recording projects. By the time I arrived at UCLA as a music student, I was convinced I was through with professional music practice. After some time, I came to the conclusion that the music industry was exploitative and sometimes downright dangerous for women. I was, however, content in knowing that being a part of the ethnomusicology department would still allow me to be close to music somehow. Soon thereafter I was introduced to Quetzal Flores, the founder of the band Quetzal. As the founder and musical director, Flores committed the band's name and resources to a movement of artists and musicians concerned with social justice. My experience in the band and in this community would forever change my view of the function of music and art.

Before meeting Flores personally, I had seen the band Quetzal perform at Troy Café a year prior. Troy Café was a hole-in-the-wall coffee shop and Chican@ artist hangout in the outskirts of Little Tokyo. Now extinct, the coffee shop had become a site of refuge for Chican@ artists and musicians after the historic space Self Help Graphics and Art closed its doors to music events.[10] As the influential artist and Asco member Willie Herrón recalls, the creation of the Vex club at Self Help Graphics was meant to foster the experimental music as it related to his art in Asco.[11] Formed in the early 1970s, Asco was a group of young Chican@ renegade street, visual, and performance artists who created art as a means to critique and incite dialogue within the community. Notable members were the artists Harry Gamboa Jr., Gronk, Willie Herrón, and Patssi Valdez. Although Asco were virtually ignored by the mainstream art institutions in the late seventies, they are now considered one of the most innovative Chican@ artist collectives of their time, as their innovative multimedia artwork has been featured in various prestigious art institutions across the country. They have also been discussed in academic publications. Most notably, their work was featured in *Asco: Elite of the Obscure; A Retrospective, 1972–1987*, published in 2011 in collaboration with the Los Angeles County Museum of Art and the Williams College Museum of Art.[12]

Troy Café became an important place to be, and I had been invited there by a friend to listen to Quetzal. I remember being captivated by the then singer Lilia Hernández, as well as Rocio Marron, who was an impressive violinist. One of the songs that caught my attention was "Agua de la manguera" (Water from the hose). The clever lyrics spoke of hot summer days in East LA:

> Blue skies. Sunny eyes.
> Walking down the street of life.
> Tattered buildings, broken streets.
> Clothes lines drying in the heat . . .
> Eating *raspados*, making water balloons, drinking *agua de la manguera*!

All at once I felt a sense of nostalgia and pride. I could relate to this song. I too had lived through those hot summer days as a child. Hot asphalt in the peak of summer is common in East LA. And water from the hose *was* the most gratifying experience after a hard day at play. The title, the topic, as well as the use of Spanglish (Spanish/English code-switching) made me feel right at home. I could relate to the experience and the poverty described. Quetzal's energy filled the small café. Absent was a sense of pity, as the overall sentiment in the song was one of dignity, pride, and hope.

Troy Café in Little Tokyo

Troy Café in the early 1990s was an important place to encounter discussions on the function and social relevance of music, art, and culture.[13] The cofounder and owner Sean Carrillo was a veteran of the previous generation of Chican@ artist movements and a former member of Asco. Carrillo's reputation as an artist as well as his friendships with Chican@ artists populated the small coffee shop. Quetzal Flores recalls spending quite a bit of time there and states that his formation as a guitarist and songwriter was a result of the plethora of Chican@ artists, musicians, poets, and intellectuals who gathered in this space to discuss, critique, and support each other's work. Troy Café was a small space. The greater part of the room was a long, narrow corridor with a small corner stage and red brick walls that frequently displayed local artists' work. Black, glass-paned doors marked the entrance

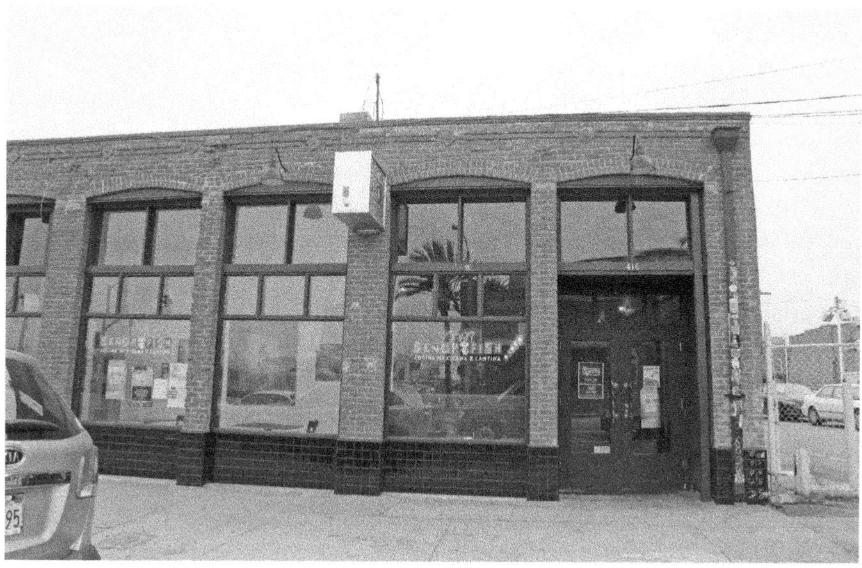

Troy Café building in Little Tokyo at the corner of Alameda and First Streets. This space has since been demolished to make space for a new Metro entrance.

into Troy Café that faced First Street. If you peered in from the outside, you could see the bar where baristas served coffee and baked goods. A long corridor led back to a small cobblestone patio that led out to a view of Alameda, Little Tokyo, and a potholed parking lot. Although Troy Café served coffee and other edibles, the food was not what drew crowds. It was the music, art, and performances.

The most interesting part to me about Troy Café was the patrons. The artists, musicians, and organic intellectuals who frequented the space were fascinating. Their manner of dress, the unique Chicana hair and makeup, set an atmosphere of creativity. Most of all, the conversations were engaging and interesting to be around. On any given night, there was some band or theater group utilizing the space to perform or rehearse. Music was always playing over the sound system or live onstage. People were supportive and conversed about their works in progress, made plans to collaborate, or just sat at the many small tables in the V-shaped room to plot their next *movidas*. Among the music groups I had the fortune of listening to at Troy Café were Las Tres, Goddess,[13] Lysa Flores, Sol, Brown Eyes, and Boca de Sandia. I remember meeting the legendary Chicana punk rock musicians Alice Bag, Angela Flores, and Teresa Covarrubias, who together were known as Las Tres. I had never seen three Chicanas sit side by side with their guitars in hand. I was amazed by their songwriting and talent.

The Chicana feminist music theorist Michelle Habell-Pallán notes how Troy made an important impact in a historical moment of "shrinking public outlets."[14] Troy Café would eventually close, and although its closing slowed the row of the creative work, it did not kill the will of a community that would soon regroup and erupt elsewhere. Nevertheless, displacement is a crisis that communities repeatedly contend with, especially in highly coveted real estate markets like Little Tokyo, downtown LA, and Boyle Heights. This still prompts questions: Can we think our way out of physical space as an essential variable that is needed to generate social movement? How are we to build momentum and relationships with each other without public spaces to meet? And what about the body? What about our sense of selves and our creative work? Do artists exist without capital markets to proliferate their work? What is an artist without an audience or a market to sell to? Troy Café succeeded in creating a space to gather a community of artists. But the ideas that flowed from that space nevertheless exalted what Quetzal Flores recognized as "a complex and continued reliance on capitalism and ideas of upward mobility."[15] Ultimately, under the current social relations of music, we are ideologically trapped in the transactional, where all that the body produces can potentially be for sale—the body as capital. Our labor, our creativity, our spirituality are all a potential sale.

According to Linda Tuhiwai Smith, one of many postcolonial tasks is an analysis of the "reach of imperialism" into our heads.[16] In this regard, Smith suggests that we must "decolonize our minds, to recover ourselves, [and] to claim a space in which to develop a sense of authentic humanity."[17] The following is meant to open up a discussion on the body in relation to capital. The body is, after all, the material vehicle from which we operate and move about society, and empire constitutes itself in relationship to its colonial subject. Furthermore, divisions and binaries imposed on the human body as the body politic / body of the state are organized around gender, color, class, sexuality, ability, and nation.

The Body and Capital

Understanding the brown body and the regulation of its movements is fundamental in the reclamation of narrative and the development of radical projects of transformation and liberation.

Cindy Cruz, "Toward an Epistemology of the Brown Body"

As the Chicana feminist Cindy Cruz notes, one must understand the brown body and the regulations of its movements, which is "fundamental" to "transformation and liberation."[18] In this way, all the delineations and abstractions are constituted in relation to each other and for the benefit of nation-state interests. African enslavement was central to the wealth and foundation of the United States. Aside from the hauntings of the unthinkable physical, ideological, and labor violence African people and their descendants have had to endure, slave labor has also left a lasting legacy on how we think of the body more generally. All bodies produce some kind of labor. All bodies must offer something for sale in our hypercapitalist society.

The African theorist Bibi Bakare-Yusuf argues that the material practice of violence was a tool used by the slave economy to produce two kinds of bodies: the body of knowledge and the body of labor. As a way of extracting capital and wealth through slave labor, the tools of torture and violence were ways of inducing terror and horror upon the body. Torture was an "active and systematic deconstruction" of the African body.[19] Bakare-Yusuf clarifies that the point was not to destroy the body but to "deconstruct the body in pain" as torture became an "imitation of death" or a "sensory equivalent."[20] She continues, "The violent subjection of the slaves was a way of transforming their bodies into an entity that could produce and reproduce the property necessary for accumulating wealth."[21] In this way the enslaver and victimizer "needs the victim to create truth, objectifying fantasy in the discourse of the other."[22] The ultimate goal was to deconstruct all traces of humanity, civilization, and freedom, which ensured the slaves' subjection but all at once created the enslavers' subjectivity. A disembodiment, an "active and systematic deconstruction" of the African body, had to be ensured to secure the extraction of capital.[23]

Although Bakare-Yusuf articulates this practice in the context of African slavery, one can gather from other colonialist accounts that the tools of torture have been a multisited and age-old practice.[24] "The use of terror was a national sport during the period of slavery" and Latin American colonialism, states Bakare-Yusuf, noting that "it was the logic underpinning the creation of colonial reality and identity";[25] thus, "it serves as the mediator *par excellence* of colonial hegemony."[26] Based on Bakare-Yusuf's analysis on the deconstruction of the black body in pain, one can gather that the knowledge base built around the material consequences of torture and slavery continues to reproduce black and brown bodies' objectification both systematically and through consent. One can also gather that these practices have structured and have had an impact on societal behaviors to this very day.[27]

Bakare-Yusuf's analysis on the materiality of the black body is not void of agency or hope. Despite the troublesome history of slavery, she reminds us that the "flesh" that is transformed to "body as property" is never annihilated. It is "hidden from the violation of the body."[28] The "counter-memory" enables "the slaves and their descendants to construct a different kind of history, a different kind of knowledge, a different kind of body that is outside the control of the dominant history and knowledge production."[29] Bakare-Yusuf invokes the importance of cultural production as a voice and a tool in the articulation of "counter-memory": "What cannot be spoken in language is evoked through other cultural representation such as dance."[30] She goes on to cite the work of the scholar Paul Gilroy, stating that "while the experience of the middle passage and the diasporic plight might be resistant to (verbal) language, it is not resistant to representation."[31] "The most elemental expression" of this traumatic experience "can be found in the music and dance of the black diaspora[,] which produced new cultural meanings of the African past, present and future."[32]

Bakare-Yusuf gleans further assistance from the African American writer Toni Morrison, who articulates agency, or "site of memory," through the metaphor of a river, stating that although humans straighten out rivers in order to create livable acreage, flooding occurs from time to time.[33] Morrison argues that the "flooding" of these spaces is precisely the act of remembering by the river. Water, having the "perfect memory," is thus always trying to "get back to where it was."[34]

For black and brown bodies, our "rush of imagination," or our "flooding," is precisely the tracing back to *our* humanity, communicating whole and unbroken. The "rush of imagination" is what preoccupied so many artists who frequented Troy Café in the early 1990s, with the many music, poetry, and art events that took place. Through their art, participants would address many issues concerning Chican@ and Mexican communities, from Governor Pete Wilson's racist practices to neoliberal policy and their general understanding and history of oppression in this country.

The Political Economy as a Social Institution

A great deal of human behaviour is not the result of individual preferences. Rather, it is governed by institutional rules, norms and conventions that have powerful material effects on people's lives.

Naila Kabeer, *Gender Mainstreaming in Poverty Eradication and the Millennium Development Goals*

Liberal neoclassical economies play a central role in the evolution of development thought and practices, where the primary goal and meaning is placed on economic growth.[35] Economics, as the "science" that studies human behavior as a relationship between competing ends and scarce means, assumes that all agents within society universally have the same interests, which are to maximize their individual utilities.[36] In *Reversed Realities: Gender Hierarchies in Development Thought*, the feminist development theorist Naila Kabeer maps a history and intellectual narrative discourse concerning women in development practices. Kabeer's project in *Reversed Realities* became a useful way of understanding how gender inequalities take on varying meanings in the development world. Kabeer urged a look at the social structures in women's lives. A structural perspective on women in development adheres to a social relations analysis that extends an interconnected understanding of gender position in any given society. Rather than an analysis strictly on women or men as isolated categories, Kabeer urges a look at the interconnecting relationships that include other social inequalities, such as class, race, and sexuality, as important in understanding the "concrete conditions" in both women's and men's lives.[37] An awareness of the social, economic, cultural, and kinship structures that allow or negate women's mobility, and thus their access to finances, has been an important intervention in development practitioners' thought processes. In addition, an understanding that there are regional differences in culture, language, and social practices has made development practitioners and theorists more aware of the concrete conditions women experience in their respective cultures.

Relevant to my project concerning music are the categories by which Kabeer identifies social institutions as key components in the naturalization of varying gender roles and patriarchies, and how they vary across space. Kabeer identifies social institutions as markets, states, civil society, religion, and kinship/family. To conceive of markets (economic policies) and states as *social* highlights the humanity that is affected by the practices and history of these institutions. She concludes that these categories intersect and inform societal rules that ultimately affect individual subjects and the decisions they can make. After all, social institutions organize social and political life by "creating and regulating ideologies,"[38] which lead to social practices that have concrete effects on subjects. In this way social institutions inform the extent of one's access, mobility, and opportunities in society.

One of the most common arrangements societies have instituted across the globe is, of course, gender. Although they vary from region to region, "women" or "men" are roles and meanings that social institutions give to visible biological difference. It is now well known that gender in this sense is a performance that describes how identities, namely those of "woman" and "man," should move about society and in relation to each other. To this end, gender identities are described, maintained, and disciplined to the point of naturalization in society. Moreover, many now recognize that these roles are relational, in that men are often constructed as superior to women, more able, and more "logical."[39] "Woman" and "man" may also describe rights and privileges, depending on the society. Kabeer asserts that social institutions define the "rules of the game."[40] She goes on to state, "The rules may be written or unwritten, explicit or implicit, codified in law, mandated by policy, sanctified by religion, upheld by convention or embodied in the standards of family, community and society."[41] Ultimately, Kabeer contends that gender rules "play a powerful role in shaping human behaviour, in terms of both what is permitted and what is prohibited."[42] Gender is a familiar example of how social institutions (markets, states, religion, and kinship/family) create and demarcate difference to regulate and control behavior.

Much like gender conceptions and their logic, our relationship to music has also been arranged over time and by way of social institutions, primarily through the impetus of market capitalism. Through force or consent, in most "modern" societies, music is seen mostly as a commodity. Participatory practices are by most social accounts nonexistent, and music practice is regarded as either an incidental hobby or a professionalized practice. Rarely does society conceive of music as a participatory community practice. Over the next couple of years, my involvement with the Popular Resource Center, as well as the Big Frente Zapatista, would begin to alter that conception.

CHAPTER 3

The Popular Resource Center and Centro Regeneración in Highland Park

By 1996, there were rumors that Troy Café would permanently close its doors. The scene at Troy's was fading, and it seemed as though, yet again, a welcoming creative space was succumbing to financial hardship. But just as Troy was closing down, other spaces had slowly been brewing and had begun to organize events. Such spaces included the Aztlan Cultural Arts Foundation housed in the old city jail and the Peace and Justice Center in downtown Los Angeles; even Self Help Graphics in East LA had begun to reopen its doors to bands after a short hiatus. Troy Café patrons and youth scattered to these varying spaces, and although we played or attended events at all the other spaces, Centro Regeneración was the place we did most of our organizing. Quetzal Flores of the band Quetzal states that the first person to invite him to Centro Regeneración was Mark Torres. Torres had just developed and begun hosting *Travel Tips for Aztlan* with Pacifica Radio on 90.7 KPFK. Torres was committed to exposing the airwaves to local Chican@ and Latin@ groups and was searching for new Chican@ and Latin@ artistic talent. Having met during early Troy days, Torres invited Flores to a music concert at Regeneración to listen to an emerging Chicano reggae band called Quinto Sol.

To be clear, Regeneración was the physical space. The Popular Resource Center (PRC) was the nonprofit organization that worked out of the Regeneración warehouse. Community members referred to the space as either the PRC or Regeneración, but regardless of how you referenced the warehouse, you ended up at 110 S. Avenue 58 in Highland Park off of Figueroa Street in northeast LA. Regeneración was named after a radical Mexican newspaper published during and following the pre-Revolution Porfiriato. Ricardo Flores Magón and his brothers founded the popular newspaper that espoused revolutionary ideas of its time. The organizers of this new space chose the name Regeneración in admiration for and in solidarity with the efforts by Flores Magón. It was well known that Zack de la Rocha, front man and MC for the up-and-coming hip-hop rock band Rage Against the Machine, was a cofounder of Centro Regeneración. Rage had just been signed by a

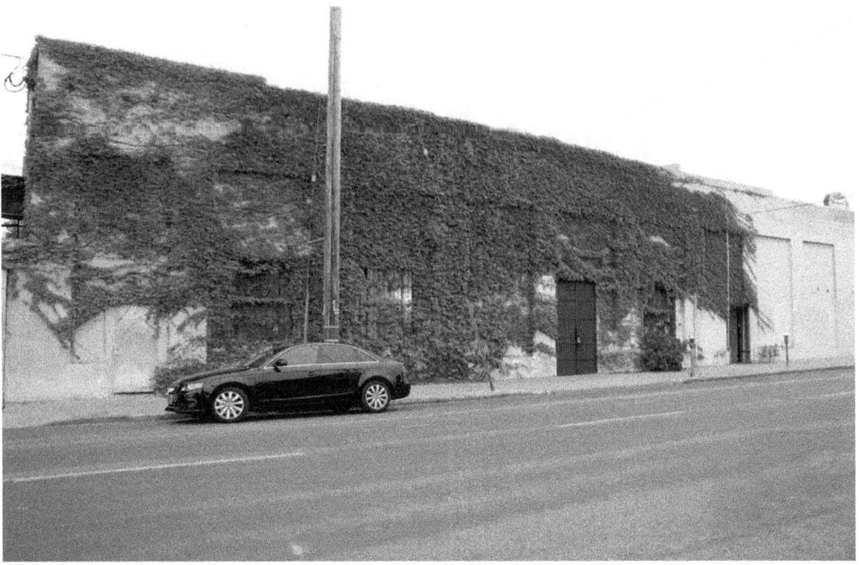

Popular Resource Center (PRC) on Avenue 58.

major label and was touring aggressively all over the world. For this reason, de la Rocha visited the space sporadically but was generous enough to cover the rent when needed.

The space itself was not much to look at. It was a gutted warehouse with a small kitchen and a single bathroom. There was a side room that housed an artist-resident who supervised the grounds and made sure that the people who came and went were respectful of the space. No drugs or BS were allowed, and the artist-resident made sure of that. Many people shared this responsibility over the years, but the person I remember being there the longest was Rudy "Rude" Ramírez. Also a musician, Rudy Rude was a drummer for a Chicano rock/hip-hop band called Aztlan Underground. He was a quiet guy with strong, attractive features. Being one of the founders, he was dedicated to Regeneración's well-being. Ramírez did not drink or smoke. If he saw someone unknown in the space, he was sure to ask what they were doing there and who they came with. Artists utilizing the space had to clean up after themselves and refrain from doing anything illegal or dangerous that could bring harm to themselves or others in the space. These actions, after all, could pose a risk to Regeneración and result in it being shut down or subjected to harassment by the cops. Things were pretty peaceful, but you knew not to fuck with the rules lest you deal with Rudy, and if he ever asked you to leave you'd best move quickly.

Overall, there was a zeitgeist revolving around music, community, and art. Quetzal Flores was immediately inspired by the space and energy the night Quinto Sol played.[1] Shortly after, Flores approached Rudy Rude and de la Rocha about utilizing the space to organize an artist collective. Flores had simultaneously been attending meetings and study groups conducted by the National Commission for Democracy in Mexico (NCDM) focused around the recent Zapatista uprising. Flores's father, Roberto Gonzalez Flores, was a central figure in these study groups. The purpose of the NCDM meetings was to study the Zapatista communiqués and teachings. Quetzal Flores soon invited Aida Salazar, Zack de la Rocha, and Rudy Ramírez to the study group.

Flores claims that NCDM meetings were somewhat disappointing in that they approached the Zapatistas solely as a political movement. He states that NCDM's approach was a canonized form of organizing—in the guise of 1970s early Movimiento days—where formal intellectual discourse was prioritized over art, music, and culture. Some members of the artist collective similarly felt that this approach was stagnant and that it failed to have a significant reach or an impact on the local community. Flores elaborates, "We were armed with art and wanted to approach and explore neoliberalism, government, and empire via the tools of art and cultural production."[2] Aida Salazar states that, via this new space, they started planning events for the NCDM and began to gather the participation of as many artists as possible.

In the Red and *Caught between a Whore and an Angel*

Although they never officially named their group, the first manifestation of the artist collective consisted of José Quetzal Flores, Rudy "Rude" Ramírez, Patricia Valencia, Antonio Willie García, Joe "Peps" Galarza, and Aida Salazar. The discussions revolved around music, art, and culture beyond capital gains. According to Quetzal Flores, "Some of the talks were about the kind of impact we wanted to have as artists. We were throwing around initial ideas concerning art and community engagement."[3] With time and youth's energy, in 1999 the group organized their first show, titled *In the Red*.

In the Red consisted of music, performance art, poetry, and visual art that challenged ideas concerning race, class, and sexuality. The show was fashioned in a variety show format. A charismatic MC named Humberto, known as "El Hache" (The *H*), hosted the show. The event engaged the audience in many formats that ranged from visual art, poetry, music, and participatory installation art.

One such installation featured the artist and painter Joe Galarza covered in gold iridescent paint wearing nothing but a loincloth. The image of Galarza covered in gold paint invoked Jesus of Nazareth, for his arms were

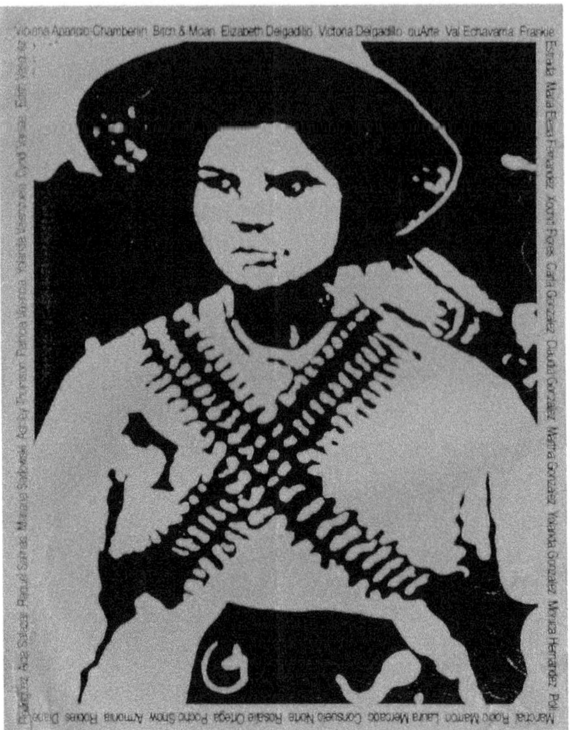

Flyer for *Caught between a Whore and an Angel* show at the PRC.

extended on a wooden cross, simulating a crucifixion. A tube protruded from underneath his loincloth. When sucked, the tube fed an audience member a libation that tasted of water. Television sets were placed on the floor surrounding Galarza's crucified body. Around the golden Christ were a number of American flags soiled with blood.

Throughout the show, members of the artist collective, as well as many audience members, approached the golden Christ and drank from the spout protruding from Galarza's groin. They would then proceed to pick up sledgehammers and destroy the television sets on the ground. I suggest that this interactive art installation had little or no antecedent, but it was indeed reminiscent of and inspired by the Asco days. The countless symbolic images and gestures that cited religion and media as tools of empire and oppression invoked important dialogues in the audience that night. For all intents and purposes, *In the Red* was a success. Flores recounts, "From there, all the crazy organizing started happening."[4]

Shortly after *In the Red* came a show entitled *Caught between a Whore and an Angel*. This night was a powerful testament to the strong female artistic presence within the community. It was also a testament to the emerging gender discussions taking place within the artist collective. The body as a site of contempt, sacredness, and desire within Mexican and Chican@ culture was the foundational theme. Chicana artists such as Rachel Salinas, Patricia Valencia, and Aida Salazar, as well as other musicians, poets, and artists, came together again in a variety show format to engage in discussions on the concepts of "whore" and "angel." The theme of the show prompted discussion on how these titles disciplined us, as women, through various means.

Zapatista teachings were an important source of inspiration for the artist collective organizers that consistently encouraged community dialogue based on race, class, gender, and sexuality.[5] A powerful moment in the show that reflected this influence was a collaborative piece between Aida Salazar and Patricia Valencia. Their piece was titled "A Tribute to Comandante Ramona." This piece was dedicated to Ramona, a prominent Zapatista commander who had been stricken ill with cervical cancer. Salazar recounts, "She was the figure who really spoke to us. It was ironic to us . . . her struggle . . . her fighting for equity for women in her community . . . the world, really . . . but she was dying from [a] cervical ailment when she had never even had children."[6] Salazar had written a poem about Ramona, while Valencia had built a metal female rib cage with dangling wax baby dolls on the sides. While Salazar recited her poem, the two of them, wearing nightgowns, threw guts and animal organs about the stage. Valencia also occasionally hammered away at a cow's heart. Salazar claims that many people had to leave the room for the graphic nature of it. I remember the piece clearly. It felt violent. There was strong silence or gasps as onlookers moved through the piece. I had never seen women portray such strong character presence.

As part of this show, I performed a song related to the theme with Quetzal's violinist at the time, Rocio Marron. *Caught between a Whore and an Angel* was well attended. It brought to the surface many female artists within the community and prompted important dialogue among all artists, especially the women. Most importantly, *Caught between a Whore and an Angel* inspired other female artist collectives, such as Mujeres de Maiz (MdM), which continue to organize multimedia art shows and dialogue to this day.

The Body as Knowledge and Ideological and Physical Site

According to Chela Sandoval, Chicana modes of theorizing epistemologies, praxis, and styles of resistance bear a historical trajectory (i.e., colonization, sexism, racism) that has given birth to ways of being and thinking needed not only to survive but to thrive amid a Eurocentric hegemony.[7] As the above artistic examples demonstrate, Chicana artivistas center the body in community art discourse. The "brown body" as a source of knowledge is done through a strategy of what Sandoval calls "differential consciousness."[8] Influenced by the queer Chicana scholar Cindy Cruz, I acknowledge that an understanding of the "brown body" and regulations of its movements are "fundamental in the reclamation of narrative and the development of radical projects of transformation and liberation."[9] Art allows the body to articulate "that which is linked to whatever is not expressible through words."[10] This mode of consciousness is precisely the mode by which Chican@ artivistas engage their art to prompt community dialogue. *Caught between a Whore and an Angel* created a night of dialogue around the discourses that concerned the reception of women's bodies. The PRC warehouse became a safe space for introspection, dialogue, and critique. The artistic work absorbed the unease associated with "whore" and "angel" and allowed people to reflect on the art and to discuss the power of the pieces.

The Body and Space

Through various means of creative expression, female artists and scholars of color have been able to articulate how power is constituted in relation to bodies. The claiming of space through art and poetry is a common strategy for women of color in the deconstruction of power. One of the most prolific theorists in this regard is Gloria Anzaldúa, who effectively utilized poetry to imagine and claim spiritual, physical, and ideological space in the academy and elsewhere. Anzaldúa introduced "border consciousness" in her ground-breaking 1987 work *Borderlands/La Frontera: The New Mestiza*. Border consciousness as a physical and an ideological space articulates an embodied experience for the Chican@. This concept has been an important addition to the Chican@ theoretical vocabulary, and an innovative theory that articulates the psychosocial and material effects of being Chican@ amid a Eurocentric hegemony.[11] In this sense, Chican@ reality as experienced through the brown body gave way to an entire social theory metaphorically tied to the geopolitical site—the US-Mexican border. The brown body was the impetus surrounding an entire field that catapulted a theoretically groundbreaking Chican@ feminist analytic tool: border consciousness.

The discourse and trajectory that has been inspired by border consciousness is a prime example of the ways in which Chicana embodied knowledge can generate a theoretical space from which to counter Eurocentric paradigms of a mind/body split. In this way, Anzaldúa's poetic inscriptions and correlation of a *mestiza* consciousness to the physical US-Mexican border as *una herida abierta*, an open wound, or "the liminal space," has been an important intervention in academia.[12] Although Anzaldúa's intellectual project has been critiqued for not abiding by academic paradigms, she nonetheless broke through traditional epistemology and methodological rules by introducing a project that refuses a positivist framework or mind/body split. Anzaldúa's *Borderlands / La Frontera* creates a space from which to elaborate an embodied existence. The brown body is centered and becomes a site where alternative modes of theorization may take place. To date, border consciousness is a powerful contribution to theoretical vocabularies that have since been utilized across academic and artistic disciplines.

With all the activity at the PRC, Troy Café had become a distant memory. Here we were, in a new space, enacting new visions. Mary Pat Brady theorizes on the discursive creation of space in *Extinct Lands, Temporal Geographies: Chicana Literature and the Urgency of Space.* Specifically, Brady excavates the intent of capitalist language in reference to geography and descriptions of landscape, claiming that geopolitical spaces via borders, architectural structures, capitalist development projects, and housing displace people as well as their memories. Brady registers these changes as "performative," concluding that space is processual and "goes extinct."[13] Brady suggests, citing Doreen Massey, that "space depends on the notion of articulation."[14] The idea that space is "produced" linguistically unsettles the assumption that space is simply something that is tied to "natural terrain."[15] Brady continues, "The process of producing space, however quotient or grand, hidden or visible, has an enormous effect on subject formation, on the choices people can make and on how they conceptualize themselves, each other and the world."[16]

So it was in the PRC that the transformative events began to shed light on greater discussions. In this way, Chicana artivistas claimed a space through their art. And the innovative programming spoke to various modes of understandings. The Chicana feminist scholar Chela Sandoval states that a "differential consciousness" is accessed through "poetic modes of expression: gestures, music, images, sounds, words that plummet or rise through signification to find some void—some no-place—to claim their due."[17] Art fed quite literally into intellectual discussions that permeated all areas of our lives. Sunday afternoon study meetings of Zapatista philosophy were sure to generate some sort of creative interpretation that would eventually be shared with an audience, prompting further reflection. The old warehouse was like a beehive of ideas that were artistic, intellectual, and hope driven. In what follows, I discuss the significance of indigenous pedagogy in Chican@ artivistas' creative work, as well as the process and organization of one of the most important and formative transnational encuentros of its time.

CHAPTER 4

The Big Frente Zapatista

USING ART AS A TOOL OF CRITICAL DIALOGUE

Chicana/o musical culture and its political work offers us invaluable bottom-up perspectives on the terrain of counterpolitics and cultural creation at the beginning of the twenty-first century.

VICTOR HUGO VIESCA, "The Battle of Los Angeles"

In October of 2018, I curated a panel for *Regeneración: Three Generations of Revolutionary Ideology*, an exhibition at the Vincent Price Art Museum at East Los Angeles College. The exhibition was curated by Pilar Tompkins Rivas, who had initially reached out months before about having me write an essay related to the show. The goal of *Regeneración* was to map three generations of transnational activist networks in the greater East Los Angeles area, beginning with the Flores Magón brothers. The exhibition then covered the classic 1970s Asco *Regeneración* publication and activities and ended with the 1990s artist-activist network that took place in the Centro Regeneración and Popular Resource Center (PRC) warehouse in Highland Park.

Although the Flores Magón and Asco sections were informative enough, the section of the exhibition on the Centro Regeneración and PRC was an undertheorized, simplified, days-of-yore depiction of what art kids from the neighborhood could do if they set their minds to it. I was not surprised to see the gratuitous name and image of one Zack de la Rocha on the walls, as if he were the sole engine that drove the movement and politics in the space. To Tompkins Rivas's credit, she vetted the material as best she could, but a museum could not contain all that had truly taken place in the gutted warehouse. Over the years there had been many attempts to narrate what truly happened, via websites, scattered academic side mentions of the space, and such. The organizing that took place at the PRC had, after many years, been quite contentious, as the initial fallout and eventual closing of the space was generated by hostile instigations by people outside of the community, to the detriment of the various relationships and working groups that organized within it. In retrospect, I feel that there was indeed an infiltration—a calculated takeover toward the goal of slowing the momentum and eventually annihilating the transformative work that had been taking place. The fallout continues to resonate within the community and among some peers. To be sure there are many versions on what happened to the PRC and who or what group was most significant. Some artists have felt cheated and downright offended by how some authors and scholars remember the space and whether or not they were mentioned in the historical telling. Although some narratives may be marred by egos and such, I think all accounts are ultimately valid, for all espouse the same sentiment. They share youth's hope and passion for a past that, although subjective, has nevertheless been impactful. Whether we produced art for vanguard's sake, organized a march, undertook an action, or curated an art exhibition or concert, we all created in this time and space in East Los Angeles and beyond. All of our memories are significant in their own ways.

As I walked out of the exhibition, I considered the glaring absence of the Big Frente Zapatista efforts, but I was not surprised, and I refuse to blame Tompkins Rivas. The Vincent Price space, like all museums, emphasizes artifacts frozen in time, organized in such a way so as to tell a particular kind of idealized romantic story that has little to no consequence to a now or distant future. But what happens when your community work lay at the heart of process-based practices that have continued to evolve and inform new movements? What happens when you have never remained still enough to be captured? Perhaps your work may be illegible to institutions such as museums precisely because it is not based on product or artifact.

By 1996, Quetzal was gigging on a regular basis. We worked tirelessly but didn't necessarily make money. "Work" usually meant free gigs and presentations all over the city of Los Angeles. Quetzal was one of many bands that played anywhere for little to no pay. In many ways, Chican@ artivistas were part of a vast network of musicians that became a resource to community organizers and organizations that could draw upon them for fundraisers and events. The content of Quetzal's musical work adhered to the struggles of our communities. We were consistently asked to play at rallies against local and federal legislation harmful to immigrant and Latin@ communities, such as Prop 187. We played benefit concerts and performances for the Bus Riders Union, Justice for Janitors, National Commission for Democracy in Mexico, Self Help Graphics, Office of the Americas, PRC, KPFK 90.7 FM, local and national MEChA organizations, Rigoberta Menchú, and the Zapatista struggle—to name just a few of the local, national, and international causes we supported and participated in.

The network of Chican@ artivistas also relied on each other for support. Artivistas who worked in all genres and mediums would donate their time for group fundraisers or future recording projects. This arrangement came with an understanding that the beneficiary would eventually return the favor. Ozomatli, Aztlan Underground, Ollin, Quinto Sol, Quetzal, Lysa Flores, and the Blues Experiment are but a few of the music groups that supported each other. Also central to this network were poets, graffiti artists, painters, muralists, filmmakers, and theater groups, including Teatro Chusma, Jose Ramirez, Omar Ramirez, Nuke, Smoking Mirrors (a filmmaker collective), In Lak Ech,[1] and the newly formed Mujeres de Maiz. The social energy revolving around the artistry could be felt at the PRC and across the city.

Victor Hugo Viesca is one of the few scholars who have written on the Chican@ artivista scene in East LA. Viesca focuses on the historical and sociopolitical groundwork that set off the grassroots movement, particularly the music scene in the 1990s. Although he does not use the term *Chican@ artivistas*, he nonetheless repeatedly highlights how music, in both content and production, was a tool in the struggle for social justice. Viesca makes reference to the ways in which the music was also a *relational* tool amongst the groups and highlights the ways in which the resources within the community were shared. He recognizes the Eastside scene, one that is grounded in the "new spatial and social relations generated in Los Angeles in the transnational era," as a "floating site of resistance, a mechanism for calling an oppositional community into being through performance."[2] Indeed, the community of artivistas was equally a product of and a way of countering "the impact of globalization on low-wage workers and aggrieved racialized populations."[3] Important to the work of artivistas are the many physical spaces that allowed artists and musicians to gather to create music, art, and culture together. These spaces, however fleeting, included Candelas Guitars in Boyle Heights, Troy Café in Little Tokyo, Luna Sol in Pico Union, the Eastside Café,[4] Peace and Justice Center in downtown LA, Centro Regeneración in Highland Park, and the Aztlan Cultural Arts Foundation in Lincoln Heights.[5]

An ongoing discussion and questions around sustainable models of community building and organizing continued to resurface as Quetzal Flores asked, "How [do you] create an identity as a way to build a foundation so that you can communicate and collaborate with other communities?"[6] Flores's question resonates with a self-reflexive exercise recognizing the importance of what Shawn Wilson refers to as *relationality*. Wilson's scholarly efforts have attempted to maintain, transmit, and clarify indigenous ways of doing and being in the world and the academy. With an understanding that we cannot remove ourselves from our realities to examine the world, relationships and relationality become central in indigenous research methods. As Wilson states, "The concepts or ideas are not as important as the relationships that went into forming them. Again, an Indigenous epistemology has systems of knowledge build upon relationships between things, rather than on the things themselves. It is important to recognize that the epistemology includes entire systems of knowledge and relationships."[7]

Relationality is part and parcel to Zapatista philosophy, which inspired Chican@ artivista praxis.[8] Not surprisingly, the Zapatistas stressed the importance of building relationships with other aggrieved communities across the globe, and we became one of many communities to answer the call.

Zapatista + Artista = Zapartista

The Ejército Zapatista de Liberación Nacional (Zapatista Army of National Liberation, or EZLN), commonly known as the Zapatistas, was the first postmodern revolution that was *not* seeking governmental power.[9] On January 1, 1994, the day the North American Free Trade Agreement (NAFTA) was to go into effect, indigenous Mayan communities in Chiapas, Mexico, took over four municipalities in the state, including the city of San Cristóbal de las Casas. Mayan communities claimed grievances with the Mexican government and the neocolonial forces of globalization. Their uprising was an attempt to bring focus and attention to their struggle. Their tactics also significantly relied on building alliances with other communities in struggle around the globe.[10]

Most unusual was the way in which Zapatistas consistently appeared masked in the media. Concealed by *pasamontañas*, or *pañuelos* and *paliacates*, or scarves, at no time did they allow their full facial features to show in public. The Zapatistas expressed to the world their struggles. The language in which they chose to communicate was not conventional political jargon. It was poetic prose, and they often made their claims through *dichos*, or sayings, such as "¡No tenemos que pedir permiso para ser libres!" (We don't have to ask permission to be free!) and "¡Detrás de nosotros estamos ustedes!" (Behind us, we are you!).[11] These kinds of *dichos* attempted to express defiance and indigenous ontologies. In addition, they boldly and repeatedly declared their *mal gobierno*, or bad government, was corrupt. In this sense, they avoided the traditional discourse of power and spoke to the heart and from the heart.

Among the constituency of indigenous *comandantes*, or leaders, was a gentleman who called himself Subcomandante Marcos. The media frenzy soon turned its attention to this charismatic spokesperson. Everyone wondered, who was Subcomandante Marcos? In attempts to discredit and shame the Zapatistas, the frustrated Mexican government published speculation that Marcos was a gay man from San Francisco. The Zapatistas responded as follows:

> Marcos is gay in San Francisco, black in South Africa, an Asian in Europe, a Chicano in San Ysidro, an anarchist in Spain, a Palestinian in Israel, a Mayan Indian in the streets of San Cristóbal, a gang member in Neza,[12] a rocker in the National University, a Jew in Germany, an ombudsman in the Defense Ministry, a communist in the post–Cold

War era, an artist without gallery or portfolio[,] . . . a pacifist in Bosnia, a housewife alone on Saturday night in any neighborhood in any city in Mexico, a striker in the CTM [Confederation of Mexican Workers], a reporter writing filler stories for the back pages, a single woman on the subway at ten p.m., a peasant without land, an unemployed worker[,] . . . an unhappy student, a dissident amid free market economics, a writer without books or readers, and, of course, a Zapatista in the mountains of southeast Mexico. So Marcos is a human being, any human being, in this world. Marcos is all the exploited, marginalized, and oppressed minorities, resisting and saying, "Enough!"[13]

The poetic yet politically charged statement reached into the public imagination. Understanding the way they might be read by the media, and in an attempt to engage the world to imagine beyond the masked indigenous subject, the Zapatistas released the above statement. Behind the *pasamontañas*, Marcos was and could be "any human being in the world."[14]

By articulating multiple moments and varying global subjects in the midst of oppression—the "Palestinian in Israel," the "gay in San Francisco," the "black in South Africa"—the Zapatistas evoked a common struggle against neoliberalism. Furthermore, by articulating the common oppression through poetic prose, the Zapatistas invoked the humanity in us all. The most important thing behind the mask was the "marginalized, exploited human being in this world."[15] The Zapatistas made their point by refusing to let the media take control of their collective resistance and single out "the one" charismatic leader. Instead, they boldly declared, "¡Todos somos Marcos!" (We are all Marcos!).

The world would come to realize that this kind of prose would become an important tactic for the Zapatistas. The Zapatistas unapologetically took to an exploration of subjectivities and discussions on economic and social oppression via multiple dialogues, poetry, encuentros, and other social technologies.[16] Furthermore, emphasizing a cosmic view of relationality, the Zapatistas requested an engagement and a dialogue with other struggling communities around the world. They called for people and sites of resistance to come to the table to dialogue without false government language and discourse. With a new language, Zapatistas believed then, as they do now, that encuentros were important, self-reflexive exercises that engendered community building and incited critical consciousness.

Zapatismo at the Popular Resource Center

I learned about the Zapatistas through my involvement with the PRC and in conversation with others in the Eastlos artivista community. What was initially striking to me was how they would repeatedly use poetry-like expression to communicate their ideas. But subjectivity is an embodied reality, and both the conscious and subconscious are more effectively articulated through creative expression. According to Laura E. Pérez, poetry and writing are, from Gloria Anzaldúa's perspective, for example, "image-making practice[s] that can shape and transform what we imagine," what we "are able to perceive," and what we "are able to give material embodiment" to.[17]

The historian Lisa Lowe has also emphasized the importance of culture production: "This is not to argue that cultural struggle can ever be the exclusive site for practice; it is rather to argue that if the state suppresses dissent by governing subjects through rights, citizenship, and political representation, it is only through culture that we conceive and enact new subjects and practices in antagonism to the regulatory locus of the citizen-subject, by way of culture that we can question these modes of government."[18] And indeed, we were beginning to question more and more as the events grew in participants and attendants at the PRC and Centro Regeneración. Art and culture production as mediums to articulate Chican@ identity and struggles were an important political force in Movimiento times.[19] But art or cultural work was sometimes not centralized or taken as seriously as the "political work." Indeed, one can think of producers of public art, including mural painters, community musicians, songwriters, and the quintessential group El Teatro Campesino, as prime examples.[20] But even in Movimiento times there was still a predominant performer/audience divide. The Zapatista uprising was an inspiring moment in the Chican@ East LA art scene for reasons concerning both its methods and its tactics. Zapatista tactics were unconventional, filled with compelling questions, and open to possibilities. Music did not have to be the "soundtrack" to the movement but rather became a movement tactic itself. In this way, an artist could include others in the process, not just those who kept up with the latest political or theoretical material.

The Zapatista approach also centered community and embodied knowledge through the encuentros. Rather than conceive of our communities as deprived and lacking in resources, we began to acknowledge and value the relationships and ways of being we already inhabited. An asset-based assessment of our communities changed our perspective and highlighted the tools we might have been overlooking.

Unique to the Zapatista movement was the degree of intimacy we were able to have with the communities. Although Marcos served as the spokesperson and seized almost every opportunity to speak about the Zapatista struggle, the power was never centralized in him. Instead, Zapatista organizing was done through *comandantes* in various regions. Quetzal Flores comments that "unlike other indigenous movements we had a direct relationship with the Zapatistas. Not with Marcos but with the direct communities and the local *comandancia*. . . . We chose the Zapatistas because it resonated with our struggle. Their ideas of not taking state power but rather building a new world were all new to us."[21] As Gustavo Esteva asserted, "They are not a fish that swims in the sea of the people, as Che Guevara would define a guerilla. They *are* the sea, not the fish: the uprising was the collective decision of hundreds of communities not interested in power. And they are not a revolutionary group in search of popular support to seize power."[22] We began to see Zapatismo as an essence, an "attitude," a way of being and seeing the world.

Besides the worldwide circulated communiqués that the Zapatistas would publish via the internet, there were also various community members who formed study groups to discuss Zapatista philosophy. One of the most important figures in my learning process was Roberto Gonzalez Flores. The director of the National Commission for Democracy in Mexico (NCDM), Lydia Brazon, was also a central figure, but her activities with the NCDM prevented her from participating regularly with us.

In 1996, Gonzalez Flores was granted a Fulbright research grant to study the organizing methods of the Zapatistas, particularly the gendered movement within it. Gonzalez Flores was an avid reader of the Zapatista philosophy and formed study groups through the NCDM or independently in his home. He was an organic intellectual and teacher with years of experience as an organizer in the Chicano movement.[23] Gonzalez Flores lived close to the PRC and participated in and frequented the events there, witnessing and contributing to the energy that repeatedly manifested in the space.[24] In this regard, the artivista efforts did not solely revolve around artists or young people. The movement included an older generation of thinkers and community organizers from previous generations who mentored, but were also challenged by, the current youth organizers and ongoing dialogues and community efforts. Gonzalez Flores examined the gender struggle within the Zapatista uprising; gender issues were a central part of the Zapatista movement. As recognized by many Zapatista scholars, such as Maylei Blackwell and Alex Khasnabish, the adopting of the Women's Revolutionary Laws was an important step within Zapatista communities. Prior to coming out to the world, the women within the movement had an uprising of their own and demanded basic rights for women within their own social structure. The laws stipulated the right to choose marriage partners, to determine how many children to have or not have, and to join the army if they so wished. The Zapatista women, as important advocates of indigenous women's rights, gained international attention with the Women's Revolutionary Laws. Gonzalez Flores's Fulbright research experience, which later became a part of his dissertation, focused on the informal transnational learning networks between the Zapatistas and Chican@s.[25]

The Chicana feminist historian Maylei Blackwell maps how the presence of women's participation in the EZLN has had a significant impact on various political scales. Blackwell states that "by weaving in and between local, national, and transnational spaces, indigenous women have forged their own forms of differential consciousness and political subjectivity based on a fusion of experiences and discourses from those multiple locales."[26] The Zapatista movement managed to challenge static representations of indigenous people and culture as pure, pious, and unchanging, at the mercy of modernity and progress. The strong woman presence in the Zapatista movement, and in particular Comandante Ramona's visibility, and dissident poetic prose were inspiring. They defied the discourse on indigenous women in government, on national and international scales, as well as within their own kinship and community discourse. Their multiple strategies decentered hegemonic "feminist" and "leftist" understandings of what it means to be a woman in the fight for social justice and instead confronted the relations of domination present at various scales of power.[27] Zapatista women also took to exploring new forms of citizenship, rights, and responsibilities, specifically indigenous autonomy and self-determination. Many will agree that the gendered movement within the Zapatista uprising has been crucial to the success of the EZLN. Despite their international acclaim, however, they are not free of challenges in the interpersonal sphere. To this day Zapatista women continue to struggle for equality within their own communities.[28] The gendered struggle within the Zapatista movement, in conjunction with the use of creative expression to inform the world of their struggles and their desire to connect across borders into other sites of struggle, all contributed to inspiring new hope and imagination in the Chican@ artivista mind-set.

Building Zapatista Relationships in East Los Angeles

The Mexican activist Javier Eloriaga was the head of "El Frente Zapatista" in Mexico City. The Frente Zapatista de Liberación Nacional (Zapatista Front of National Liberation, or FZLN) was the nonclandestine political arm within the Zapatista movement and was in direct contact with the Zapatistas.[29] The NCDM informed LA's community of organizers and supporters of the Zapatistas that Eloriaga would engage in a speaking tour to raise money for Comandante Ramona's medical bills. Comandante Ramona was a leading member of the clandestine movement and had fallen ill with cervical cancer. The PRC had produced art shows to raise money for Comandante Ramona's medical bills, and at one such event Eloriaga bore witness to the community of artivistas and the level of organization we had achieved. Eloriaga was so impressed with the community that he asked for some of the members to visit Chiapas, Mexico, and proposed an encuentro with the *comandancia*.

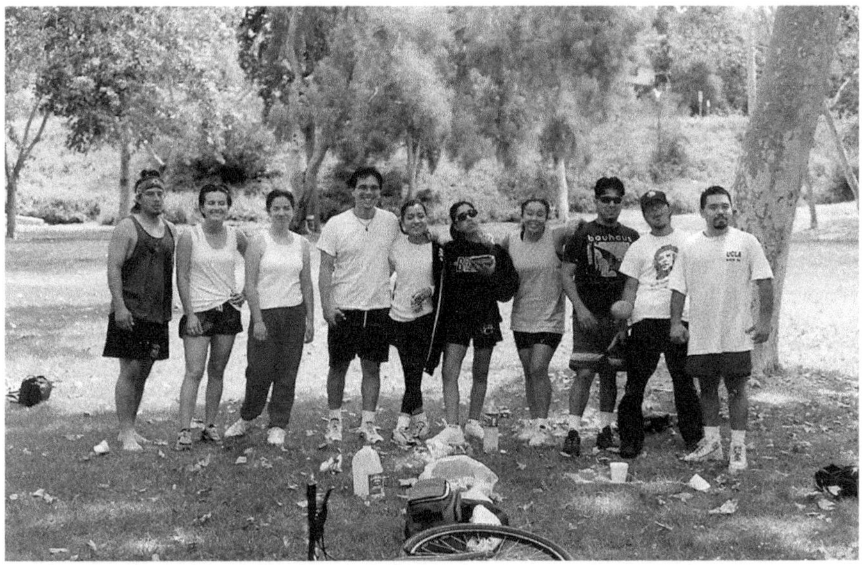

Some of the Zapatista Run participants at the finish line in Arroyo Seco Park. From left to right: Javier Lujan, Suyapa Portillo, Lucy Castro, Mark Torres, me, Claudia Miranda, Emily Martinez Toledo, Raul Baltazar, Joe "Peps" Galarza, and Mario "Chivo" Valenzuela.

Per Eloriaga's request, in December of 1996, a small contingency embarked on a trip to Chiapas. Quetzal Flores, Jose Ramirez, Gabriel Tenorio, and Roberto Gonzalez Flores made the trip, which entailed visiting two different communities—Oventic and La Realidad. Quetzal Flores recalls, "In Oventic, we met with Comandante David and proposed an encuentro Chicano in California. He suggested we do it in Oventic instead, due to the fact that it was the community that was the most organized."[30] Flores continues, "So we went to La Realidad and we met with [Subcomandante] Marcos and he told us exactly the same thing. Almost word for word."[31]

While on the 1996 trip to Chiapas, the group was invited to meet Ramona after a successful surgery. During this meeting, Ramona expressed the same sentiment as her comrades. Ramona had been born and raised in Oventic, and she thought it would be the right community for such an encuentro. The small group returned to East LA energized and ready to deliver the news. After being informed of the trip and the comandante's wishes, the groups began to meet once a week at the PRC to plan the possibility of having a cultural encuentro with the Zapatistas. We began to devise ways of fortifying our relationships in order to have a coherent, well-organized encuentro, one that would center music, art, *teatro* (theater), and dance as the tools of dialogue.

The Big Frente Zapatista

Chicana art . . . has responded, in greater or lesser measures, to the rise of particular social, economic, and political forces. Some of the most salient of these have been the rise of postindustrialist, digital-based production and distribution systems enabling accelerated, transnational flows of information; the restructuring of business and labor; the disempowerment of workers and the growing relocation of unskilled manual labor jobs in manufacturing industries from the United States to the third world and elsewhere, including the Mexican side of the border.

LAURA E. PÉREZ, *Chicana Art*

The term *artivista*, the conflation of the words *artista* and *activista*, coincides with Laura E. Pérez's recognition of Chicana artists as "intellectuals whose work embodies theories of resistance and visionary ideals of social change."[32] We began to use the term more frequently, sometimes interchanging it with *zapartista* (Zapatista + *activista* + *artista*). With everybody's eye on the Zapatista movement, a call was put out inviting whomever was interested in planning for an encuentro between Chican@s and Zapatistas. Most of the people who answered the call were college students between the ages of eighteen and twenty-five.

The Big Frente Zapatista (BFZ) became the organizing body for the proposed encuentro. It was a playful title based on the Frente Zapatista de Liberación Nacional. As previously mentioned, El Frente was a civil society organization in support of the EZLN. The BFZ assumed the Aztlan connection. We quickly formulated a callout to the community that read:

El Big Frente Zapatista invites you to participate in the First Cultural Gathering for Humanity and Against Neoliberalismo. This Encuentro will take place in Chiapas, Mexico, between August 5–10. . . . The Big Frente is a collective of artists, students, youth, workers, and cultural promoters from various communities and organizations. We work with all those who have been excluded and marginalized by neoliberalism and who have been inspired by the Zapatista movement. We are members of civil society, uniting in the efforts of Zapatismo, not only to support the EZLN in Mexico, but also to actively participate in our own transformation "desde nuestra propia trinchera" [from our own trench]. The BFZ is dedicated to promote the work of the EZLN, FZLN, and any other organization working towards the creation of just societies for all humanity. In order to engage in this process we have organized the following Cultural Encuentro for Humanity and Against Neoliberalism.[33]

The BFZ flyer invitation also included the goals and objectives of the encuentro, to be achieved "through dialogue and collective cultural and artistic creation":

* Begin the process of building a strategic alliance between the Chicana/o community in the US and the Zapatista Indigenous community in Mexico.

* Develop a process for self-reflection that will deepen our understanding of our history and our present situation, in order to facilitate the development of democratic and inclusive forms of organizing within our communities.

* Develop a deeper understanding of the Zapatista model of organizing for building a just society towards the goals of true democracy and autonomy.[34]

The call was circulated by word of mouth, early primitive email, and fax.

The Organizing Process

Organizing meetings were scheduled every Sunday for about a year and were mostly held at the Centro Regeneración in Highland Park. The informal network consisted of artists working in various genres and mediums, including visual and graffiti art, spoken word, music, dance, artisan craft, poetry, and filmmaking. The BFZ also consisted of community organizers who might not have practiced artistic expression but who acknowledged the value in creative and artistic work and the inherent power in the practice. Among the talented body of community organizers were Laura Palomares, Suyapa Portillo, and Miguel Rodriguez. Organizers held countless meetings and fundraising events that in retrospect strengthened the alliances between the groups and artists.

Sunday meetings were primarily about collectively discussing Zapatista philosophy and communiqués. We were also adamant, however, about building trust within the collective. Although most of the artists were not "formally" trained, we each had the responsibility of facilitating creative ways of engaging group dialogue for our weekly meetings, such as icebreakers or trust exercises from our respective disciplines. The group Chusma, for example, shared various theater exercises. As the weeks progressed our discussions became more intimate. Sometimes the conversations brought up childhood memories of violence and sexual abuse. Some of the women and men shared experiences with spousal abuse or battery. The instilled trust initiated a kind of sharing that could have been incriminating or shameful for some of the participants; however, there was a space of forgiveness and a know-how among us that allowed these moments to come up without fear or shame. In these trenches we were safe. Artivistas attempted to expand the boundaries and possibilities of communication. Stuart Hall has stated that "without language meaning could not be exchanged in the world."[35] Indeed, abstract theories speak to nonlinear sensibilities capable of shifting consciousness and thus invoking critical change. Artivistas enacted this through communal creative interactions.

The weekly meetings were also an opportunity to plan concerts and events to generate funds for the trip. We wanted all who wished to attend the encuentro to do so. The fundraising was constant as events, concerts, and art shows filled our weeks. There was a "Zapatista Run," where the community sponsored runners whose partial route took place in the LA River Basin. Visual artists designed and sold merchandise. Omar and Jose Ramirez, for example, designed T-shirts that displayed self-designed images on the front, with the Women's Revolutionary Laws or the Himno Zapatista (Zapatista anthem) printed on the back. Once we raised enough funds, the community organizers Laura Palomares and Suyapa Portillo left two months earlier than the rest of the encuentro participants to make arrangements and to ensure that we had personal contact with Zapatista organizers on the Mexican side of the border. The BFZ sustained Palomares and Portillo as they prepared for our arrival in Chiapas and kept us appraised of the food and lodging logistics. Funds for the encuentro had to be given to the Zapatistas ahead of time so they could purchase food supplies from their own networks and communities. Recycling of money within the communities was important to the overall Zapatista emphasis of autonomy throughout the region. On August 5, 1997, one hundred and twenty Chican@ artivistas, mostly from the Los Angeles area,[36] set out for Chiapas, Mexico, to partake in the Encuentro Cultural Chicano/Indígena por la Humanidad y contra el Neoliberalismo.

La Neza

Before arriving in Oventic, we had some business to take care of in Mexico City. The BFZ were scattered among different hotels and hostels across the city, but we were able to plan mini encuentros with the FZLN and Zapatista supporters and artist collectives in Mexico City. We also managed to raise funds for an autonomous school in the infamous colonia Nezahualcóyotl, or La Neza.[37] Barrio Neza had been founded as a squatter town and was known for rampant crime and violence. We had been in contact with the organizers of a Zapatista-inspired school in the region. Quetzal, along with Aztlan Underground and Chusma, were invited for the school's inauguration. The trip into La Neza was to deliver the funds we had raised and also to play and to participate in the festivities associated with the school's opening.

The morning of our trip into La Neza, a group of us were assaulted on the subway near the Palacio de Bellas Artes. At knifepoint Gabriel Tenorio's and Dante Pascuzzo's money and passports were taken. Quetzal Flores was stabbed on the right side of his rib cage and taken into La Cruz Roja, the Mexican federal health facility. He was released that same afternoon and insisted that we continue our journey into barrio Neza. We all thought he was crazy but figured the worst had happened, and we proceeded to make our way.

The trip into La Neza would be difficult. The barrio was infamous for its assaults and violence, and many *taxistas*, taxi drivers, would not entertain the idea of driving near it. Once they learned where we were headed they would immediately respond, "No. ¡Yo no voy 'pa ya'!" (I don't go there!) and race off. One taxista finally took a moment to ask, "Why would you all want to go there? Do you know how dangerous it is?" The taxista then explained to us that even if we were to get into La Neza, we would have a difficult time getting out since no taxista in their right mind would be caught dead in that part of the city after dark. We offered more money and asked if he could take us *and* bring us back. He agreed on one condition. On his return to pick us up he would drive by the school. If we were not outside with our instruments and ready to go at the exact time we agreed, he would drive off and we would be left to find a place to stay overnight. We agreed, paid him half the amount, and began our journey into barrio Neza.

Every group made their way into barrio Neza on their own. Our band, Quetzal, all rode in the same taxi. Taxistas in Mexico are aggressive drivers. Rather than witness the madness I closed my eyes and quietly prayed that we would all arrive safely. There were fires on the street corners and tattered homes and squatters.[38] As we drove deeper into La Neza, not only was the degree of poverty visually present but there was also a tangible desperate energy. But when we finally made it to the concert and dialogued with the founders of the school and community members, we were floored. We shared some of our music, and community members and parents shared with us their struggles—the origins of the school and how they had managed to build it. It was impressive and inspiring.

The celebration had not officially ended, but our time was up, and we waited outside the school with our bags and instruments in hand. The Los Angeles–based graffiti artist Nuke and some Mexico-based artists were tagging up the outside school facade wall. There was also a bustle of women and children of all ages coming in and out of the school as the smell of food and music was blaring. As we waited outside, the taxista slowly drove by and recognized us. He then circled around and stopped. He got out of his vehicle, looked around, and asked, "¿Qué está pasando aquí?" (What is going on here?). He was impressed and had never imagined something like this could happen in a place like La Neza. He took a moment to enjoy the scenery and felt comfortable enough to go inside to use the restroom while we loaded up. Once we were all in, the taxista informed us that he was going to try and make it out of La Neza as quickly as possible, so he asked us to duck out of view. Although his car was visibly marked as a taxi, he wanted to appear as if he had no passengers and thus diminish the risk of being held up. We took his advice and lay down, ducked, or hunched out of view. The taxista then began his skillful maneuver back. He sped, ran red lights, and barely slowed down for fear of being ambushed. Although it sounds dangerous, he had a way of making you feel safe. He was a funny chilango fast-talker and told us about his life and the hustle of the city. He had been held up various times on the job and seemed to enjoy recounting all his adventures and close calls. Thanks to him we arrived quickly and safely. We paid him the remainder of the money and mentioned we planned to go to Chiapas the next day. He happily offered to take us to the central bus station in Mexico City. The following morning, he was leaning on his VW Bug, sipping coffee, waiting to take us to La TAPO.

Encuentro Cultural Chicano/Indígena por la Humanidad y contra el Neoliberalismo

Too much time has gone by, and the taxista's name escapes me. He, like many people in Mexico City, had been curious about us. Quetzal members were a racially mixed group, and we stood out everywhere we went. Dante Pascuzzo is Italian American, Tylana Enomoto is of Japanese and Thai descent, and Danilo Torres is half-Nicaraguan and half-Mexican. The only group members of Mexican descent were Gabriel Tenorio, Quetzal Flores, and me. Once we opened our mouths to speak, however, we were clearly identifiable as Chican@. Our *pocho* Spanish as well as our way of dressing were dead give-aways. Pascuzzo decided not to continue the trip into Chiapas. My youngest sister, Karla, who was with us, also decided to go home after the two days in the Distrito Federal. Those of us left from the group were Enomoto, Torres, Tenorio, Flores, and me. There were so many others from the BFZ who were making their way into Chiapas that we chartered a bus. It was a long and windy eight-hour trip into San Cristóbal de las Casas, and most everyone on the bus was from the BFZ contingent.

In preparation for our trip we were advised not to reveal that we were heading to Chiapas for the encuentro. Commiserating with a "rebel army" on Mexican soil was, after all, a crime. If we were stopped or questioned, we were instructed by the *comandancia* to state we were there as "ecotourists." This came in handy, as our bus was stopped often, and some of the women and men were escorted off the bus for questioning.

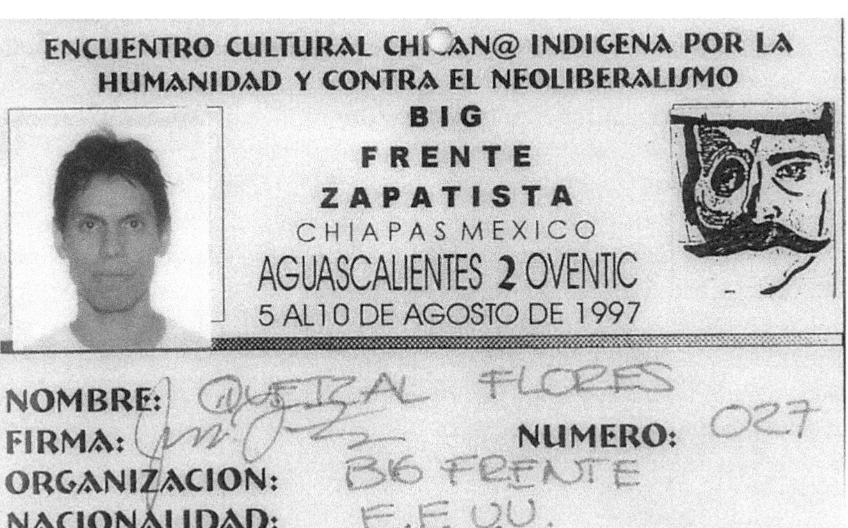

Quetzal Flores identification for the Encuentro Cultural Chicano/Indigena por la Humanidad y contra el Neoliberalismo.

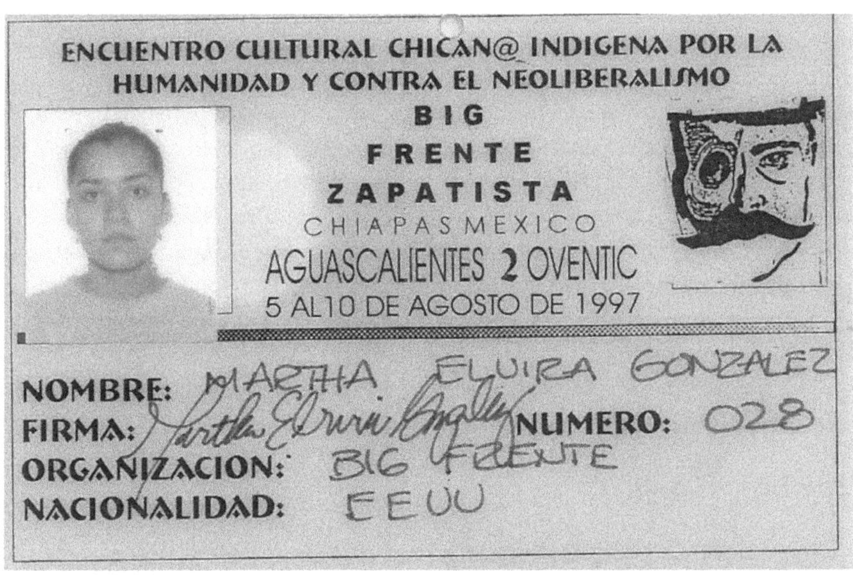

My identification for the Encuentro Cultural Chicano/Indigena por la Humanidad y contra el Neoliberalismo.

Once we arrived in San Cristóbal, we spent a day preparing and acquiring our *credenciales*, or credentials, as issued by the Zapatistas in order to step foot onto the autonomous community of Oventic. Walking through the streets of San Cristóbal, we would repeatedly bump into BFZ members or other Chican@s from Los Angeles, San Diego, or Long Beach. Some of the shops or restaurants would blare their radios, many of which were tuned to local or clandestine radio stations. The night before we were to travel into Oventic, we heard a radio announcer say, "Le damos la bienvenida a los chicanos de Los Ángeles que vienen al primer Encuentro Cultural Chicano/Indígena por la Humanidad y contra el Neoliberalismo!"[39] Sitting at the dinner table, we smiled at each other and tried to look inconspicuous. The following day at dawn, a chartered bus filled with BFZ members took the final trip into Oventic, Aguascalientes II.[40] It was August 5, 1997.

"Nos Encontramos"—"We Have Found Each Other"

We arrived at Oventic a bit after sunrise. Comandante David greeted us. In order to keep their communities safe, they needed to make sure we were not carrying arms, alcohol, or drugs. Alcohol and drugs were strictly prohibited in Zapatista communities, and we were asked to respect their laws. Once we had all been searched, we were greeted by the community of masked Zapatistas, who lined up on the side of the road in a *Soul Train*–like formation. As we walked down toward the *cancha* (athletic court), the Zapatistas clapped and yelled, "¡Bienvenidos!" Many Chican@s from our group cried, overtaken with emotion. We danced all the way down to the basketball court or jumped and clapped along. It was an amazing moment. When we reached the bottom of the *cancha*, there was a small marimba band of masked Zapatista musicians who were playing *porra*-like tunes.[41] The Zapatistas outnumbered us as they filled the stadium seating. At least a thousand indigenous people were in attendance the first day.

The format of our visit to Chiapas and the encuentro had been previously discussed with the Zapatistas and was outlined for all participants as follows:

    ** August 1, 1997
    ** 1) - Tentative - CONCERT IN El D.F. - "Todos Somos Zapatista" - Several Chicana/o and Mexicana/o artists will be performing for the purpose of attracting the attention of the media as well as civil society to the Chicana/o Indigena Encuentro Cultural and the Zapatista struggle against neoliberalism and for humanity.

    ** August 4, 1997
    ** 2) - SAN CRISTOBAL WELCOMING - This is an effort to help

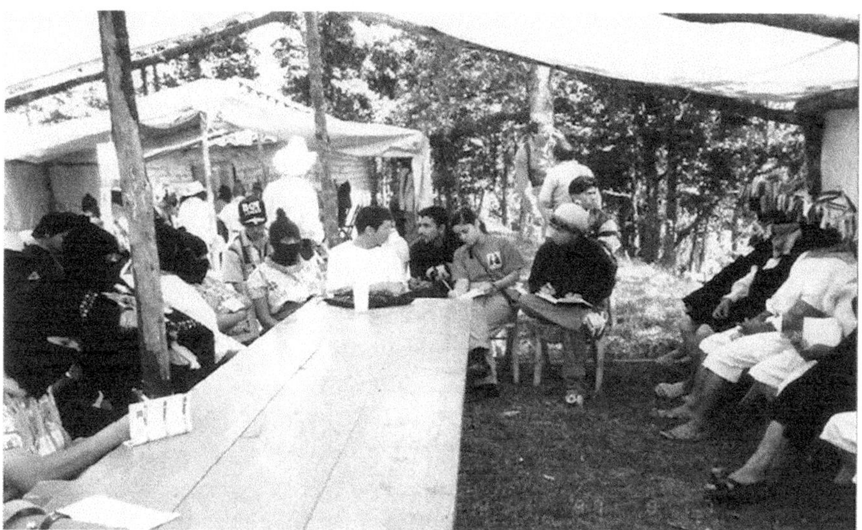

One of many Encuentro tables on the Dia de La Mujer, where participants discussed health issues in communities. In attendance were Zapatista women who spoke Tzotzil, Tzetzal, Tojolabal, and Nan. Also present were Dr. Michael Wada, Gabriel Tenorio, Lisa Rocha, and me. Courtesy of Javier Martinez.

establish a broader support base for Zapatismo and to develop stronger relationship with the Zapatista community in the City of San Cristobal de las Casas.

** August 5, 1997
** 3) - BIENVENIDOS A OVENTIC - An opening ceremony/welcoming event, as a chance to settle in and hear Zapatista representatives address all participants (indigenous community members, and Chicana/o community members) from the main stage.

** August 6, 1997
** 4) - NOS ENCONTRAMOS - A day dedicated to presenting the realities of our respective lives as communities and establish a better understanding of/for each other and ourselves.

** August 7, 1997
** 5) - LA MUJER - Artistic expression and dialogue focused on the implementation of the EZLN Revolutionary Laws for all Women in order to ensure the full participation of women in all aspects of community reconstruction and redefinition. This day is also focusing on the role of men in the implementation of these laws.

** August 8, 1997
** 6) - ART & CULTURE AS A TOOL OF RESISTANCE AND RECONSTRUCTION - A day to focus on the use of different artistic media for the purpose of political action, education and reconstruction; together we will learn from each other and create strategies through art.

** August 9, 1997
** 7) - AUTONOMY - A day to examine the concrete areas of political, economic, cultural, and educational autonomy as a necessary foundation for rebuilding and redefining community.

** August 10, 1997
** 8) - CLOSING CEREMONY - A day of self-reflection. This is not a day of good-byes, but a day of welcoming the birth of a new organized effort towards the reconstruction of our communities through the process of autonomy in the US. This is also a day for the creation of the first Chicana/o Artist Declaration for Humanity and against neoliberalism.

** August 11, 1997
** 9) - FUNDRAISING CONCERT IN SAN CRISTOBAL - A closing ceremony in the Plaza de Toros to begin the process of a united front between Mexican artists and Chicana/o artists from the US. "Rompiendo el Cerco."[42]

As the schedule reflects, we agreed that the days would each have a theme, or a *dicho*, and all activities would revolve around the theme. We began with breakfast. We then had the *mesas de diálogo*, or table discussions; followed by lunch; and then *talleres*, or workshops. We then had dinner and shared what each group had worked on.

The Creative Process

The first day was titled "Nos Encontramos" (We have found each other).[43] The goal was to get to know each other and to share our respective cultures, challenges, and survival strategies. Dialogue was slow. The Zapatistas are not a homogenous group, as they are made up of various Mayan cultures and languages. Some of the languages we heard spoken in the encuentro were Tzotzil, Tzeltal, Tojolabal, and Mam, among others. The translation from these languages into *castellano*,[44] or Spanish, and vice versa was a tedious process. We were, however, invested in and dedicated to being present for each other and were dedicated to the *convivencia*. I believe that whatever was lost in translation was partly recovered in being present and interacting with each other and the overall creative process.

After the *mesas de diálogo*, participants had to choose a creative workshop. The goal was to engage in the creative process as a community. Encuentro participants could choose workshops conducted by artivistas in *teatro*, poetry, music, graffiti and mural painting, and dance. The dancer Janelle Gonzales and I were in charge of the dance workshops. On certain days, I was also able to participate in the music workshops. Alberto Ibarra, Marisol Torres, and Danny Torres of Chusma and Richard Montoya of Culture Clash facilitated the *teatro* workshops. Felicia Montes, Liza Hita, and Cristina Gorocica conducted the poetry workshops. Nuke, Omar Ramirez, Arnoldo "Zeta" Vargas, and Rachel Negrete Thorson were in charge of the mural painting workshops. And finally, Rosa Marta Zarate, José Quetzal Flores, Gabriel Tenorio, Tylana Enomoto, and Claudia Gonzalez conducted the music workshops. Additional members of the BFZ floated around to different workshops, depending on where they were needed the most. Yaotl, Joe "Peps" Galarza, and DJ Bean from Aztlan Underground were among the multitalented musicians and artists who were able to partake in more than one medium. The organizers Laura Palomares and Suyapa Portillo floated around making sure logistics were set and that we stayed on schedule.

Teatro Workshops

The *teatro* presentations produced multiact plays that were powerful and informative moments. The day dedicated to *la mujer* (the woman) was most inspiring. Participants of the theater workshops decided to create something that addressed indigenous women's health and the abuse of power by government doctors and clinics. The morning dialogues informed the creative process, and the plays mirrored the testimonios and discussions that took place at the dialogue tables.

One particular one-act play portrayed the perils of an indigenous woman trying to seek medical attention in the city. Directed by members of Chusma, the play had a *rascuache*-like feel.[45] The doctor was played by the Culture Clash member Richard Montoya, who wore a vaudevillian half mask. Montoya was animated and loud in his portrayal of the money-hungry government doctor. The act began with an indigenous woman walking into a town clinic, seeking help for discomfort in her abdomen. Her accompanying male partner communicates to the doctor in *castellano* that his wife is in pain. The doctor quickly issues her contraceptives and ushers them out. The scene continues with other indigenous women coming into the clinic and complaining of various ailments but repeatedly being sent out of the office

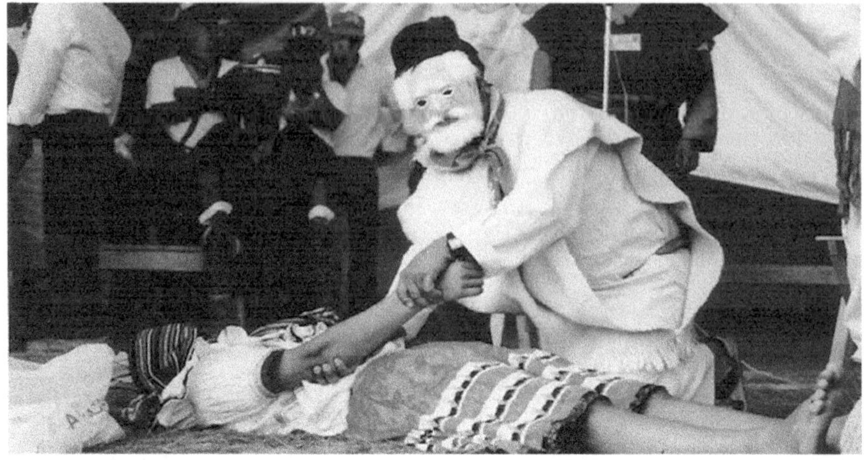

Teatro workshop participants performing their theater piece for the community. Courtesy of Laura Palomares.

with contraceptives in hand. In the end, the first *indígena* woman's pain becomes so severe that she gives birth to a healthy, strong Zapatista baby in the doctor's clinic. Upon hearing the news, the evil government doctor runs out in the middle of the *cancha* and drops dead of a heart attack. The stadium of *indígenas* cheered as the Zapatista women and their partners boarded the imaginary bus and playfully ran over him as the scene concluded. The audience laughed at the many jokes and slapstick antics. The skits always ended with powerful resolutions.[46]

Teatro Chusma members were effective facilitators in the workshops and had a way of bringing out the best in all the participants. The plays reflected many perils that indigenous women experienced in the city. Indeed, government clinics are not concerned with the health of indigenous women. Quality care is hard to find or completely lacking. If *indígenas* receive care at all, it is with reluctant indifference, and they are repeatedly prescribed contraceptives regardless of their ailments. This is of course a deliberate attempt to lessen the growth of their population. As Chican@s in the United States, we could relate to inferior healthcare and to the indifference. The discussion and skits prompted us to think of the many ways *our* relationship with the US healthcare system and its doctors was strikingly familiar to that of Mayan men and women.

Collective Songwriting Workshops

The process of writing song lyrics was tedious. "Nos Encontramos" was the topic of the day, and we had spent an hour composing lyrical ideas. The *cabaña* was filled with chatter as the participants attempted to come up with the next line to the composition. Rosa Marta Zarate was a former nun who was invited by the Zapatista women to participate in the encuentro. Zarate was a talented singer and guitar player and facilitated the songwriting workshops. She was an effective leader as she encouraged and moderated the various silences and outbursts of ideas in the midst of creative energy. The workshop was filled with masked indigenous people and Chican@s who all focused their attention on a poster board mounted on the wall of the *cabaña*. It was chaotic as the plethora of languages filled the room: Chican@s speaking English and broken Spanish, Zapatistas speaking *castellano*, Tzotzil, Tzeltal, and Tojolabal, and Mexican observers speaking Spanish and broken English. Rosa Marta Zarate, however, kept everyone on task.

Zarate had a comedic way of diffusing opposing ideas on wording and phrasing. We showed our consensus by a show of hands, and Zarate would affirm our collective visions by writing the final lyric on the poster board. Some Zapatistas wanted a corrido-like form, and the Chican@s wanted a hip-hop feel. Other Zapatistas felt our song should be more festive and danceable. In the end we titled the song "El grito de alegría" and chose to make it a danceable cumbia. Our band, Quetzal, later recorded this song on our debut album. "El grito de alegría" has since been played in venues all over the United States, Mexico, Japan, and Canada. The lyrics state:

El pueblo con paso lento va ganando la lucha
La tristeza que hoy llevamos será un grito de alegría.

El gobierno manipula encarcela y asesina,
Nosotros los Zapatistas romperemos las cadenas.

Zapatistas somos todos y luchamos por la tierra.
Dignidad, paz y justicia, libertad son nuestras metas.

Si nos robaron la tierra, si nos quitaron el pan,
El pueblo que marcha unido, lograra la libertad.
¡El pueblo que marcha unido vencerá!

The contents of the song reflect the day's topic, which included our respective histories of colonization, war, disease, enslavement, and loss of ancestral lands. "El grito de alegría" is a rearticulation of the more common phrase "war cry." "El grito de alegría" was instead "the cry of happiness," a celebration of the present, the process, and the hope we felt in each other's presence. Importantly, through the collective songwriting process we continued the dialogue that we began in the *mesas*. For the most part, both the dialogue and the creative work fostered a space to share one's testimonios

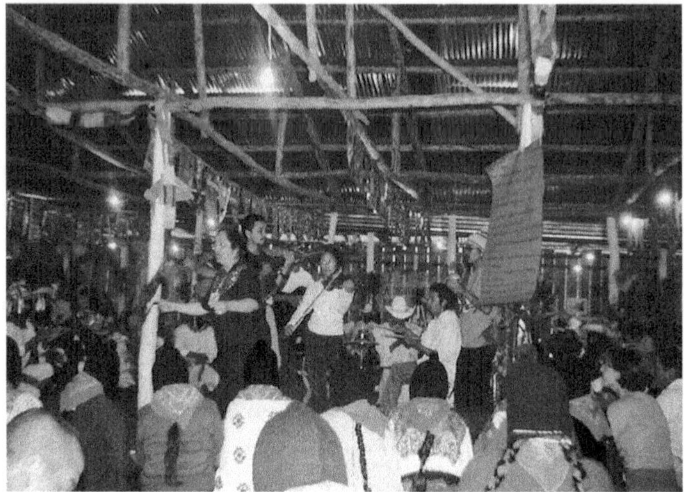

Rosa Marta Zarate and members of Quetzal facilitating a collective songwriting workshop.

and experiences that intrinsically brought us closer as community and led us into greater critical consciousness.

Conflict and Citation through Creative Expression

It is inevitable for discussions on race, class, nation, and sexuality to arise in the dialogue and creative process. One such moment arose on a day dedicated to *la mujer*.

Covered with flowering cornstalks, Oventic is in a small valley that leads down to a river between two steep mountains. Every walk down to the base of camp meant a steep walk back up to the different landings that held the *talleres*. I had walked down to base camp to speak to one of the organizers, and as I made my walk back up to the music workshop, I decided to take a detour to see what the muralists were creating. The side wall of Oventic's community hall was prepped and they were ready to paint. They had spent the morning dialoguing and had ideas for the mural. Mayan women in Chiapas engage in creative expression on a daily basis. For example, they take great pride in the design and fabrication of their clothing. It is a coming-of-age ritual for a young woman to weave and embroider a *capa* (cape) with unique flower motifs that will identify her for the rest of her life. The reiterative and citational practice in the embroidery of self-designed flowers culminates in womanhood.[47] When asked to paint on the mural wall, there was little to no apprehension. Due to the fact that it was an encuentro between Chican@s

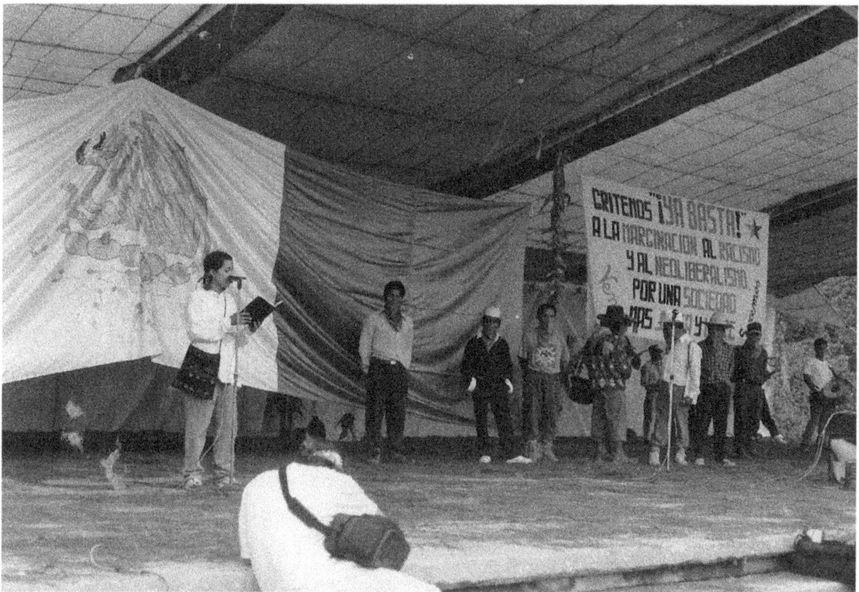

Giving a closing reflection. Courtesy of Javier Martinez.

and *indígenas*, most observers—many who were Mexican nationals, Spanish Europeans, and Australians—were generally conscious about not interfering in the dialogue. But two women from Spain interfered on this day and urged a Mayan participant to paint the sign of Venus on the mural wall. They went so far as to insist by guiding the Mayan woman's hand, helping her to draw the symbol. Chicana participants painted their interpretations of womanhood, drawing moons and cornstalks, but never once attempting to impose their ideas on Mayan participants. The Mayan participants were kind and appeared not to have a problem with the Spanish women's insistence. The Chicana mural participants, however, were furious about the audacity and imposition, and a conflict ensued.

Sex performativity varies from culture to culture. When varying performativities come together in encounters such as these, versions of what gender is can clash, inform, or influence others. When confronted by the Chican@ participants for imposing their symbols, the Spanish observers felt unwelcomed and attacked. They felt that creative expression constituted a sharing of ideas, views, and influences and saw no problem in sharing their symbols with the Mayan participants. What was important to the Chican@s, however, was to be present—the idea was not to convert but rather to dialogue. The Chican@s were suddenly demonized by the Spanish women for not being "in the spirit" of the encuentro. The discussions that ensued revolved around competing notions of "woman" symbolism, race, colonization, and privilege. The Spanish women felt silenced, the Chican@s felt transgressed, and the *indígena* women felt indifferent—not necessarily bothered by the request—and felt unthreatened by the Spanish women's insistence. For the Chican@s, their histories and understanding of their own struggles in the United States, including white privilege and histories rooted in colonization, came to the surface. Why had the Spanish women interfered in a conversation that was not about them? By the same token, if this gesture did not bother the Mayan women, why did the Chican@s feel the need to speak up? Did the Chican@s feel the need to "protect" the Mayan women from the Spanish? I venture to say that the answers are not as relevant to the situation as much as the questions themselves. My point is that the conflicts during a moment of collective creative expression generated a fruitful discussion that is best articulated through an intersectional lens. Issues of race, class, nationality, and privilege are all embedded in the conflict that was generated through collective creative expression. This is a perfect example in my attempt to convey how convening through art for the purpose of social change plays out "theory in the flesh" via the collective as well.[48]

The legal scholar Kimberlé Crenshaw repeatedly addresses intersectionality as an important tool, not for some grand "totalizing theory of identity" but rather as an attempt to account for what Crenshaw refers to as the "multiple grounds of identity."[49] Art and creative expression highlight embodied knowledge, which can also bring about the "multiple grounds of identity" and how they are shaped, are negotiated, and exist amid economic, political, and cultural worlds.[50] With art or creative expression, intersectionality requires a personal introspection and a look at specificity that positivist traditions discourage. In this sense, intersectionality is, in effect, a creative analytic tool that has the ability to cut through institutional thought and structures embedded in positivist disciplines and laws, highlighting their blind spots. Collective creative art process is a parallel analytic tool.

The conflict at the encuentro brought about many discussions. I agree with Judith Butler when she states that there are no essential norms or laws of sex performativity.[51] Yet, at this stage in the neocolonial game, the kinds of performativity one engages in can be loaded with power. Which bodies mattered in the conflict? Which bodies imposed their symbols to be cited above all others? Who has the power to be cited, and who was being excluded by this act? Had the Spanish women considered the specificity of place they might have realized we were in the mountains of Chiapas in solidarity with the Zapatista struggle for economic, spiritual, and cultural survival. We were in the mountains distanced from all that represented colonial order, such as the city, industrialization, and endangerment of indigenous culture. Notions of universal sisterhood were questioned and dispelled.[52] As far as we were concerned, a relational view of each other did not mean overlooking or citing one another's symbols; it meant bearing witness to each other's expressions.

In the end, the Spanish women took their complaint against the Chican@s to the *comandancia*, who listened to both sides of the conflict. The *comandancia* asked if the Spanish women had understood that this was a Chican@ and Indigenous encuentro. The Spanish women asserted that "art" had to be an all-inclusive expression. In their view, they were not interrupting a dialogue but rather contributing to a piece of "art." The *comandancia* then asserted that the creative expression was also a part of the dialogue and invited the Spanish women to leave if they did not wish to abide by the encuentro arrangements. Because Portillo, Palomares, and the Chican@ muralists refused to issue an apology to the Spanish women, they packed their bags and left the following morning. Nevertheless, important points of discussion took place in the creative moment and well after the Spanish women departed.

Indigenous Pedagogy and Chican@ Artivista Praxis

We could not *be* without *being in relationship* with everything that surrounds us and is within us. Our reality, our ontology is the relationships.

The land is paramount for all indigenous societies. Their relationship to that land, their experience on that land shapes everything that is around them. . . . Land is another word for place, environment, your reality, the space you're in.

Shawn Wilson, Research Is Ceremony

As Shawn Wilson states, "Our ontology is the relationships."[53] The encuentro clearly demonstrates how relationship building through artistic expression was central to its purposes. Both Linda Tuhiwai Smith and Shawn Wilson advance an understanding of research by stressing the importance of relationships and accountability in the researcher and the research process. Research, its foundation in colonialism, and the practice that upholds its early beginnings are of course ethically troublesome.[54] Although I was not a formal researcher at the time of the encuentro, nor in my early years as a member of the artivista community, I have slowly engaged my community of artivistas as an indigenous researcher and ongoing observing participant. The indigenous scholars Smith and Wilson offer analytical tools that have kept me from falling too much into a colonialist framework even when speaking as an "insider" in the artivista community. As Smith asserts,

"Research is one of the ways in which the underlying code of imperialism and colonialism is both regulated and realized."[55] I understand that the academy is the "knowledge" engine for capitalism and that institutions are encouraged to uphold capitalist interests and in turn are rewarded through financial endorsement (e.g., tenure).

Wilson, being from the Cree nation, explores Canadian and Australian indigenous ontologies. Wilson comes to find that relationality and even geometric shapes like the circle are a common thread among many indigenous people's belief systems. "It's egalitarian," Wilson writes, "it's relational, it's a structure that supports an inclusion, a wholeness."[56] He continues, "Right or wrong; validity; statistically significant; worthy or unworthy: value judgments lose their meaning. What is more important and meaningful is fulfilling a role and obligations in the research relationship—that is, being accountable to your relations."[57] Indigenous pedagogy extends a relational view of the self as part and parcel to many other relationships—human and cosmic. The Zapatistas' call to dialogue with other struggling communities around the globe imparts a similar philosophy. Through twenty-first-century tools, they communicate indigenous relationality via the internet and other forms of social media.

Conclusion

So, I mark this as a beginning, but it is a beginning that affirms a profound term that Maldonado Torres has called the "decolonial turn." The questions proliferate at this time and the answers are difficult. They require placing, again, an emphasis on methodologies that work with our lives, so the sense of responsibility is maximal. How do we learn about each other? How do we do it without harming each other but with the courage to take up a weaving of the everyday that may reveal deep betrayals? How do we cross without taking over? With whom do we do this work? The theoretical here is immediately practical. . . . How do we practice with each other engaging in dialogue at the colonial difference? How do we know when we are doing it?

María Lugones, "Toward a Decolonial Feminism"

The processes of creative expression as tools of dialogue are promising ways of reaching the fundamental questions María Lugones poses. As a participant observer in the 1997 encuentro, I witnessed how conviviality became an important language to speak in the neoliberal age, or as Lugones states, in "the decolonial turn."[58] The process of collective artistry during the 1997 encuentro helped participants (Chican@, Spanish, and Mayan) draw out and encounter multiple subjectivities. Through artistic processes, our differences were highlighted and deconstructed, while existing in multiple and intersectional ways in our daily lives. Encuentro participants produced multiple multimedia works that were not made for profit nor made in competition among participants. Painting a collective mural or writing songs in community, along with other works produced via artistic conviviality, fostered interactions and conflicts that gave way to important discussions. The negotiation of multiple grounds of identity was key in articulating the importance of not ignoring nor attempting to theorize that our differences were insignificant or that one was more important than the other; but rather, we began to collectively imagine, just as the Zapatistas urged, "a world where many worlds could exist."[59]

The moments of convivencia were in essence excavating ways that had long ceased to be relevant or had been obliterated in the neoliberal world. Beginning with colonization and well into the promises of modernity, human life has been slowly stripped of creative communal interactions, such as collective songwriting and other forms of participatory creative expression. Except within families, there are very few communal creative efforts free of ties to nation-state agendas or economic transactions. Most often, autonomous community efforts are unimaginable in the "first world." Upon witnessing creative expression as a convivial tool, one is inevitably led to question capital market arrangements of one's own creative expression and in relation to one's community. With an emphasis on process, the 1997 encuentro generated a deep reflection on the status of creative expression in our lives and gave way to an even bigger question: how to engage more people in collective creative expression, especially in our own trenches. In this way an arena of hope opened up, a hope that came with a clear genesis and praxis and that allows an active imagination. I suggest that, ultimately, experiencing convivencia, or the praxis of conviviality, through music, art, poetry, and *teatro* in this encuentro was a step toward building both individual and collective critical consciousness.

I cannot negate how love was an important motivating factor in these processes. Many social scholars have identified "love as an important source of empowerment" for social activists.[60] The Chicana feminist theorist Chela Sandoval discusses the hermeneutics of love as a "set of practices and procedures that can transit" all subjects.[61] Sandoval identifies love as something that can break through oppression to find "understanding and community."[62] Much like love, creative expression, especially when exercised in community, is something that can "puncture" through "narratives that tie us to social time and space, to the descriptions, recitals, and plots that dull and order our senses insofar as such social narratives are tied to the law."[63] In this historic encuentro between Chican@s and Zapatistas, art and creative expression transcended the law of narratives. Combined with "risk and courage," we began to imagine that love could "make anything possible."[64]

CHAPTER 5

Fandango Jarocho as a Decolonial Tool

"Aesthetic" here refers not to culturally and historically specific elitist European and Euroamerican values in narrowly defined notions of taste or beauty but, more generally, to the conceptual and formal systems governing the material expression of the activity within societies that we refer to as artmaking.

Laura E. Pérez, *Chicana Art*

It was January of 2003. A thick fog engulfed the cold morning in Veracruz, Mexico, as men of all ages arrived from the southern and northern part of the state. Holding worn wooden instruments, farmers, luthiers, butchers, and taxi drivers by trade huddled in a small café in central Xalapa to dialogue with the Chican@ musicians and artists who had traveled from Los Angeles to be present on that day. The meeting, now referred to as the Encuentro Chicano Jarocho, marked an important moment in our collective histories when the musical relationship between Chican@ and Latin@ communities in the United States and *son jarocho* fandango communities in Veracruz, Mexico, transformed into a translocal dialogue I will refer to here as *fandango sin fronteras*, or fandango without borders.

In this chapter, I explore the multiple translocal community efforts of *fandango sin fronteras*, or the US-Mexican fandango community. I will demonstrate the many liberatory veins in the enactment of *fandango jarocho* in the United States, and how convivencia inherent in the practice has enabled a critical consciousness for practitioners. The sounds of the *son jarocho*, specifically the relationships built in and around the ethics of fandango, have generated a sonic transmigration to and fro that has enabled a moral, political, economic, and musical economy that, I suggest, contributes to the lexicon of social movement. I delve further into an analysis of convivencia as aesthetic. I refer to convivencia as an aesthetic due to the fact that it is precisely the formal and valued system governing the material expression of fandango. I will recount how fandango practice succeeded in redefining

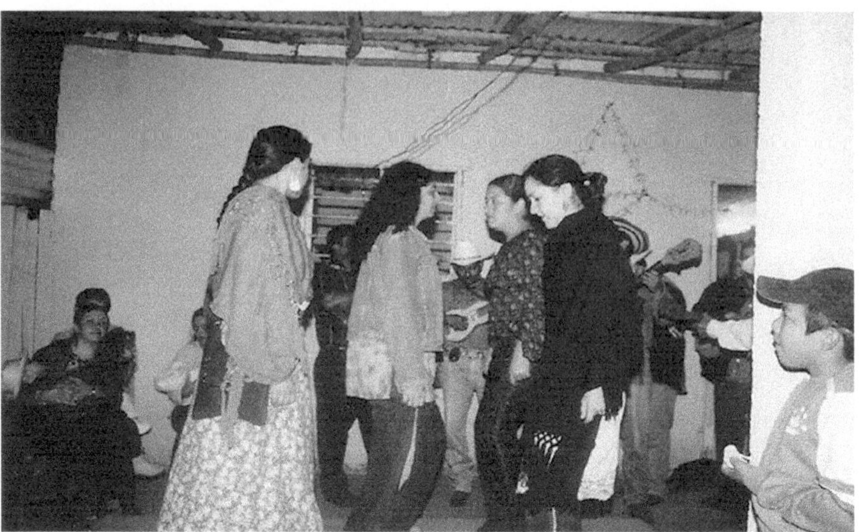

Fandango in El Háto, Veracruz, circa 2000.

music conception, not only for me but also for an ever-growing number of practitioners in the United States, Mexico, and beyond. Fandango practice intrinsically articulates the importance of convivencia in the music-making process, as it is independent of capitalist conceptions of music as a concert, a service, or a commodity. In addition, fandango praxis, and the community it has inherently built across the country and transnationally, has generated discussions among practitioners that have enabled a critical consciousness. For all of these reasons, I suggest that fandango as a social tool has become *the* language utilized across borders between Chican@ artivista communities and musicians in the United States and fandango practitioners in Mexico. It was after experiencing art as a tool of dialogue in the mountains of Chiapas that I came to experience this important practice, and it steadily changed what I thought I knew about the power of music.

A Brief History of *Son Jarocho* and Fandango

Rooted in a history of colonization, labor exploitation, and resistance, the music, poetry, and dance of *son jarocho* fandango emerged as a unique cultural mixture of African, indigenous, and Spanish (Andalusian) influences. Prominent in southern Veracruz, Mexico, fandango is currently exercised as ritual celebration in honor of a town's patron saint or as part of other community celebrations, such as weddings, baptisms, and funerals. From fandango emerged the music, dance, and poetry known as *son jarocho*. *Son jarocho* is manifested and maintained through everyday practice of the *jaraneros* (musicians who play a small, eight-string, five-course, guitar-like instrument called a *jarana*), *versadores* (poets), and *bailadoras* (dancers). As a point of reference, the most well-known *son jarocho* in the fandango repertoire is "La Bamba."

Communities within Veracruz and across the Mexican republic currently practice fandango, but although some communities never stopped the practice, this wasn't always the case. In the 1930s and as a result of the grueling Mexican Revolution of 1910 to 1920, Mexico went through a period of codifying its various music, food, and dance from every region in the republic. With the intent of promoting ideologies around modernity and progress, the national project took shape through the promotion of literature, tourism, and federally funded research of indigenous dances throughout Mexico. The consolidation of cultures and creation of staged spectacles came to be performed in Mexico and abroad through *ballet folklórico* touring groups but was mostly popularized through film (specifically La Época de Oro del Cine Mexicano, or the golden age of Mexican cinema) and sound recordings. Indigenous music, culture, and traditions were altered to fit the attention spans of theater, film, and radio audiences. Over time and by default, the constructed and efficient staged "folklore" began to replace the community practices from which it had emerged. In the case of *son jarocho*, the original communal culture, particularly the fandango and participatory aspects (the transgenerational, multilevel, spontaneous, community-oriented music-making process), nearly disappeared in the consolidating effort.

Quetzal after the 1997 Encuentro

Upon returning from the 1997 Zapatista encuentro, Quetzal continued to play in Los Angeles and throughout the state of California. The events we participated in revolved around sharing our experience of the Zapatista encuentro, as well as continuing to foster the network of musicians and artists in LA's Eastside community. The year was 1998, and upon returning from this life-changing trip, most of the Chican@ artivista work revolved around Zapatista philosophy and teachings. We took the Zapatistas' advice of "helping ourselves" and consistently found ways to engage our community as much as we could through music concerts and other public events. As a musical group, Quetzal remained active in local community events but also began to branch out professionally.[1]

Our music was developing somewhat professionally, but we remained tapped into community struggles. Our local community relationships and the Zapatista struggle had changed our worldview. In 1998, we recorded our self-titled debut album, produced by John Avila on Son del Barrio Records,[2] and a second album in 2001, entitled *Sing the Real*, produced by Greg Landau with Vanguard Records.[3] Shortly thereafter, in 2003, we released our third album, *Worksongs*, produced by Steve Berlin of Los Lobos.[4] Within the span of the three albums, we toured throughout the United States, Canada, Japan, Mexico, and Moscow.

The content and sound of our music were reflective of our community experiences and philosophies. Quetzal's work soon became known for its unique sound and political message. Our music was entrenched in topics concerning the upliftment of and accountability to our community and other communities in struggle, the empowerment of women, as well as unapologetic commentaries on modernity and neoliberalism.[5]

Quetzal had its share of changes in personnel. Gabriel Tenorio and Tylana Enomoto left the band shortly after the release of our debut album. The new members' influences filtered into the compositions. *Worksongs* continued to feature Dante Pascuzzo (bass), who had a jazz background; and added Rocio Marron (violin), who returned to the band and added her classical University of Southern California training; Edson Gianesi (percussionist) from Brazil, who studied music composition at the California Institute of the Arts; Kiko Cornejo (trap drums/timbales), a Chicano from San Diego whose musician father had instilled in him the music and rhythms of Latin jazz and *son cubano*; and Ray Sandoval (guitarist), who was Japanese and Mexican and had rock, classical, and jazz training. My brother, Gabriel Gonzalez, was also an important member, as his singing and songwriting style was elemental to the energy of Quetzal.

As the primary musical director, Quetzal Flores was adamant about welcoming varying members' backgrounds as well as their sonic upbringings, which included both formal and informal training. The influences of the varying members organically filtered into the sounds. Understandably, the varied experiences could not be articulated in categorical genres. For all of these reasons, we were not interested in sticking to a certain industry sound. We consistently explored the many sonic experiences we had grown up listening to.

The Quetzal Sound: Joining the Trajectory of a Chican@ Music Experience

Quetzal's music and our way of writing and producing music is not unique to Eastside Chican@ music culture. In general, Chican@ music historically has not adhered to genres or fit into market-defined categories. As mentioned in earlier chapters, the community of Chican@ artivista musicians in 1997 was a varied sonic field. Quinto Sol expressed their concerns and ideas through reggae, dub, as well as a mix of cumbias. The Blues Experiment had a classic rock feel in the style of the Doors. Aztlan Underground played hip-hop/punk rock but also melded traditional Mexican indigenous instruments, like the *huehuetl* and *sonajas*. These groups expressed themselves according to their experiences and not in terms of genres or categories implemented by music market systems. As George Lipsitz has stated:

> In many areas of cultural production, but especially in popular music, organic intellectuals within the Los Angeles Chicano community pursued a strategy of self-presentation that brought their unique and distinctive cultural traditions into the mainstream of mass popular culture. Neither assimilationist nor separatist, they played on "families of resemblance"—similarities to the experience and culture of other groups—to fashion a "unity of disunity." . . . In that way, they sought to make alliances with other groups by cultivating the ways in which their particular experiences spoke with special authority about the ideas and alienations felt by others. They used the techniques and sensibilities of postmodernism to build a "historic bloc" of oppositional groups united in ideas and intentions if not experience.[6]

Quetzal's music was no exception. We consistently worked with and among other musicians who were not directly tied to our own communities, which generated Quetzal's unique sound.

Despite our many influences, most of our albums were released amid the new "world music" craze and thus were often catalogued in this "genre." On the business end, we refused many liquor and tobacco sponsorships. I must admit, turning down large amounts of money from alcohol or tobacco companies seemed like professional suicide. In many respects it was. Music groups often survive on this money to fund their tours or other aspects of band business. But Quetzal Flores in particular was adamant in holding every aspect of the Quetzal business workings accountable to Zapatista philosophies—or as much as possible, anyway. We would have long band meetings or discussions and would agree, some reluctantly, that liquor- and tobacco-related sponsorships were not the way to go. These were, after all, addictions that our families and communities were plagued by, and Flores expressed that Quetzal as a group should refrain from building our career on these monies. Due to our unconventional choices, we continued to ebb and flow in financial hardship. It was a creative yet difficult time. Despite the hardship, we continued to play and collaborate with musicians and artists who had similar concerns.

María Elena Gaitán and *Son Jarocho*

One of our most memorable collaborations was with a performance artist and cellist named María Elena Gaitán. Gaitán was creating a solo piece titled *The Adventures of Connie Chancla* and invited Quetzal Flores and me to accompany her. We decided to play a couple of *son jarocho* pieces. The *son jarocho* we knew was based mostly on what we had listened to via the popular 1950s recordings. We had learned and imitated the most popular renditions of the *sones*. These recordings were fast-paced, virtuosic, condensed versions of the most popular *sones*, such as "La Bamba" or "La Guacamaya." Interpretations popularized by *jarocho* musical greats such as Lino Chávez and Andrés Huesca through films and recordings were classic interpretations that became codified in the popular consciousness as *the* only way to play *son jarocho*. Flores and I naturally followed the canon and emulated this style of playing as much as we could.

During one of the rehearsals Gaitán gave us a cassette tape by a group from Veracruz called Mono Blanco. Gaitán had just returned from trips to the Guadalupe Center in San Antonio, Texas, where she had the pleasure of working with Gilberto Gutiérrez, the founder of Mono Blanco. Gaitán wanted us to learn a *son jarocho* piece called "El perro" (The dog). We had never heard about this *son* and were anxious to listen to it.

When we listened, we heard a very different *son jarocho* from what we had grown up with. At first it was slow and the verses were sung in a "call-and-response" fashion.[7] There was something about the playing, however, and the intimacy of the recordings that moved us. Shortly thereafter we received a CD recording of the group Son de Madera from a musician mentor and colleague named Russell Rodriguez. In contrast to Mono Blanco, Son de Madera's sound seemed to be more experimental, but it had the same call-and-response structure to most of the *sones*. The call-and-response, the pace, the verses, were all unique. Son de Madera's CD also consisted of composed original works. Both of these gifts would change our music world forever, for both Mono Blanco and Son de Madera were rumored to be part of *el nuevo movimiento jaranero*, the new *jaranero* movement.

We lived with the Mono Blanco cassette tape and the Son de Madera CD for nearly a year, and listened to them over and over again. In 2001 Quetzal was invited to play in Veracruz for the annual Festival Afrocaribeño. This was thrilling for us. The festival organizers had scheduled us to play in both Xalapa and the port town of Veracruz, so we made sure to set aside time to seek out both groups; Son de Madera was based in Xalapa, and Mono Blanco was based in the city of Veracruz. When we arrived we were unable to meet either of them but left messages and contact information at their respective addresses. Once we returned to the United States we were contacted by both groups, which allowed us to establish continued correspondence and make plans for the future.

El Movimiento Jaranero

Put another way, participatory music and dance is more about the social relations being realized through the performance than about producing art that can somehow be abstracted from those social relations.

Thomas Turino, *Music as Social Life*

In the late 1970s Gilberto Gutiérrez, a young musician from Tres Zapotes, Veracruz, initiated the *movimiento jaranero*. This movement consciously strayed from the institutional and commercial canons that had previously represented the state of Veracruz to inform today's global society that the *son jarocho* was vibrant, born in fandango, and should be practiced by communities at large. *Movimiento jaranero* efforts marked the resurgence of fandango in rural and urban communities. Furthermore, Gutiérrez, with the help of his *son jarocho* group Mono Blanco, continuously perpetuated a discourse and recognition of the indigenous, Spanish, and in particular African roots in the music and culture of Veracruz. Gutiérrez was one of the originators of Mono Blanco, a group that was partly responsible for the resurgence of fandango and that initiated the *movimiento jaranero*. A Veracruz native, he, like many others, had moved to the capital city of Mexico to find work after sugar plantations closed down in the southern part of the state.

In the mid-seventies, Gilberto Gutiérrez, along with his brother José Ángel Gutiérrez, Andrés Vega, and Juan Pascoe, looked to the legendary Arcadio Hidalgo. Hidalgo was a proud veteran of the Mexican Revolution of 1910 to 1920 and one of a handful of surviving early *fandango jarocho* practitioners. The Gutiérrez brothers, Vega, and Pascoe learned and documented the stories, protocols, *sones*, and *versadas* (poems) that Don Arcadio's memory was able to conjure up.[8] In this way, Hidalgo was their key to the past. He was also the trusted elder who allowed them access to all of the ranchos they subsequently visited for years in search of other elders who remembered the *sones*, the instruments, and the old dances of this nearly forgotten pastime—the fandango.[9]

Besides Mono Blanco's professional ventures and staged music presentations of the *sones* in the vein of fandango, Mono Blanco spent a great deal of time reconnecting rural communities to fandango practice by encouraging the elders, the *señoras* (older women), and especially the youth to *convivir* in these nearly forgotten and undervalued ways. Through Don Arcadio they were welcomed into the communities. Without Hidalgo's presence, the bunch of hippy-looking youngsters would have had trouble acquiring the trust and rapport needed to gain access to the older generation of men and women in rural communities. The community of *fandangueros* now refer to this time period as the *rescate del son*, or rescue of the song and dance form.[10] The Gutiérrez brothers, Vega, and Pascoe moved through various rural communities in search of information. The *movimiento jaranero* went precisely against the grain of what the state had already established in the 1930s and the construction of what was supposed to be the canon of Veracruz. Most importantly, Mono Blanco generated a discourse about the importance of convivencia in fandango.

Importantly, fandango practice redemocratized music and summoned the community to partake in playing the *son jarocho* through fandango ritual. In this way, it challenged the nation-state canon not only in its representation of what was "Veracruz" or "jarocho" but also by the ways in which the music was generated—the fandango. One needn't be a "musician" to play in fandango. One could be the *señora* across the street or the *viejito* who lived on the *cerro* (hillside). Either way, the communities' participation in fandango was essential, for the sake of convivencia.

This reconceptualization of music as an activity rooted in convivencia is an important disruption in how we think of music in this day and age. The musicologist Christopher Small has noted the importance of this distinction, stating,

> Music is not a thing at all but an activity, something that people do. The apparent thing "music" is a figment, an abstraction of the action, whose reality vanishes as soon as we examine it at all closely. This habit of thinking in abstractions, of taking from an action what appears to be its essence and of giving that essence a name, is probably as old as language; it is useful in the conceptualizing of our world but it has its dangers.[11]

Convivencia as an aesthetic extends Small's analysis, both his concept and his introduction of "musicking" to alleviate abstraction.[12] Rather than focusing on the "activity" of fandango and the convivencia inherent in the practice, the act of "abstracting" the music of the *son jarocho* from the people and relationships that give it meaning, as it was given meaning in the past, fails to understand the power inherent in it. Convivencia, or the deliberate act of being with and present for each other as community, is a moral, social, and political aesthetic of fandango practice and a central reason for the gathering. The reconceptualization of music as an activity rooted in convivencia is an important disruption in how music is thought of in our present age. My treatment of convivencia as an aesthetic in community music practice aims to bring focus on relationships and process rather than sounds, outcomes, or products. Because music is more often than not considered something you buy or sell, but rarely something you participate in with others in community, treating convivencia as an aesthetic places value and meaning on the relationships that are producing the music rather than on the music itself. In short, learning about the liberatory practice and becoming a part of the transnational community illuminated new possibilities.

Diversity of Fandango Communities in the United States

In 2002 the former Troy Café and Centro Regeneración artist collective member Aida Salazar, as well as the local organizers Lalo Medina and Marco Amador, proposed a concert titled "Fandango Jarocho" for the Ford Amphitheatre summer series.[13] Marco Amador had previously fostered a relationship with both Mono Blanco and Son de Madera, and Amador and Quetzal Flores suggested these groups for the annual Ford Theatre series. The groups Quetzal and Los Jardin were also scheduled to play.[14]

The concert was a success. Our band had been on tour and flew in from New York to make the concert date. Besides the Ford Amphitheatre concert, Flores and Amador also resolved to have an event that was more accessible to Eastside residents. They organized a concert at East LA's own historic art space, Self Help Graphics, days after the Ford Amphitheatre concert, to raise funds for El CaSon, a cultural space Mono Blanco was attempting to jump-start. El CaSon would become Mono Blanco's space, where the community in Veracruz could take *son jarocho* workshops.

The energy of the Self Help concert was especially powerful, as many Chican@ artivistas were present and sharing their time, music, and organizing efforts with the *jarochos*. Aztlan Underground, Domingo Siete, and Quetzal were but a few of the bands and artists that donated their time on this night. The former Mono Blanco member César Castro recalls,

> Estábamos en el Este de Los Ángeles . . . no sabíamos lo que se trataba esta cosa de Chicanos, no? Gilberto sabia un poco porque vivió en la Bahía.[15] Pero eso fue diferente. La música era muy ruidosa, pero también tenia el elemento mas acústico.
>
> Eran varios grupos, ustedes [Quetzal], El Aztlan Underground . . . de ellos los seguí escuchando. El Domingo Siete me impresionaba por su capacidad de poder reproducir un sonido caribeño. Según nosotros veníamos de cinta negra pero al escucharlos pensé, no espérate estos

le pegan bien bonito, no? Siempre muy chistoso cuando pronunciaban ciertas palabras[;] es decir que no pronunciaban bien que diga-
mos . . . era nomás un toque donde te recordaba que . . . ah sí . . . son
Chicanos.[16]

We were in East Los Angeles. . . . We didn't know what this Chicanos
thing was about, right? Gilberto knew a little because he lived in the
Bay [Area] for a time. But that was different. The music was very loud,
but it also had some acoustic elements.

There were several groups, you [Quetzal], and Aztlan Underground.
. . . I kept listening to them. With Domingo Siete I was impressed by
their ability to produce a Caribbean sound. According to us, we came
as black-belt level musicians, but when I heard them I thought, wait a
minute, they hit hard [sound good], no? Always very funny when they
pronounced certain words[;] that is to say that they did not pronounce
certain words well. . . . It was just a hint that reminded you that . . . oh
yeah . . . they are Chicanos.

Castro's comments illuminate an important point. He was, in short, surprised at the level of musicianship and community that thrived in East LA.
Some Mexican scholars and musicians have identified Chican@s as "huérfa-
nos de la cultura," or orphans of culture. Indeed, great Mexican writers such
as Octavio Paz have openly lamented Los Angeles's "vague atmosphere" of
Mexicanism, which, they have commented, is "never quite existing, never
quite vanishing."[17] George Lipsitz, however, has rightfully noted, "Paz's static
and one-dimensional view of Mexican identity prevented him from seeing
the rich culture of opposition embedded within the Los Angeles Chicano
community."[18] The general understanding is that Chican@s are in deficit;
that is to say that as a result of being born and raised in the United States,
Chican@s have no culture of their own and will forever look to the "mother
country," Mexico, for cultural foundation. Thus, these ideas have sometimes
established a paternalistic understanding in the relationship between *jarochos* and Chican@s in that Mexicans provide the culture while Chican@s
strive to emulate and or imitate being "Mexican."

At the end of the night and in the presence of the towering mosaic of
the Virgen de Guadalupe, Gilberto Gutiérrez stood in the Self Help parking
lot, impressed with the level of musicianship and organizing. In witnessing
the crowd, the level of commitment, and the love of music, art, and culture, he thought the fandango might also thrive in this space. This was an
affirmation for us. As I have stated, Chican@ cultural and historical legacy
reflects an interest in connecting with other communities in struggle
in the United States and elsewhere. In this sense the affinity to the fandango for many is not so much to "become" and emulate being *jarocho* as

much as it is about connecting with the *jarocho* communities in solidarity and cooperation.

Finding Fandango

From 2002 to 2004, Quetzal Flores and I made extended trips to Veracruz, where we received invaluable musical direction and hospitality from members of the fandango community and from groups like Son de Madera, Mono Blanco, Los Utrera, Chuchumbé, and Los Cojolites. Flores and I were newlyweds and childless at the time, and therefore had the leisure to travel. When we were not touring we saved our pennies to be able to make these trips every summer and winter season. On one of many trips, we were guided across the state and into the Sotavento (the region along the southern part of the Papaloapan River) to visit various communities, musicians, and luthiers. We made our way to a region called Los Tuxtlas and into various ranchos, like Apixita, El Hato, and Boca de San Miguel. Town after town, we moved by way of old noisy buses and beat-up taxis. Winding roads under big skies led us through gorgeous tropical greens. Traveling for hours throughout the day, we always managed to arrive at our destination before sundown. What the *jarochos* were most eager to show us was the fandango practice.

As the anthropologist Antonio García de León notes, the term *fandango* is derived from the Bantu word *fanda*, meaning *fiesta*.[19] Indeed, as long as there is reason to commemorate or celebrate, there is reason to *fandanguear*. These festive moments can be familial or community events, such as weddings, baptisms, New Year celebrations, Christmas festivities, and fiestas for La Candelaria, Reyes Magos, and the arrival of a visitor or the departure of one.[20]

One of the most noticeable aspects of fandango for me was the absence of an audience. In fandango, there is no formal audience but rather all present are considered participants.[21] The absence of a formal "audience" therefore calls for an almost circular formation in the gathering of people, musicians, and friends. Another unique attribute of fandango is the transgenerational aspect of the fiesta. From the oldest practitioner to the youngest, the fandango community welcomes people in all stages of life.

In the midst of fandango, I quickly realized that there was an unspoken protocol. The *requinto jarocho* instrument "declares" the melody, *declara el son*, signaling the *jaranas* (five-course, eight-string guitars) of all sizes and the *leona* (bass-guitar-like instrument), the *quijada*, (donkey or horse jaw percussion instrument), and the *pandero* (tambourine) to begin. Only recently have other instruments, such as the *cajón* and the *marimbol*, been reintroduced.[22] The *tarima* (a wooden platform where the percussive dance is executed) is the heart of fandango, as it is the vortex of the festivity on which the dancers and percussionists set the pace, choose the *sones*, and keep time for the musicians around them. Women dance *sones de a montón* in pairs. The *sones de pareja* are danced by opposite-sex couples.

Bailadoras, or dancers, are respected and praised for their ability to maintain a balance between timing and grace while improvising to the music. *Bailadoras* dance in continuous rotation on the tarima. When they have completed a cycle of *verso* (verse) and *estribillo* (refrain), they are immediately followed by waiting dancers, who gently tap them to indicate that their time is up. A single *son* can last for hours at a time as *bailadoras* rotate on and off the tarima throughout the night. There are many *sones* in the fandango repertoire, all of which are tied to nature, love, animals, or customs of the rural areas.

The older women in the communities are highly respected fandango practitioners. I spent most of the initial trips to Veracruz fascinated and in awe of the female dancers of all ages, most of whom were dancing *sones de a montón* (*sones* for many). After observing a few *bailadoras*, I had only begun to assimilate the complexity of the fandango style of *zapateado* footwork. When I worked up the nerve to get on the tarima, I realized it was much harder than it looked. I found that the improvisational aspects of the dance were the most challenging. *Zapateado* uses stomps, strikes, slides, shuffles, and rests of the shoe in positions that are fully flat on the toe and the heel to create sounds on the tarima. Technically, there is but one main step, which some *jarochos* informally refer to as *café con pan*.[23] This basic step was not difficult for me to grasp,[24] but rather it was the *cadencia*, or cadence, of the step depending on the *son* that I struggled with. I simply did not understand the feel of the *zapateado*, and as much as I wanted to dance, I sat and listened instead.

Experiencing the 1997 Zapatista encuentro had taught us enough to recognize the social, political, and revolutionary implications of fandango. We learned that we had to build relationships in a particular way, and that relationships could be built through music, art, and culture as tools of dialogue. I was humbled by fandango and the communal music-making process. These early fandango experiences were near magical, and we came home to East LA once again inspired by the convivencia we had experienced in the communities of practice.

Post-Xalapa Meeting: Chican@ and *Jarocho* Translocal Ripples and Waves

If the production of space is a highly social process, then it is a process that has an effect on the formation of subjectivity, identity, sociality, and physicality in myriad ways. Taking the performativity of space seriously also means understanding that categories such as gender, race, and sexuality are not only discursively constructed but spatially enacted and created as well.

Mary Pat Brady, *Extinct Lands, Temporal Geographies*

Fandango communities have since developed in multiple ways across the United States and yet are part of an extensive informal network that includes support and development of fandango instruction workshops, fabrication of instruments, instrument maintenance, supplies, music collaborations, and even independent radio shows dedicated to the music and culture of the *son*.

In East Los Angeles, early efforts to establish fandango praxis in communities revolved around teaching the basic elements and protocols of fandango. The initial instruction allowed for an understanding of the basic elements and ethics of the practice while we simultaneously planned and fundraised to bring fandango elders and more experienced practitioners to teach for an extended period of time. The goal was not to become *son jarocho* "experts" but rather to impart enough information in order to participate comfortably in fandango on some level. Individually and collectively, organizers and musicians in Los Angeles, such as Marco Amador, Russell Rodriguez, Carolina Sarmiento, among other Chican@ artivistas and East LA bands, artists, poets, and musicians, contributed to the early implementation and dialogue. The Encuentro Chicano Jarocho in the cold morning in Veracruz was precisely the moment when the informal dialogue was officially acknowledged. These efforts directly or indirectly began to catch fire. From 2003 and on, the fandango practice spread. In southern California, a group of Chican@ and Mexican youth organizing out of El Centro Cultural de Santa Ana became a particularly strong force in the dissemination of fandango in California. Fandango communities at present abound across the United States. In California you can find fandango communities from the northern to the southern part of the state, including San Jose, San Francisco, Fillmore, Los Angeles, Santa Ana, and San Diego. Other fandango communities across the United States include Seattle and Olympia in the state of Washington, Phoenix, Oregon, Wisconsin, Chicago, New York, South Philadelphia, and Washington, DC. Although they all range in duration and level of experience, most communities have a connection to and varying points of entry into the informal networks with the practitioners and communities from Veracruz.

Fandango Communities To and Fro

It is important to recognize that, at present, the musical dialogue, resources, and ideas flow in both directions. That is to say, *jarochos* in Mexican communities have also enthusiastically initiated dialogue and music projects with Chican@ communities by drawing on fandango practitioners from Los Angeles and elsewhere to participate in events held in Veracruz during important holidays and at fiesta times, or simply to collaborate on new recordings or performances. From grassroots efforts to state-funded concerts, Mexicans and Chican@s and Latin@s have collaborated and performed extensively.

Communities in the Bay Area cities of Oakland, Berkeley, and San Francisco have developed relationships with the *jarocho* musicians Liche Oseguera, Patricio Hidalgo, and Andres Flores, enabling multiple formal and informal residencies. With funding from Jose Ramirez and Xochi Flores, Quetzal Flores, Dante Pascuzzo, and I produced Son de Madera's *Las orquestas del día* (2003). Producciones Cimarrón, led by Rubí Oseguera, Marco Amador, and Liche Oseguera, produced and recorded the first ever Encuentro de Leoneros in Chacalapa, Veracruz. The East LA–based, former Guadalupe Custom Strings co-owner Gabriel Tenorio coproduced, arranged, and musically directed Patricio Hidalgo's *El regreso de la conga* (2012), which featured many Chican@ and Latin@ artists from Los Angeles.

Over the years many Chican@ and Latin@ musicians, such as La Marisoul Hernandez, Jacob Hernandez, Juan Perez, Federico Zuniga, Russell Rodriguez, Anna S. Arismendez,[25] and I, have participated as core or invited members in Mexico-based touring groups, grassroots community cooperatives, and countless Mexican-produced *son jarocho* sound recordings. Our band, Quetzal, has pulled on the fandango community of musicians for multiple recording projects beginning with *Worksongs* (Vanguard, 2003), *Die Cowboy Die* (independent, 2006), *Imaginaries* (Folkways, 2012), *Quetzanimales* (independent, 2014), *The Eternal Getdown* (Folkways, 2016), and the soon-to-be-released *Puentes sonoros* (Sonic bridges) on Smithsonian Folkways.

In addition to the music projects and performances, multiple practitioners and scholars have published literature, reflections, and analysis on the current US-based fandango community and culture. Most prominently, Daniel Sheehy, Russell Rodriguez, Micaela Díaz-Sánchez, Alexandro Hernandez, Ruben Hernandez-Leon, and Rafael Figueroa, among others, have contributed multiple perspectives, speaking to the diversity of thought and dialogue that is reflective of the spirit and convivial nature of fandango.

In 2005 the musicologist Alejando L. Madrid organized at Cornell University one of the first conferences dedicated to the translocal movement. Fandango scholars, practitioners, and varying representatives of fandango community sites near and far attended the two-day conference. Funded by the Atkinson Forum in American Studies, it featured a performance from Tembembe Ensamble Continuo from Mexico, scholarly presentations, workshops, dialogue panels, as well as a fandango.[26] Conferences and panels dedicated to the movement, as well as interest in the fandango, continue to develop. Events such as the yearly Encuentros de Jaraneros in California and Chicago and the prominent yearly Son Jarocho Festival in San Francisco also give the translocal fandango community opportunities to gather, discuss, and engage in fandango.[27]

Held in the early days of February, in 2018 the Son Jarocho Festival in San Francisco hosted by the Brava Theater memorialized Don Andres Flores, who had unexpectedly died. Andres Flores was a prominent and well-respected *jaranero*, percussionist, *laudero* (luthier), and maestro of the *son*. Originally from Coatzacoalcos, Veracruz, over the years Andres Flores had traveled throughout the United States as an invited maestro for his skills as a singer, percussionist, dancer, and *jaranero*. As a longtime member of the prominent Veracruz-based group Chuchumbé and a maestro of the *son*, he had a unique pedagogy in teaching that intrinsically instilled the spirit of convivencia into any space he occupied. His short illness and sudden death also had a way of making the vast network of fandango communities across Mexico and the United States known. Through social media, friends and family kept everyone apprised of his illness. All networks immediately rallied around his family and parents to support them emotionally and financially.[28] Upon his death various sites paid tribute to him and the legacy he left behind as a performer, an award-winning *laudero*, and a generous teacher.

Transborder "Meshworks" as Social Movement: A Method to the Madness

Chican@ artivista and *son jarocho* community-building methods are reminiscent of what the anthropologist Lynn Stephen refers to as transborder community; transmigrant communities have always crossed "racial, ethnic, linguistic, and class boundaries between Mexico and the United States" in both northern and southern directions.[29] *Transmigration* and *meshworks* are useful terms to describe *fandango sin fronteras* networks because they disrupt the social science focus on binaries (global/national, local/transnational) and instead make visible the material survival strategies within the various communities. *Transmigrants* can generally be defined as people who, "having migrated from one nation-state to another, live their lives across borders, participating simultaneously in social relations that embed them in more than one nation-state."[30] We can understand that the interlinked networks of migrant communities are developing as a result of globalization, for both transmigration and meshworks emphasize fluid forms and ever-changing strategies of survival. The transmigration between Mexican and US fandango communities has been extensive, often erratic, and has indeed grown in unplanned directions. This has made all fandango communities unique at present, not only in terms of origin and respective histories but also by the ways in which they organize among themselves and between varying sites. From San Diego to the Bay Area, every major city in California is now linked in one way or another to a community or performance group of fandangueros in Mexico. The vast fandango network has been beneficial to both US and Mexican communities. Master practitioners or groups can book entire tours, traveling from one city or state to the next, via the informal networks that communicate through social media or email.

The network has grown so extensively that, most recently, fandango community practitioners in Chicago managed to organize a grassroots, nationwide tour and discussion via their Jarochicanos ensemble in December of 2016. Their Facebook page explains their origins and purpose: "Jarochicanos formed in 2008 as a youth workshop with the desire to learn the musical tradition called Son Jarocho. This tradition we live, we breathe and we share. We use this music as a tool to create community based projects like Talleres en la 18, Jarana All Stars, and La Tiendita de la 18. We also participate in Son Chiquitos and Son y Arte Summer Camp as musicians and instructors."[31] The group's December tour was a search for dialogue and connections across the multiple fandango community sites. The results, reflections, and photographs by the matriarchal-driven group—led in part by Maya Zazhil Fernández, Gina Pacheco-Gamboa, Jackie Rodriguez, Stephanie Rodriguez, Laura Cambron (a transplant from Santa Ana, California), Camilo Rincon, and Raul Fernandez—were shared in an exhibit that debuted in Chicago in August of 2017. According to Maya Zazhil Fernández, the tour made visible "the crazy impact the fandango has had across the nation."[32]

Although most activities occur in local contexts, the networks reach out to other cities and groups across the United States. For transmigrants, there is never a permanent "state of being" between two or more locations.[33] In this way, social expectations and cultural values are being shaped by more than one political and economic system. Such is the case with the *jarocho* transplant César Castro, who married Xochi Flores, a Chicana from Los Angeles, had a daughter, and now resides in El Sereno, Los Angeles.[34] Having relocated to LA, Castro began to feel nostalgia for his place of origin, Veracruz. Castro, however, has found ways to remain connected to the fandango community and musicians in Veracruz by creating a YouTube podcast series, *Radio Jarochelo*. According to Castro, he created *Radio Jarochelo* not only as a way to bind the multiple scattered sites of fandango practitioners all over Mexico and the United States, but also as a way to remain connected to the thriving fandango community in Mexico. The content of *Radio Jarochelo* is dedicated to everything and anything having to do with *son jarocho* and fandango. The show is self-produced and airs every fifteen days. For Castro, conceiving and creating *Radio Jarochelo* was a way of being in two places at once. Once he began to create and air his show regularly, Castro commented, "Yo sentía que yo salía, tenia vida otra vez" (I felt like I would leave, [like] I had life again).[35]

In addition to producing *Radio Jarochelo*, Castro founded Cambalache in 2010, which has since become one of the most respected traditional *son jarocho* groups in Los Angeles.[36] In addition to performing, Castro, along with his group, continues to conduct fandango workshops in community centers, elementary schools, and universities in the LA area. Castro is also known for being an accomplished luthier who is sought out by most US-based fandango practitioners for *son jarocho* instruments and repairs.

Chican@ Contributions and Innovations in the *Son*

Although fandango has its origins in Veracruz, Mexico, some US-based fandango musicians have revolutionized how *son jarocho* is played in both the United States and Mexico. East LA–based musicians such as Juan Perez, Dante Pascuzzo, and Jacob Hernandez have had an influence on the *son jarocho* genre, especially in performance.[37] Juan Perez, a prolific bass player, was invited to play with Son de Madera in 2003. Perez's years with Son de Madera include two studio albums as well as tours in the United States, Canada, and Europe from 2003 to 2010.[38] According to the cofounder and musical director of Son de Madera, Ramón Gutiérrez, "Pérez tiene algo; entiende el son y todas sus posibilidades sin salirse demasiado" (Pérez has something; he understands the *son* and all of its possibilities without going outside [the genre] too much).[39]

Another East LA native who has made an impact on the *son jarocho* world is Jacob Hernandez, who was a key member of Los Cojolites from 2003 to 2009 and again in 2012. At present, Hernandez is known as one of the most proficient *marimbol* players in the world of *son jarocho*. Octavio Rebolledo Kloques, a musician, an authority, and a scholar on the origins of the *marimbol*, has also commented on Hernandez's distinctive and highly developed style of playing the instrument: "Me gusta mucho como toca; ha desarollado algo propio, es uno de los mejores" (I like very much how he plays; he has developed something of his own, he is one of the best).[40]

With a growing interest in fandango comes a demand for instruments and *jarana* strings. Founded by the legendary musician Francisco "Pancho" Gonzalez, Guadalupe Custom Strings has been a one-stop string shop for many musicians in the East LA area. Jacob Hernandez became Gonzalez's apprentice and later acquired the business. In Hernandez's early tenure with the shop, and as the fandango boom continued to grow, Hernandez and Gonzalez developed what became known as the "mifren" string for the *requinto jarocho*.[41] It was an important contribution and a replacement for the string tuned to G, which was difficult to find. In addition, and according to César Castro, Guadalupe Custom Strings helped refine the sound of the mosquito (a small *jarana*) and *chaquiste* (the smallest *jarana*) by providing the correct .002 and .018 caliber of nylon string for the respective instruments.[42] The *jarochos* had previously resorted to utilizing fishing wire or strings intended for *charangos* (stringed instruments of Andean origin), which stifled the sound of the instruments. Guadalupe Custom Strings is currently one of the most well-respected and sought-after string manufacturers in both the United States and Mexico. Although making a profit by producing a product from raw materials is nearly impossible in the United States, the shop has managed to stay afloat. Jacob Hernandez married a Mexican woman and now lives a translocal life between Mexico and East Los Angeles.

Although Chican@ artivista musicians have historically used the tools of music, art, and other forms of creative expression for political purposes, through fandango we were able to engage with community on a level outside of Western "performance" culture. As a professional musician, I acknowledge the effects a great concert or sound recording can have on an audience, community, or society as a whole. Performance in the most traditional sense has the ability to incite critical thought, which can eventually lead to social change. But fandango as a transgenerational participatory music, poetry, and dance practice enacts individual and communal empowerment in a most exceptional way. The physical and ideological formation democratizes music in a way that disrupts how music functions in capitalist societies. Fandango, in essence, is *the* social movement.

Fandango, and particularly the convivencia inherent in the practice, incites dialogue among its constituents, which can lead to greater analysis of society and one's role in it. It is no coincidence that more than one fandango site uses the tools of the music, *son jarocho*, and fandango to build understanding and community around issues and struggles; for fandango practice, and the embodiment of the practice, is able to instigate dialogue and critical consciousness among its practitioners. In Santa Ana, California, for example, Son del Centro has utilized *son jarocho* and fandango practice in support of immigrant rights, May Day marches, the Immokalee workers' strike, antigentrification, and other related local and international struggles. In Seattle, Washington, the Seattle Fandango Project organizes fandango events and workshops in women's shelters, at food justice events, and at preschools, elementary schools, middle schools, and high schools.

Some enactments of fandango are more outright political than others. In San Diego the Fandango Fronterizo, or Border Fandango, is a yearly event initiated in 2008 at the US-Mexican border, wherein two tarimas are placed on each side of the US border fence.[43] This event in particular is a powerful enactment of fandango. By managing to hold a fandango at the border, the sociality of sound temporarily wills the border out of existence. Indeed, in the case of the Fandango Fronterizo, embodied practices are "an episteme, a praxis, a way of knowing as well as a way of storing and transmitting cultural knowledge and identity that is not adherent to political or nation-state boundaries."[44] Although the event has been spearheaded by Jorge F. Castillo, various Santaneros have been instrumental in the organizational activities and development of this powerful yearly event, including Roxana Bernal and Carolina Lamar.[45]

FandangObon: All Things Connected!

The body [is] . . . unconsciously re-performing invented traditions in order to reduce them to a singular grammar that awaits liberation from the silence of historical violence.

The body's arc of traumatised movement thus strives to create a singular metaphorical community, inventing and defending a collective self, yearning to create solid identities, common legacies and attachments.

Bibi Bakare-Yusuf, "Scattered Limbs, Scattered Stories"

In Los Angeles fandango has also been utilized to reach across communities and ethnic racial groups in order to incite critical dialogue and cultural collaboration. In 2013 the Japanese American artist and activist Nobuko Miyamoto participated in a fandango workshop Quetzal Flores and I conducted at Plaza de la Raza in northeast Los Angeles. As Miyamoto observed, *obon* and fandango are strikingly similar, and she urged us to emphasize the important connection between the Mexican celebration and the Japanese *bon odori*. Under Miyamoto's guidance and urging, FandangObon was born and has been enacted for nearly six years now.

The title of the event stems from the words *fandango* and *obon*. *Obon* is an abbreviation of a Buddhist sutra called the Urabongyo or Ullambana sutra in Sanskrit.[46] *Bon odori* literally means "the death gathering of joy," and the celebration is about remembering those who have passed. In the United States the celebration season takes place over the course of several weekends during the summer months of July and August. Japanese American Nisei, Sansei, and consecutive generations convene to remember their dead by way of dancing together as community. The most inspiring aspect to witness in an *obon* celebration is the concentric-circle formations around the *yagura* (a large, wooden platform tower) as they are lined with people of all ages dancing. Traditional fans move together in unison formation, simulating ocean waves that rise and crash. Young and old bodies move together to a chosen repertoire of prerecorded traditional Japanese songs that are accented by the *taiko* drummer or *fue* (Japanese flute) player on the *yagura*.

Importantly, and in keeping with the social justice imperative of the gathering's philosophy, FandangObon has since expanded to collaborate with African American communities via the most recent participation of the master drummers and dancers Najite Agindotan, Francis Awe, and Omowale Awe, and the South-Central LA–based West African dance and drumming group Le Ballet Dembaya.[47]

Nobuko Miyamoto and the initial FandangObon efforts have since led to six years of FandangObon programming by the Great Leap nonprofit in and around September and October. The Japanese American Cultural Center (JACCC) and the Aratani Theatre in Little Tokyo have hosted the FandangObon for several years since its inception.[48] What is striking to me is Miyamoto's insistence on teaching the traditional respective repertoire but also creating new works in preparation for the annual gathering.

The first FandangObon, for example, inspired the collaborative piece "Bam butsu no tsunagari,"[49] meaning "all things connected." Drawing upon the many things fandango and *obon* have in common—from the wooden platforms centered in the celebration, to the circle formation around the platform, as well as the shared belief in convivencia and transgenerational participation—"Bam butsu no tsunagari" was born. The lyrics written in English, Spanish, and Japanese express FandangObon's central purpose for community connection and participation:

> In the circle we dance
> No beginning, no ending
> In the circle we dance
> I am you, you are the other me
> Bam butsu no tsunagari . . .
>
> Carácter ceremonial
> el fandango rompe el orden
> Celebración especial
> en donde las almas borden
> Con sus ritmos, melodías
> Que al día de hoy celebramos
> Ancestral sabiduría
> con la cual nos abrazamos
>
> Ceremonial character
> Fandango breaks with order
> A special celebration

Where souls intertwine
With its rhythms and melodies
From which we celebrate today
Ancestral knowledge
Which we used to embrace

The movements were also an important contribution to the overall prayer the composition invokes. The choreography was carefully created by the *obon* master Elaine Fukumoto and Nobuko Miyamoto. The choreographers were deliberate about incorporating aspects of traditional fandango, "Guacamaya" arm movements and footwork, as well as *obon* fan technique. And like most *obon* dances, the movement mirrors the lyrics, bringing attention to the importance of the circle.[50]

As a board member for Smithsonian Folkways, Quetzal Flores helped facilitate and bring attention to the work Great Leap was doing with FandangObon, which led to an invitation to the annual Smithsonian Folklife Festival.[51] As participants, our respective legacies of celebration and resistance came together on the National Mall the week of June 26, 2016, for the *Sounds of California* exhibit.[52] The Smithsonian Folklife Festival gathered fandango musicians from Veracruz, Mexico; Los Angeles; and the Bay Area, such as Quetzal Flores (*jarana*, vocals), Russell Rodriguez (*requinto*, *jarana*, vocals), Tylana Enomoto (violin), and Juan Perez (bass). From Veracruz, Ramón Gutiérrez (*requinto*, vocals) was in attendance. *Obon* practitioners from Los Angeles were also present, including Nobuko Miyamoto, Elaine Fukumoto (dancer and choreographer), George Abe (*fue*), and Sean Miura (*shamisen*). The local DC *taiko* player Mark Rooney was also present. Our entire group was presented by Asian American scholar and ethnomusicologist Deborah Wong. Her thoughtful and conscientious presentation illuminated the work's artistic and political importance.

The celebrations, workshops, and countless panels were a great success with the festival's audiences. Men, women, and children of all ages were able to participate in the discussions, and the Smithsonian Folklife organization and staff produced a number of web links and media that documented the historic moments during the festival. This was much more than a gathering to partake in each other's music and dance. The air of celebration could not take the place of the seriousness that this gathering implied both politically and historically for both groups; for the intent to establish cross-cultural traditions of music and dance in the United States is, in its simplest terms, a pushback on the persistent isolation capitalist society inflicts on us all. Through a radical lens, FandangObon and cross-cultural convening methods such as these can be considered new healing practices that might remedy the wounds of colonization, war, mass incarceration, discrimination, and physical and emotional violence, while creating new generative forms of resistance. FandangObon introduced the nation's capital to a new California-based cross-cultural tradition of empowerment via participatory music and dance practice. Using the cultural convening methods of *obon* and *fandango*, FandangObon is attempting to get all communities back to where we once were—to our humanity, back to the circle, whole and unbroken.

Challenges of Fandango

The "social field" of *fandango sin fronteras* is vast and has stretched across nation-state boundaries and linguistic and cultural borders. Fandango as a protocol and a social tool has assisted in the formation and strengthening of communities in various parts of the United States and the world; however, the cultural logic of capital often finds its way into the convivial space of the fandango. The essentializing of fandango and of what it means to be "jarocho" is often idealized as community subjects begin to discipline each other on how to be "jarocho." Thus, the imitation in *jarocho* performativity begins to take precedent, rather than the practice that leads one to convivencia. In addition, the convivencia in fandango and mutual sharing on all levels decentralize power, yet they fail to deconstruct the ingrained notions of what it means to be an "authority" and a "student" in capitalist society. The sharing of minor to major skills in fandango practice empowers the person imparting the knowledge, oftentimes to the point of corruption. Furthermore, the impetus to perform the community practice of fandango as formal presentation is also epistemic. Fandango practitioners, often with little to no knowledge of the practice, begin to aspire to be on the stage as "performers" and "authorities" of *son jarocho*. Thus, the formation of performance groups becomes a way for subjects to reach a level of prestige, social status, and economic capital. These are challenges that both Chican@s in the United States and *jarocho* communities in Mexico share. For although fandango has been used as a democratic tool that instills in communities the possibility of mutual participation, it nonetheless fails to undo the social logic of capitalism.[53]

Despite these challenges, fandango practice is ever growing in communities and inspiring new generations. Through the efforts of the *movimiento jaranero* and Chican@ artivistas in East LA, Chicago, and other parts of the United States, *fandango sin fronteras* continues to thrive. It is through the efforts of *fandango sin fronteras* that a new generation of fandango practitioners can readily fathom music as more than just another product to buy or to sell in our society. Music can also be pastime, critical convivencia and the language of one's community.

CHAPTER 6

Los Guardianes de la Convivencia

Esta obra esta protegida por los guardianes del fandango jarocho.

Patricio Hidalgo Belli, *Piedras y flores*

In 2010, after years of traveling throughout the state of California and engaging in dialogue with multiple fandango communities, the poet and *sonero* master Patricio Hidalgo published a poetry book titled *Piedras y flores* (Stones and flowers).[1] The final page of this self-published book reads, "Esta obra esta protegida por los guardianes del fandango jarocho" (This work is protected by the guardians of the *fandango jarocho*). Rather than use industry copyright symbols, Hidalgo invokes "los guardianes del fandango jarocho," the guardians of the fandango, as those who will protect his work. Along with the many beautiful *versos, decimas,*[2] and other poems that inhabit the pages of *Piedras y flores*, I was particularly moved by this simple statement, for it reaffirmed to me the communal essence of fandango communities in Mexico and abroad. With this statement, Hidalgo addresses communities that partake in, maintain, and live amidst *convivencia fandanguera* and thus understand the importance of protecting both collective knowledge and individual legacy by taking responsibility, protection, and vigilance of Hidalgo's poetry into their hands.

As one of many *guardianes* of the *fandango jarocho*, and as a *testigo* (witness) to the 1997 encuentro, I demonstrate in this chapter how the lessons learned in the midst of varying translocal community struggles and triumphs translate into artivista praxis by way of two examples: Entre Mujeres and the Seattle Fandango Project. Chican@ artivista praxis ultimately operates to produce, instigate, and plant seeds that bring about a new understanding of the social relations of music and art. Through these projects, I demonstrate how methodologies learned in the 1997 encuentro and in fandango praxis have been utilized and shared with others, and how these moments of convivencia have continued to instigate critical consciousness within our lives and the lives of others.

The translocal feminine composition project Entre Mujeres was formally initiated in Veracruz, Mexico, from September of 2008 to June of 2009. Entre Mujeres fostered a new way of music engagement that actively took women and their multiple responsibilities into consideration. Low-cost,

portable recording equipment facilitated transnational music dialogues between US-based Chicanas in Los Angeles and *jarocha* musicians in Veracruz.
Furthermore, I engage in a theoretical analysis of the collective songwriting process learned in the 1997 *encuentro*, which was utilized in the Entre
Mujeres project. I came to find that convivencia, testimonio, trust, healing,
and knowledge production are the principal epistemologies in the collective
songwriting method. Through Entre Mujeres, among other collective songwriting efforts, I have witnessed time and again how the collective songwriting method creates space, builds community, challenges multiple patriarchal
systems, and can potentially produce knowledge that is accessible beyond
the academy. I believe that eventually songs as texts, or what I introduce
here as "sung theories," can be accessible archives that communicate important embodied knowledge across time, disciplines, borders, generations, and
other ways of knowing.

The second example recounts the inception and initial development of the
Seattle Fandango Project. Having left our tight-knit family and artist community in East Los Angeles in 2008 to commence my graduate studies at the
University of Washington, teaching and sharing of fandango praxis became a
way for my partner, Quetzal Flores, and I to connect with others. This effort
flourished into the Seattle Fandango Project, which continues to hail an ever-
growing number of practitioners of all races and backgrounds. At present, the
project is one of the most influential and active fandango communities in the
United States. The community's self-awareness and ongoing critical analysis
of social and economic power as sites of contention for community well-being
have established an informal system of checks and balances within the community. Importantly, I demonstrate how Seattle Fandango Project community members navigate activities ranging from grassroots efforts to paid gigs
and University of Washington–related functions and endorsements. In this
way, I show how the collective efforts of the *guardianes de fandango jarocho*
in the Pacific Northwest underscore the importance of participatory music
and dance practice as a way of building and maintaining community health.
Additionally, I explore how these important forms of convivencia through participatory music and dance practice usher communities into critical consciousness that translates into multiple areas of their individual and collective lives.
I am especially proud to be part of this community of *fandangueros*, for participating in and witnessing the project's developing community-organizing
methods continue to reinforce my belief in the true power of music.

Entre Mujeres: Women Making Music across Borders

As a professional and community musician and an active practitioner in the
translocal, community-based, participatory music and dance practice known

as fandango, I was moved by the significant participation of women, children, and the elderly the first time I witnessed fandango in Veracruz in 2003. Women's presence is seen and felt in every aspect of fandango—from *son jarocho* music, dance, and poetry that give currency to the practice, to the organizational aspects of events. Women play important roles as dancers and percussionists on the *tarima*, a wooden platform. A Mexican anthropologist and a *bailadora de fandango* from birth, Rubí Oseguera Rueda, from Coatzacoalcos, Veracruz, has documented the significance and presence of women in fandango in her 1998 book *Biografía de una mujer veracruzana*. Oseguera's important work was the first to document women's testimonios in fandango culture. With this publication Oseguera urged the fandango community to take note of all labors generated by women in the kitchen and in the music making, especially on the tarima. The tarima is the vortex of fandango, where all musicians gather around the dancers, who strike their feet on the wooden platform in a percussive manner. It is here where women execute perhaps the most important musical contributions to the fiesta in the intricate percussive dance that is the pulse and drive of the *son jarocho*.

Inspired by the broad participation of women and children in this practice, I initiated the translocal music composition project Entre Mujeres between the fall of 2007 and the summer of 2008. The goals of the project were to document women's role in fandango practice, to engage in musical dialogue with the women in the practice, and, if possible, to create original music compositions with those who were willing and able to participate. With support from the Fulbright–García Robles scholarship program, I was able to move with my partner and child to Xalapa, Veracruz, where we spent nine months composing with various fandango practitioners.

I never initiated a formal call for the project before arriving in Xalapa. I approached women whom I knew through previous fandango celebrations. After many years of engaging in fandango, both in Veracruz and in the United States, and knowing the community well enough, I had an idea of who would be interested in participating. Some women volunteered after hearing about the project, and others were recommended. In the end, the final music project included eight Mexican and seven US-based musicians.

From Fandango Tradition to Composition

Most of the women involved in Entre Mujeres were very receptive to working on original compositions. It was still a challenge for them, however, to move comfortably beyond their social and musical understanding of the fandango and *son jarocho* music genres. Regardless, I believe that the strong, *mujer*-driven tradition on the tarima made it easier for Entre Mujeres participants to interact with one another. The fandango—specifically the *son jarocho* repertoire—offers many instances where it is solely women and girls who participate on the tarima during *sones de a montón* (songs where many are signaled to dance). The syncopated rhythmic patterns they create on the tarima are meant both to keep time and to contribute to the polyrhythmic character of the *son jarocho*. These moments in fandango offer invaluable interaction, convivencia, and dialogue, especially among women, whose bodies and feet become conduits of individual and collective expression. The female homosocial space on the tarima, especially during the *sones de a montón*, provide moments Angela Davis might refer to as "quotidian expressions of feminist consciousness."[3] Davis uses this phrase in reference to women in the blues tradition, but I extend this black feminist consciousness to fandango as a related African diasporic expression. In fandango, the tarima is a space where the "collective consciousness" of women gathers in the presence of community. Most of the women in the Entre Mujeres project had previously experienced a collective consciousness on the tarima in the midst of fandango practice. I believe this alleviated the difficulties of composing original works in the collective. Despite initial anxiety by some of the *mujeres* concerning original music composition, the musical ideas began to slowly flow.

Collective Songwriting: Testimonio, Theory, and Knowledge Production

My partner and I rented a small, furnished flat in the center of Xalapa, Veracruz. We settled in quickly, creating a kitchen, a living room, and a small, makeshift recording nook, all in the same one-room space. Most days we would wake up to Xalapa's orchestral city sounds. Being from a big city like Los Angeles, we were used to vehicle traffic noise. But Xalapa city sounds were also intermingled with the voices of *vendedores ambulantes* (mobile street vendors) announcing their goods and services, or the gas company's rhythmic metal tapping, the trash collection cowbell, and the single stroke of the knifesmith's metal pan flute. All were sonic reminders that we were far from home. My partner and I would make our morning coffee and breakfast for our son and then wait for the *mujeres* to arrive.

We had previously made arrangements and invited the *mujeres* to our little flat "para tocar"—to play music, to hang out, or to compose. Unfortunately, most of their time was completely taken up by *chamba*, or work. Despite initial anxiety among some of the *mujeres*, the musical ideas slowly began to flow. Oftentimes one of the ladies we had scheduled a session with would call and say that something had come up with family and would cancel our writing session. Other times we would schedule many women at once, everyone would show up, and we would manage to play some *sones* or jam for a while. I soon found it difficult to gather them all in one place. And even if we did manage to compose something, I knew that rehearsal and recording time would also be difficult to schedule. Technology was very helpful in this regard. We owned portable recording equipment and began to utilize it in every jam session. The technology also allowed us to record some of the impromptu lyrical ideas that were generated during the sessions.

Lyricism became a vehicle that facilitated individual and collective expression. In all instances, there were moments of testimonio and the telling of experiences that generated more dialogue and sharing during the collective songwriting process than I would have expected. As we began to compose, I encouraged an exploration of topics. Each *mujer* chose a topic that resonated with her, but this did not limit our collaboration, as we would often cowrite the lyrics or each author would write a stanza or verse. Song topics were often driven by experiences in motherhood and love or views on the state of the world. The most intimate moments of creativity in the collective songwriting process brought about discussions pertaining to participants' experiences as women, life lessons, and general life philosophies. Most participants shared and learned from other testimonios, and this process bound the group in an intimate way.

"Sobreviviendo"

As windows to the mind and soul, lyrics often focused on the women's sharing of embodied knowledge as well as their community knowledge. Mothering and the birthing process were common topics throughout the Entre Mujeres project. The sharing of community knowledge and migration experience, however, was also expressed, as in the piece "Sobreviviendo" (Surviving). The lyrics read partially as follows:

La gente vive luchando
sin saber que pasara
Con sus pasos van surcando
caminos nuevos harán
No saben si hay una mañana
pero al fin se marcharan

Sobreviviendo, sobrevivir
Solo siguiendo, ya sin sentir

Por fuerte que sean los vientos
la palma siempre será
Me doblo por la tristeza
me enderezo por amar

La raíz es lo que importa
para toda humanidad

The people live in struggle
without knowing what is to come
As they walk their journeys
new roads emerge
They don't know if there will be a tomorrow
but nevertheless they depart

Surviving, survive
Just moving, without sensing

Despite the strongest winds
the palm tree will always be
I bend to the sadness
I stand tall for the loving
The root is what matters
for all humanity

Originally from the state of Yucatán, Silvia Santos moved to Xalapa as a young college student. Santos and her husband, David, had a *son jarocho* group called Híkuri and were active participants in the fandango networks, mostly in the Xalapa area. The mother of a ten-year-old daughter, Santos came to my home whenever she had a free moment, which was usually during her daughter's school hours. "Sobreviviendo" was Santos's idea. Although there were extensive discussions on other subject matter, Santos initiated the composition and was adamant about writing on the subject of immigration. I contributed a verse and the final chorus, but for the most part Santos had a clear vision of what she wanted for the song. My partner, Quetzal Flores, also played a key role in the arrangement of the piece and final recording. Having played several tours in the United States, Santos had visited California four years prior to her participation in the Entre Mujeres project. While visiting the Santa Barbara area, Santos had an opportunity to meet and converse with various undocumented immigrants from Mexico. Aware that I was from California and that the music generated in the project might reach this community, Santos seized the opportunity to create a piece that expressed the effects migration can have on families on both sides of the Mexico-US border. "Sobreviviendo," or "Surviving," expresses the views of both those who migrate as well as those who stay but are affected by the loss of *los ausentes*, or those who are absent. Santos describes the inspiration for the song:

Esta pieza es una síntesis de algunas vivencias de una estancia en California, en donde me encontré con migrantes que me contaron su sensación de tener el corazón lejano y en la mente el lugar que dejaron a sus seres queridos. Y como eso los motivaba a seguir en un mundo diferente. En el mundo físico de las jornadas extenuantes y una cultura diferente. Creo que todos somos viajeros en este mundo, pero ser viajero con el corazón dividido es algo muy duro, y ver tantos rostros, escuchar tantas historias de desarraigo, es algo que me dejó la huella que trato de plasmar en "Sobreviviendo."[4]

This piece is a synthesis of a lived experience I had in California, where I found myself with [Mexican] migrants who told me how they felt having their hearts and minds with their loved ones far away and how this motivates them to continue living in the physical world of everyday laborers . . . away from their homeland and in a different culture. I think that we are all travelers in this world, but to be a traveler with a divided heart is something that is very difficult, to see so many faces, and listen to so many different stories of uprooting, is something that left its mark on me and I try to communicate this in "Sobreviviendo."

Santos was moved by the testimonios she heard in Santa Barbara, but also by the families she knows in Mexico whose loved ones have migrated to the United States. She utilized the testimonios of migrant workers in the United States and families left behind in Mexico as a source of knowledge from which to create song lyrics for "Sobreviviendo."

In a follow-up interview I conducted in Xalapa, Veracruz, during the summer of 2014, Santos reflected on the ways in which undocumented audience members would often approach her after a performance by Híkuri:

Con la música mucha gente se acercaba a nosotros y nos contaba sus experiencias de viaje y de migración . . . pero además es como cuando alguien de pronto no tiene como comunicarse y encuentra una vía de escape. Llegaban y nos decían, "Ay que bonita música me recuerda a mi tierra." Y entonces después de eso se les habría esta válvula de los recuerdos. Y entonces era imparable lo que surgía. Surgían minutos, hasta horas de platica. De lo que era su experiencia como migrante. Incluso habían experiencias traumáticas en medio de todo esto. Que yo no se como habían sobrevivido también ellos a esas experiencias aparte de sobrevivir físicamente. O sea no de moralmente y eran tan fuertes que, de plano, mi pareja se llevaba a la niña para que no escuchara lo que me estaba contando porque se veía que la otra persona tenia la necesidad de contar, de decir lo que le había pasado. Un poco para sanar. Realmente el hablar, cura.[5]

With the music many would approach us and tell us about their experiences, about migration . . . but it's like when someone hasn't had someone to communicate with and then they find an escape. They would come to us and say, "Wow, what beautiful music, it reminds me of my country." And then the memory valve would open up. Then it was unstoppable. There were minutes, hours of discussion and telling of their experiences as migrants. There were even traumatic moments in all of these experiences that I don't even know how they survived emotionally let alone physically. I mean like morally. And these stories were so heavy that my partner would take my little girl away so that she didn't listen to what they were telling me, because it was obvious that the person needed to speak about what had happened to them a bit to heal. In reality there is healing in the telling.

Santos states that the "válvula de los recuerdos," or memory valve, would often open to reveal painful experiences of the dangerous, often fatal, migrant trails. The people who approached Santos were survivors of the grueling journey. Indeed, the stories she was entrusted with in Santa Barbara were in her consciousness when I arrived in Xalapa and approached her about participating in the Entre Mujeres project. Santos acknowledges the healing process of testimonio as she describes the change of energy once the "válvula de los recuerdos" was exhausted. She continues:

Entonces hablas de tu proceso. Hasta que llega un momento en el que ya no lo vez como en tercera persona. Ya no es, lo que le paso a "él," sino lo que me paso a "mi," como lo asimile, y como . . . que a pesar de eso . . . sobrevivo. Por eso finalmente, el son se llama "Sobreviviendo." Por que es este proceso para mi también de reflexión como uno puede sobreponerse a cualquier circunstancia siempre y cuando haya algo por lo cual sobrevivir. Que conserves la fe en que vas a ver a las personas que quieres. Que vas a regresar a tu tierra. Que vas a darles algo mejor, a las personas por las cuales te fuiste. Y las cual estás lejos siempre. Pero estás lejos físicamente y tu mente está ahí de todos modos. Es un asunto de dicotomía muy fuerte que todos tenemos en mayor o en menor medida.[6]

You then speak of your process. Until there is a moment where you don't speak of it in third person. It is no longer what happened to "him" but rather what happened to "me," how I assimilated it, and despite it all, how I survived. That is why finally the *son* is called "Sobreviviendo." Because it was also a moment of reflection for me on how someone can survive any circumstance if and when they have someone to survive for. You maintain faith that you will see the people you love. That you will return to your homeland. That you will provide something better to those whom you left and the reason for which you left and are far away. But they are gone physically but mentally always there. It is a dichotomy issue that we all have in a greater or lesser sense.

As Santos states, to keep the faith, or to hope for and envision a successful return to one's homeland, was part of her intention and process as she wrote these lyrics with her migrant friends in mind and advocated for the song's recording as part of the project. Importantly, "Sobreviviendo" encapsulates first- and secondhand testimonio. Santos recounts people's experiences of perilous migration but most importantly their resilience to move forward regardless of what the future holds.

Testimonio has been an important intervention in an effort to decenter subjective knowledge and Western research paradigms that often "other" communities of color. Testimonio centers firsthand knowledge and experience as an invaluable resource and a place from which knowledge can be formulated. In this way, testimonio has been recognized as a powerful research praxis for people of color. Testimonio, when shared in a community, may also initiate what the indigenous scholar Shawn Wilson cites as "relationality," which results from moments of sharing and healing. Citing relationality as part and parcel to an indigenous ontology, Wilson states that "rather than viewing ourselves as being *in* relationships with other people or things, we *are* the relationships that we hold and are a part of."[7] To this end one must recognize not only the importance of sharing one's testimonio through the collective songwriting process but also the spaces that are generated in the process and thus allow for this relationality. As Gaye Theresa Johnson has articulated, "Meaningful space is essential for the survival of communities, but also for the discursive practices encoding the stories that define and redefine who people are, where they fit into the world, and what they envision for the future."[8] "Sobreviviendo," as a culmination of both primary (immigrant women in Santa Barbara) and secondary (Santos in Xalapa) testimonio sources, speaks to the impact of migration from multiple perspectives. Through the gathering of testimonios on both sides of the border, Santos's composition is an ode to immigrant people's stories in both Santa Barbara and Mexico, and all at once a synthesis of the grand effects migration can have on two communities at once. "Sobreviviendo" is a double-sided view of migration as a global phenomenon that affects those who leave as well as those who remain in their home country.

Finally, similar to theories regarding testimonio, the most important aspect of collective songwriting is not the song itself but rather its ability to "engender solidarity."[9] Testimonio was utilized in the Entre Mujeres project as a way to create knowledge and theory through personal experiences toward the goal of creating a song, or what I began to see as "sung theories." It became a space from which to discuss and create collective ideas among women, which simultaneously created a sense of community among all *mujeres* involved. Collective songwriting as an enactment of spatial entitlement, the varying ways that participants like Santos created new collectivities in the face of adversity, is not just based "upon eviction and exclusion from physical spaces, but also on new and imaginative uses of technology, creativity, and spaces."[10] With one eye on Santa Barbara, California, Santos weaves migrant testimonios into lyrical prose that reflects migrants' exodus from their homeland and the daily hardships they face in new territory. "Sobreviviendo" recounts an enduring strength and resilience.

Entre Mujeres CD Release

Five years after completing the project in Xalapa, we released *Entre Mujeres: Women Making Music across Borders* (2012) in Los Angeles, California.[11] In the end, the mothers, women, men, and children involved participated in different ways, either through lyricism, music and instrumentation, *zapateado* (percussive dance), or voice. The compositions touched on familiar musical themes, such as being in love ("Sirena lanza" [Mermaid rising]), coping with a broken heart ("Agua del mar" [Ocean water]), and hoping for a positive future ("Quien nacerá" [Who shall be born] and "Vida" [Life]). Other tracks explored more specific experiences, such as "Chocolate," which spoke on the cocoa trade from the perspective of a small child caught up in the throes of slave labor. We also explored unconventional topics; "Encinta" (With child), for example, described the final physiological stages of pregnancy.

"Sobreviviendo" has received the most acclaim. The final recording of the piece is sung by Silvia Santos (Yucatán, Mexico), Raquel Vega (Boca de San Miguel, Veracruz), and Laura Cambron, a Chicana from California. Cambron can also be heard playing *requinto* in the recording. With permission, it has been utilized by various social justice organizations both in the United States and in Mexico since the album's release. Mujeres Activas en Letras y Cambio Social, for example, utilized the song for their website and a video promo for the organization. In Mexico, "Sobreviviendo" was used to raise awareness around domestic violence. These are only a few of the many organizations and audiences that continue to approach me about the song. "Sobreviviendo" seems to resonate with many groups in struggle.

Song as Archive, or "Sung Theories"

At present, the Entre Mujeres recording project stands as an archive that documents one of many translocal dialogues between Chican@, Latin@, and Mexican communities in the United States and *jarocho* communities in Veracruz, Mexico. In order to accommodate multiple schedules as well as to engage with and document music dialogues across political borders, a manipulation of recording technology was important to the project's completion. Utilizing these technologies, Entre Mujeres, through convivencia, created a space that prompted testimonios and discussions on music, love, mothering, politics, and overall life experience. Ultimately, "Sobreviviendo" represents process and archive. Songs as archives, or "sung theories," are important elements of the Entre Mujeres project, especially when one considers them over time. Recordings, lyrics, and performances of these songs stand to be remembered, revisited, reconstructed, critiqued, or honored by future generations. Bell hooks reminds us that "as we work to be loving, to create a culture that celebrates life, that makes love possible, we move against dehumanization, against domination."[12] In this way, Silvia Santos understood that songs and the theories embedded in them can inform across time, disciplines, borders, generations, and other ways of knowing, but most importantly songs can register the hope and resilience that inspired their creation.

The Seattle Fandango Project

We arrived in Seattle, Washington, in September of 2008. Los Angeles was far behind us as we drove through downtown Seattle on the way from the airport. A mixture of excitement and sadness enveloped our little family. Like mothers before me, I had learned to make light of everything for my son's sake, no matter how I was feeling. I pointed at the vast greenery and the Space Needle as we drove through downtown. I realized that although we had been to Seattle many times over the years with Quetzal—we had played in Seattle proper as well as the surrounding areas, such as Kent and Kirkland— this time we were here to stay. I had been accepted into the PhD program in the Department of Women's Studies at the University of Washington.[13] Graduate school was the last place I had ever thought music practice would take me, but I had learned to value the years of experience in East LA Chican@ artivista communities and knew that the possibilities for analysis and documentation would be important work to engage in.[14]

Besides the rigor and pace of a graduate program, the most challenging aspect of living in the Seattle area was the weather and the lack of friends

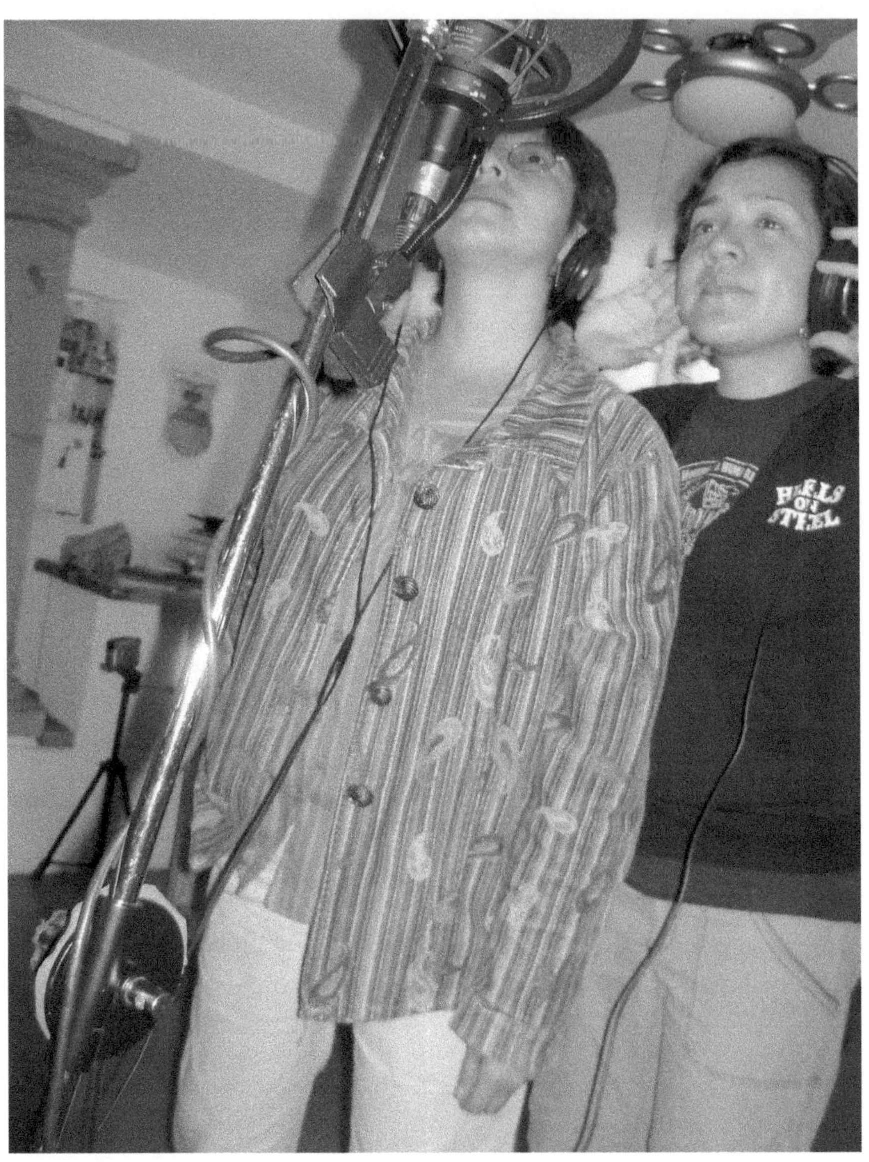

Kali Niño and I, recording backgrounds for "La Madera."

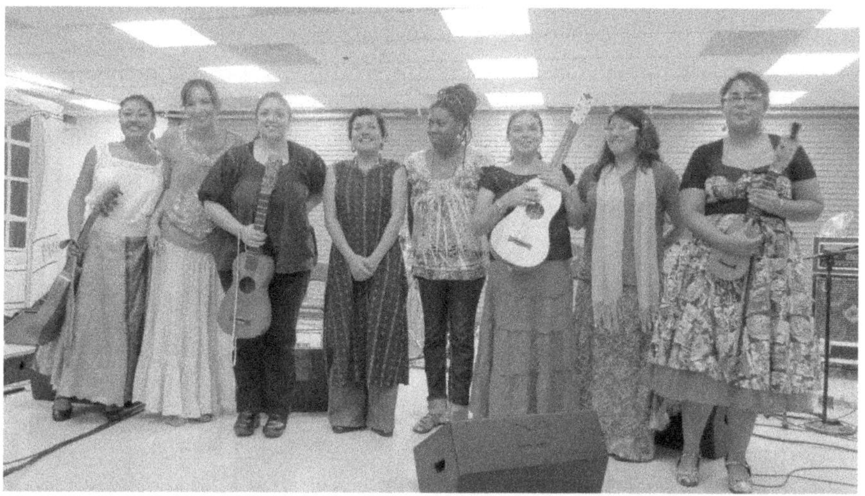

Entre Mujeres performance for Viva El Arte in Santa Barbara, California, circa 2012. From left to right: Annahi Hernandez, Rocio Marron, Laura Rebolloso, me, Niki Campbell, Wendy Cao Romero, Kali Niño, "La Marisoul" Hernandez.

and family around us. I remember feeling terribly lonely after completing my first quarter. We began to reach out to some of the people we knew lived in the area—to convene, to play, or to connect in some way. The first person we reached out to was Francisco Orozco. Orozco was a Bay Area friend and an ethnomusicology graduate student in the School of Music at the University of Washington. He had some previous experience with *son jarocho* and fandango. Orozco informed us that there were other folks in the Seattle area who knew aspects of the tradition, and we began to meet regularly in my home.[15]

In the meantime, my partner, Quetzal Flores, obtained a job as program coordinator for the American Music Partnership of Seattle (AMPS). His role was to coordinate and oversee a collaboration among the Experience Music Project, KEXP-FM radio, and the University of Washington. The School of Music professor Shannon Dudley was the chair of AMPS, and he approached Flores about implementing any kind of project that would connect the AMPS partners to local communities through music. Flores immediately suggested fandango as a community-building tool.[16]

Although there were some people in the Seattle area who had some experience with *son jarocho*, no one had formally taught the fandango protocols enough to foment a movement. Flores and I were able to impart the music, voice, and dance protocols that were needed to be able to have all the elements that make up a fandango. Through the Simpson Center for the

Humanities, the University of Washington provided some funding for Flores to buy supplies to build the first Seattle Fandango Project tarima. Once Professor Dudley had committed to providing a space in the music school, we knew we were set. The goal was to get University of Washington students and the surrounding community involved in learning the skills, but more importantly the ethics, of fandango practice.

During the spring quarter of 2009, with our son, Sandino, in tow, we gathered every Monday night to teach and discuss fandango practice. We had arrived in Seattle with a reputation as accomplished members of Quetzal. It was also well known that we were accomplished *son* practitioners and had studied with some of the most respected elders in the fandango tradition. Both through our reputation as well as through our demonstration of the practice and playing of fandango, we earned the trust of the community as we shared the basic tenets of the practice. Although the gatherings were on the University of Washington campus, it was not a registered university course. Flores and I volunteered our time and sought to create a "come one, come all" type of gathering. With the help of Francisco Orozco and other community members who had some experience with the *son jarocho*, such as Iris Viveros and Eduardo Sierra, word spread of fandango workshops around campus and in the community. Soon, a critical mass began to form.[17]

Monday nights were a relief from the loneliness we felt as non-Seattle natives. Viveros and Sierra were both Mexican immigrants and became invaluable community members. Students from different disciplines, as well as community people and families with children from the surrounding areas, began to show up to learn about fandango. My son, Sandino, soon had a flurry of children to play with, and Music Building room 313 felt like a community space, a home away from home for us on the University of Washington campus.

In teaching the basic *sones*, dances, and strumming of the instruments of the *son jarocho*, Quetzal Flores was adamant about consistently emphasizing the fandango as the *most* important aspect of the practice. During our two-month pit stop in Los Angeles before we had moved to Seattle, we had witnessed how fandango practice in LA had been somewhat abandoned. Many practitioners had been empowered by fandango, but as mentioned in the previous chapter, they began to spend most of their energies taking to the stage. Again, I believe that the impetus to learn music is enjoyable, cathartic, and empowering, especially in fandango practice; however, when the empowerment and understanding of fandango becomes distorted, novice practitioners often begin to form performance groups that solely aspire to play onstage. Suddenly, the original intention of fandango as a community practice loses importance. Fandango mistakenly becomes a logical stepping-stone toward professional music practice. Flores and I were adamant:

in our sharing of the practice with the Seattle Fandango Project, we consistently reiterated that the goal of knowing the practice of fandango, and of building on the skills and knowledge base of the practice, was to better participate in fandango as community. Our role as experienced *fandangueros* was not to teach skills of the practice to make participants "professional musicians," but rather to instill the know-how and sense of convivencia through music. The reiterative discourse of fandango as a community-building practice was thus a teaching anthem in our *talleres*, or workshops, straight away. The democratization of music practice as it is articulated in fandango is not the same criteria of the stage. Indeed, the original intention, struggle, and resurgence of fandango practice in communities by the *movimiento jaranero* had become lost in the intervening years. Novice students empowered by the practice have often soured the *movimiento jaranero* efforts by forming low-quality performance groups that seek paid gigs, notoriety, and social capital.

The University of Washington and the Seattle Fandango Project

To support and expand the work we were already doing with the fandango classes, a budget was created by Quetzal Flores and Professor Shannon Dudley in order to invite Son de Madera for a ten-week residency. In the middle of this planning, Professor Dudley had to relinquish the role as principal investigator on the AMPS grant, turning it over to the Simpson Center for the Humanities.[18] This bureaucratic move marginalized the plans and budget of the Seattle Fandango Project. The Simpson Center decided that it would make the funds available to other projects and interests across the University of Washington campus. The Seattle Fandango Project received 20 percent of the original budget.[19] With or without the funds, the *talleres* on the university campus were already in full swing, and we were still able to make plans to bring Son de Madera for a short residency.

To celebrate the last day of classes of the spring quarter before Son de Madera's visit, I suggested we hold a potluck. As we approached music room 313, I could hear the chatter of people and the strumming of *jaranas*. Entering the classroom, I saw a table full of food and drink. Participants were accustomed by then to greeting each other via warm embraces. The music, families, and children running about warmed my heart. We had our usual workshop, ate, and celebrated together. As we drove home that night, I vividly remember commenting to my partner on the complete change of energy I felt. Our lives were suddenly different in Seattle. Through the sharing of fandango practice we had become closer to many people. We had a community. We had a home.

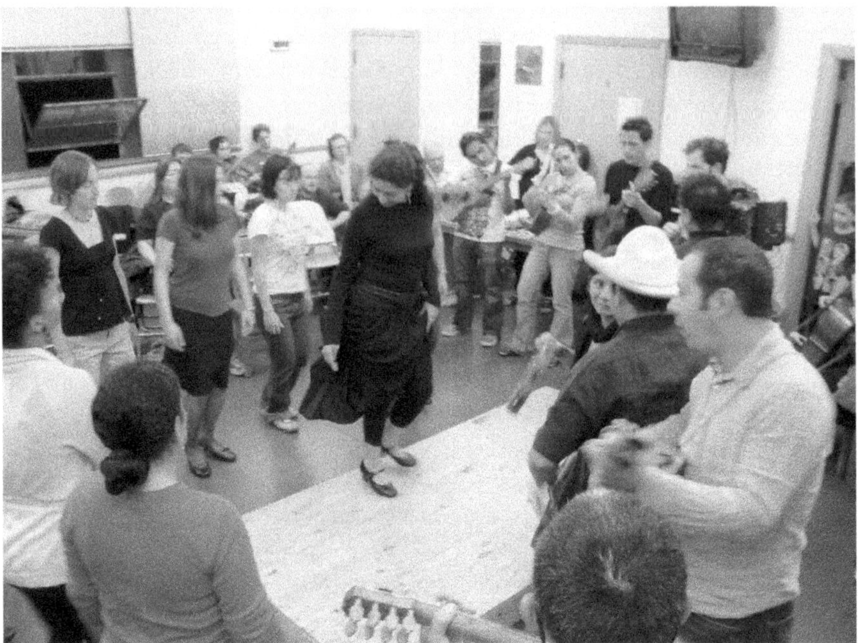

Rubí Oseguera and Son de Madera facilitating a fandango workshop in the Music Building, room 313, at the University of Washington, Seattle. Courtesy of Scott and Angelica Macklin.

School of Music and Department of Gender, Women, and Sexuality Studies

Before Son de Madera's arrival, we had committed to expanding the community. Quetzal Flores, Francisco Orozco, Iris Viveros, Eduardo Sierra, and I expanded the Seattle Fandango Project to conduct workshops in West Seattle and the Beacon Hill areas. Community centers such as Youngstown Cultural Arts Center and El Centro de la Raza quickly became sites of instruction that garnered a critical mass and attendance of multiracial, transgenerational communities. By the time Son de Madera arrived for their monthlong visit, there was a substantial interest in and curiosity about fandango practice in the area.

As the Seattle Fandango Project grew and a demand for instruments became a necessity, the project decided to spend some of its funds on instruments to meet the demand of the increasing number of participants.[20] These would be instruments that the University of Washington would own but that students could borrow and check out during the *talleres*. Flores reached out to instrument and string makers in the *fandango sin fronteras* network. The decision to "spread the love," or economic resources, was very important. Since the network involves more than one *laudero*, or instrument maker, Flores carefully selected opportunities for as many *lauderos* as possible. Additionally, having witnessed the potential of fandango as a community-building practice, El Centro de la Raza also applied for a grant through the City of Seattle Office of Arts and Culture that allowed for the purchase of a *requinto*, a *leona*, and seven *jaranas*. Again, the outgoing resources were distributed to *lauderos* and musicians within the *fandango sin fronteras* network.[21]

In addition to Professor Shannon Dudley's support, Professor Michelle Habell-Pallán of the Department of Gender, Women, and Sexuality Studies was also instrumental in advocating for the support of the project by proposing a lecture series and related events during Son de Madera's residency. Recognizing the important role women play in fandango practice, Professor Habell-Pallán secured funds for a series of lectures and events titled *Alma en la tarima*.[22] The goals of the series were to highlight the important role that women play in fandango and to reiterate the social justice implications in the praxis of dance rooted in community that extended into other areas of the panelists' respective works.[23] The series panelists included Rubí Oseguera Rueda (Veracruz), Carolina Sarmiento (Santa Ana, California), Laura Marina Rebolloso (Veracruz), Marisol Berríos-Miranda (Puerto Rico), Teresita Bazán (Oaxaca and Mexico City), Iris Viveros (Xalapa, Veracruz), and me. These events were almost always followed by gatherings at the home of Shannon Dudley and his wife, Professor Marisol Berríos-Miranda. Open to the entire Seattle Fandango Project, the potlucks with food, drinks, laughter, and convivencia strengthened the bond among the fandango community.

Seattle Fandango Project
Performance Group, Son Tequio

As part of the project, a performance group developed in order to pull practitioners into the different workshop sites taking place all over Seattle. Although this was a point of contention for Flores and me, the goal was to pique people's interest in the practice so that they would then attend the *talleres*. This helped our recruitment, but it also led to requests for more performance-oriented presentations. In all these performance moments, we collectively agreed that we needed to stress who we were as a group and our goals. These invitations ranged from political demonstrations and school assemblies to food sovereignty events and Día de los Muertos celebrations. The small amounts of pay from these events created a "cochinito" fund, which was used to advance Seattle Fandango Project goals.[24]

The Seattle Fandango Project performance group was sometimes known as Son Tequio.[25] *Tequio* was a term introduced by Teresita Bazán, a Seattle Fandango Project community member. Originally from Oaxaca via Mexico City, Teresita suggested the term, which means "work" or "tribute" in the Zapotec language, for the performance group name.

Important to note, some tensions began to surface concerning stage performances done by members of Son Tequio. The members of the project who were more experienced were often chosen to participate in Son Tequio. Beginner students, if not completely offended, were often bothered at not being considered. We had to explain that the stage and the fandango are two very different spaces with different criteria. Indeed, this created tension, and at times Son Tequio were jokingly referred to as "the VIPs."[26]

First Fandango in the Pacific Northwest

On October 30, 2009, after the month-long artist residency by Son de Madera that included Ramón Gutiérrez, Rubí Oseguera Rueda, Tereso Vega, and Juan Perez from East LA, we had the first fandango in Seattle at the Vera Project.[27] The fandango was a huge success, as it brought together various communities within the University of Washington and beyond. Students and their families from the different sites, as well as students from the University of Washington, gathered to participate in and to witness for the first time a fandango in the Pacific Northwest. *Fandangueros* from El Centro Cultural de Santa Ana (Los Santaneros) made the time and the effort to trek to Seattle from California to perform and participate in the fandango. The Vera Project fandango was a sort of baptism inducting the Pacific Northwest *guardianes* into the transnational networks via representatives from Mexico, East LA, and Santa Ana.[28]

To add to the excitement and momentum that Son de Madera's visit had generated, the Vera Project fandango was followed by a two-quarter-long visit from Laura Marina Rebolloso (cofounder of Son de Madera and former wife of Ramón Gutiérrez). Rebolloso's time in Seattle solidified the influence of master musicianship in music, *zapateado* (percussive dance), and voice instruction that Son de Madera had initiated. An experienced instructor for children, young people, and adults alike, Rebolloso undertook a visiting professorship in the School of Music that is now legendary. Her presence and generous teaching style pulled many more fandango practitioners onto the tarima. Although Rebolloso's time and teaching efforts in Seattle communities were compensated, in addition to the activities of her visiting professorship she also took the time to teach the community of the Seattle Fandango Project.[29]

Community as the Key Force in
the Success of the Seattle Fandango Project

The core reason for the Seattle Fandango Project's success, and what has continued to drive the project to this very day, has been the involvement and ethical direction that the surrounding communities of West Seattle, Beacon Hill, and White Center (to name a few) brought to the project. These communities have been the soul and engine that continue to initiate new constituencies and communities into this liberatory practice. During and well after our time in the Seattle area, the community took hold of the project and made it their own.

Without community involvement, the Seattle Fandango Project would not exist, let alone thrive. That is to say, the project would not have been as successful were it not for the community involvement and support. This awareness has led to tensions in the relationships between the University of Washington and the fandango community at large. The University of Washington provided the project with initial and important financial and logistical support to facilitate bringing Son de Madera and Laura Marina Rebolloso, as well as purchasing much-needed instruments. While there is a sense of gratitude from members of the Seattle Fandango Project, the community also understands the importance of their own presence and creative labor and how their support provides an invaluable resource that has made the project as successful as it has been. This is key to the practice and understanding of fandango. This relationship (money and institutional support versus critical mass and community involvement) has been a constant negotiation between the community and the University of Washington concerning the existence and workings of the Seattle Fandango Project. The professors, the students (like me), and others who have been connected to the university have been held accountable by the community time and again. Whether through publications, museum exhibits, demonstrations, or anything having to do with the Seattle Fandango Project, the community has manifested their right to have a voice in how they are represented. A system of informal checks and balances has been a part of the development of the project from the outset. Through email correspondence via LISTSERVs and social media, the communities of *fandangueros* not only inform each other of different gigs, demonstrations, classroom presentations, and community events, but they also bring up important issues of representation and power dynamics.

As the most visible connections between the University of Washington and the Seattle Fandango Project, the tenured professors Shannon Dudley and Michelle Habell-Pallán have often had to answer to the community for the actions taken by the university, or for publications that have surfaced that misrepresent the project's history and philosophy.[30] Although Seattle Fandango Project participants are not all on the same page in terms of what is important to check and balance, the tradition of questioning the University of Washington for its actions is part of the relationships in place that I believe reflect the ethics and understanding of fandango practice. In the end, it is the tradition of questioning that is important. Most significantly, this process has fundamentally challenged people's core beliefs concerning power, community, and personal accountability held by *all* participants.

Film and Archiving: The Invaluable Efforts of Scott and Angelica Macklin

The multiple assets that varying people have brought to the Seattle Fandango Project have had a tremendous impact on the project's success. Film and documentation are important tools that have supported the project's efforts. The then University of Washington–affiliated filmmakers and archivists Scott and Angelica Macklin have been closely documenting the Seattle Fandango Project *talleres*, performances, and efforts since the first *talleres* in Music Building room 313. Their close relationship and involvement in the community has been captured via multiple documentary clips that have made visible the struggle, beauty, and efforts of the project. The Macklins' films and photographs have been instrumental tools in proving the kind of critical mass and impact the fandango project has had on the local, national, and international community. The documentaries have served many functions: educational, recruitment, assessment (often required as outcomes by grant makers), and overall archival documentation of the development of the project.[31]

Seattle Fandango Project Still Going Strong

The community-building efforts of the Seattle Fandango Project have been recognized by grassroots communities and arts partnerships nationwide as well as the University of Washington.[32] The project was named the recipient of the 2012 University of Washington Vice President for Minority Affairs and Vice Provost for Diversity Award for Community Building. Participants in the project, as individual and active *guardianes*, have utilized fandango sharing and practice in other spaces and projects related to the surrounding community, including the City of Seattle Office of Arts and Culture, Youngstown Cultural Arts Center, El Centro de la Raza, Casa Latina, FICA Capoeira Studio, Hidmo restaurant and community center, Washington Hall, the Vera Project,

V-Me Television, Experience Music Project, KEXP Radio, KBCS Radio, K–12 schools in King and Yakima Counties, and Acción Latina.[33]

Importantly, the Seattle Fandango Project has also garnered admiration and support from various communities in Mexico, specifically in Veracruz. Besides Son de Madera and Laura Marina Rebolloso, the project has gone on to host other *son jarocho* and fandango groups or masters in the tradition, such as Los Cojolites, Patricio Hidalgo, Andres Flores, César Castro, Alfredo Godo Herrera, and the notable *son jarocho* scholar Antonio García de León.

Many of the women in the Seattle Fandango Project have gone on to higher education as a result of their involvement and experience in participatory music and dance as liberatory practice. Iris Viveros is finishing up her PhD in the Gender, Women, and Sexuality Studies Department at the University of Washington. Kristina Clark received her MFA from the same institution.[34] Finally, Yesenia Navarrete Hunter, whose four children grew up on the tarima in the early years of the movement, is finishing up her dissertation in history at the University of Southern California.[35]

In October of 2019 the Seattle Fandango Project celebrated their ten-year anniversary. They continue to go strong, and their reach continues to be felt throughout the state of Washington.

Imaginaries

THE GRAMMY AND
THE GRADUATE STUDENT

Art and culture are inseparable and symbiotic resources that live at the essence of community vitality and transformation. With art and culture we provoke critical analysis of our communities. Cultural convening practices are sites for the facilitation of power and cooperation.

Quetzal Flores, personal correspondence, 2017

Differential consciousness requires grace, flexibility, and strength: enough strength to confidently commit to a well-defined structure of identity for one hour, day, week, month, year; enough flexibility to self-consciously transform that identity according to the requisites of another oppositional ideological tactic.

So much was taken away that "the place we live now is an idea"—and in this place new forms of identity, theory, practice, and community became imaginable.

Chela Sandoval, Methodology of the Oppressed

It was June 2009 and we had been in the midst of composing a new album for the Smithsonian Folkways label. We were still living in Seattle, and I sat down to put words to a musical idea our bass player, Juan Perez, had composed. The idea Perez had recorded for me was not on his usual instrument, the bass, but rather on a Kurt Schoen Turbo Diddly. The Turbo was built from recycled parts that consisted of a wooden Cuban cigar box and a metal resonator for the body of the instrument. The resulting sound of this unlikely instrument was the epitome of man/machine balance. Like the Turbo, artivistas are creating new sounds and creative approaches from unlikely parts. Using music as tools of dialogue, our differential consciousness has allowed us to navigate between and among worlds. We have recognized how music and other forms of creative expression can be liberatory tools, and how these tools can be harnessed collectively to escape the arranged social relations of music to move into a different mode of consciousness and existence. The Turbo and the artivista are both hybrid creatures in their respective worlds.

As I sat down to compose to the sound of the Turbo, I had Emma Pérez's 1999 book *The Decolonial Imaginary: Writing Chicanas into History* bumping in my head. Having taken a Chicana feminist theory course with Professor Michelle Habell-Pallán in the fall of 2009, I was still high on the material we had been assigned. These thoughts, coupled with the feelings of the final night of the fandango *taller* at the University of Washington, inspired the lyrics to "Imaginaries":

> A shift a move a surge we feel and manifest
> Slide from uncertainty and lunge into intent
> Interminable imaginaries guided by ancestor's strength
> abide by no one's government
> "We below and to the left"[1]
> More
> We see more
> Whose life is this for?
>
> Global affinities, we work within our trenches
> We make love through local intentions
> Slow, chaotic and slow
> but that seed you forgot you sowed
> Is one day a tree guarding you from the cold and more.
> We see more
> From margin to the core.
>
> Will slowly build
> Will slowly build
> Imaginaries
> Now!

"Imaginaries" outlines a differential consciousness, a community mind-set, and a process that can range from "uncertainty" to "manifest." In the first verse, I wanted to demonstrate how experimentation, dialogue, and quite possibly fear are all intertwined in social movement processes. Multiple imaginaries and feelings of doubt and uncertainty converge and are present before the possibility of change. I reference the plurality, or "interminable imaginaries," within community that exist and must be taken into account, for dialogue and consensus are messy and must be mediated daily. This was indeed something I had witnessed in the Big Frente Zapatista, the 1997 encuentro, *fandango sin fronteras*, Entre Mujeres, and the Seattle Fandango

Project. Again, the processes or attempts to reach consensus do not adhere to uniformity, but rather consensus work helps us reach the goal of shaping "a world in which there is room for many worlds."[2]

The second verse of "Imaginaries" speaks to the importance of building alliances in other regions and across borders with other communities in struggle without losing sight of living and thriving in local trenches and at local scales. I wanted to demystify the notion that being in "community" means being perpetually harmonious and void of conflict. In reality, working intimately with a community in reaching a goal is "slow, chaotic and slow." Ultimately, the goal is to sow seeds that one day become the fruit of our labors and, as the lyrics state, "the trees guarding you from the cold and more."[3]

Indeed, as we have moved from place to place, from East LA and Veracruz, Mexico, to graduate school in Seattle, Washington, my partner and I have implemented the tools we have learned with local and translocal communities and have shared them with others along the way. As a "self-consciously organizing resistance, identity, praxis, and coalition under contemporary U.S., late-capitalist cultural conditions,"[4] Chican@ artivista method adheres nicely to a differential consciousness, or what Gloria Anzaldúa calls "la facultad." I am reminded of artivista efforts of the late nineties and how different artists and community organizers have continued to create and thrive in the present. These methods learned in our youth have not lost credibility as we have aged and been confronted with the "real world" of raising families and having to make ends meet as adults.

The Grammy Nomination

"Imaginaries" became the title track for the fifth Quetzal album, released on the Smithsonian Folkways label and subsequently nominated for, of all things, a Grammy Award.[5] Being nominated for a Grammy at this stage of our careers as musicians and community organizers was not necessarily "a dream come true"—or rather, it did not convince us that we had finally "made it." Although we were grateful for the recognition, the emotion we felt was like having Santa Claus come to your home when you don't necessarily believe in him anymore. The lack of belief is not from a place of jaded indifference. The idea of Santa Claus is still nice to think about, but the sentiment had been somewhat demystified.

Nevertheless, as word spread of Quetzal being nominated, many old friends and community people bombarded us through Facebook, emails, and texts. Streams of messages poured in. Old-school fans that had followed us from the earliest days of Centro Regeneración were taking ownership of Quetzal's nomination. The triumphant comments and sentimental reactions ushered us to celebrate it our way. Understanding the social importance of the nomination in both an industry and a community context, Quetzal Flores convinced the group that we should leverage the moment and focus on the bigger picture.

Pre-Grammys Party

Because an unprecedented number of *son jarocho*–influenced projects had been nominated, we wanted to bring attention to how these groups related to each other.[6] Los Cojolites, Sistema Bomb, and Quetzal were all part of *fandango sin fronteras* networks. Although we had been invited to attend the Hollywood Grammys galas that are held for all nominees, in attempt to celebrate with community and to acknowledge the importance of the relationships that give rise to music-making efforts, Flores along with Gabriel Tenorio organized a performance and discussion at the Eastside Café, as well as a pre-Grammys party at the newly renovated Breed Street Shul multipurpose room in Boyle Heights. The organizers' goal was to gather East LA–based musicians who had been nominated for a Grammy at one point or another in their careers. Raul "El Bully" Pacheco (Ozomatli), Louis Pérez (Los Lobos), "La Marisoul" Hernandez (La Santa Cecilia), and the *jarocho* musician Andres Flores (Chuchumbé) were some of the artists who agreed to participate.

Cultural theorists and academic scholars who write about the East LA music and art scene were also present. Russell Rodriguez, George Lipsitz, Victor Hugo Viesca, Michelle Habell-Pallán, Josh Kun, Greg Landau, and Roberto Gonzalez Flores shared their thoughts concerning music and community.[7] The crowd consisted of new and familiar faces. From the days of Centro Regeneración and the Popular Resource Center to the present-day fandangos, we filled the multipurpose room to its maximum capacity.[8] Russell Rodriguez later stated, "The night was a joyous and magical gathering of music, thoughts, food, friendship, and *convivencia*. And the desire for Quetzal to want to share their celebration with their family, friends, and neighbors, clearly demonstrates where their heart is, where they get inspiration, where they write and compose, where they represent, and where they live—in their community."[9]

The Trophy

On February 10, 2013, at 1:30 p.m., we sat in the Nokia Theater in downtown LA, waiting for the Grammy Award announcements. Days before, we had been through both a pre-Grammys fandango and the pre-Grammys party. We had also just spent hours walking down the red carpet. Needless to say,

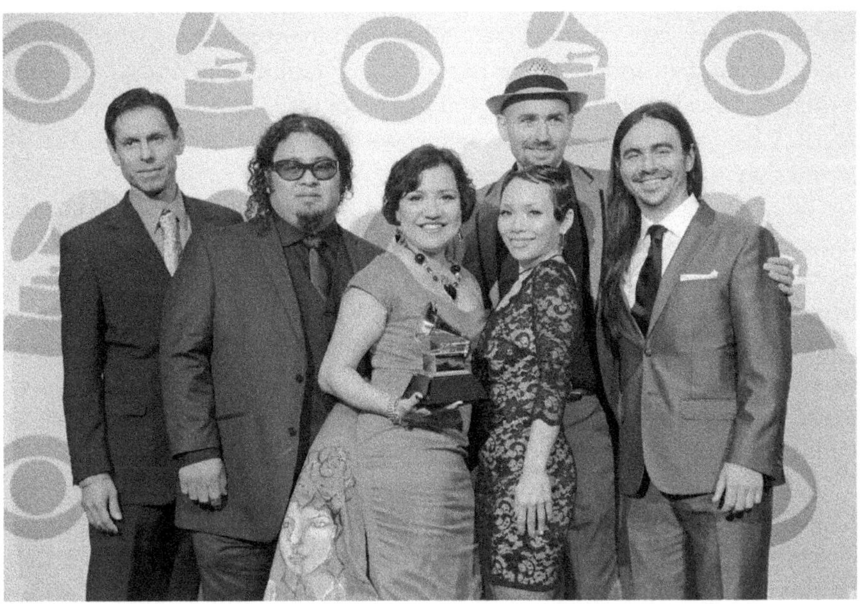

At the Grammys.

we were *desvelados* (lacking sleep) and exhausted overall. As we sat waiting for the category of Best Latin Rock, Urban, or Alternative Album, we looked around in awe at all of the great musicians that walked by. Bonnie Raitt, Esperanza Spalding, and Chick Corea were but a few of the great musicians and songwriters we ran into.

When our category finally came up the presenter mispronounced our band name and the title of the album, *Imaginaries*. As I waited to make sense of what the announcer had said, our percussionist, Alberto Lopez, stood up and yelled, "¡No mames!" We had won! As I still tried to decipher what the announcer had said, Lopez was already out in the aisle and walking toward the stage. Quetzal Flores called out, "Get up, Martha, we won!" I was in disbelief. I could not believe the announcer had mispronounced our name. Nonetheless, I slowly began to rise out of my seat and scoot out into the corridor. As we made our way down to the stage, I could hear our *jarocho* friends Los Cojolites cheering for us as we walked by. Running down the corridor, Tylana Enomoto, Quetzal's violinist, turned back to me and asked, "What are you going to say, honey?!" I was in complete shock. After all of these years, who knew this moment would come? Once onstage I was handed the Grammy, and I quickly thought about all the past Quetzal members and collective moments of struggle. I began by thanking my brother and teacher, Gabriel Gonzalez. Rocio Marron, Edson Gianesi, Ray Sandoval, Dante

Pascuzzo, and Camilo Landau were other prominent members who came to mind. I then mentioned our transnational community of musicians, such as Son de Madera, Mono Blanco, and Los Cojolites.[10] Although it felt like an eternity being up on the podium, before we knew it our time was up and we were ushered backstage.

What happened next was hilarious and a testament to the illusion the industry upholds. As we went through the wings, a well-dressed model was waiting for us. She took the Grammy from my hands and said, "This stays here. It's a prop." We were assigned a guide who walked us across the street and through a media center setup at the Staples Center. They repeatedly gave us a Grammy "prop," took photos, and then removed it from our hands. In every photograph of us taken by the media, I have a different Grammy in my hands. That night we went home without a trophy. ¡Era el colmo!

I thought about my father and what he would have thought about this moment. This process was both redemptive and sobering. It was an affirmation of what the music industry must strive to be and the great lengths they go through to construct the fairy tale to perpetuate the validity of an industry. I witnessed and walked through the well-oiled machine that day. The Grammy Awards event is highly organized. As we walked through the media frenzy, we were thrilled, honored, and mostly in disbelief that after all of these years we were standing in the Staples Center as Grammy winners. But there was also a sobering truth to it all.

I've been called a "party pooper," or a "hater," because of the way I describe this moment. I believe that these kinds of reactions are due to the fact that when we speak the truth we taint people's dreams and perceptions of a moment like this. But this is precisely the importance of respectfully speaking openly about these moments. The truth is that the Grammy Award, although recognizably important on a symbolic front, can also be seen as an illusion that the industry has constructed as a measure of "success." The reality for musicians, even the most prolific, is much different. I personally know accomplished musicians and former Grammy winners (including me) who struggle with obtaining health insurance and maintaining a steady income. If the industry really cared for the musicians, they would find a way to provide for the most accomplished and the aging musicians. In addition, the contracts they urge artists to sign should be just and fair. But the reality is that most record companies busy themselves with accruing their own wealth and trying to find new ways to gouge artists from their earnings and artistic and intellectual property rights.

Reflecting on all of the love and well wishes we have received from various community members concerning the Grammy nomination, none was as gratifying as the call we received from the community musician legend and Quetzal Flores's mentor, Lorenzo "Lencho" Martinez. In a quintessential East LA *chuco suave* accent he said,

Hey, Flaco, just want to say congratulations on your win. Welcome to the club. [He laughs.][11] We know that this doesn't change our existence. We know what we're all about. We continue to do what we do with or without it. We live, we play, and then . . . we die. Eso es todo. Nothing more, nothing less. Ok, saludos a la familia. ¡Ay te wacho, cucaracho![12]

As Lencho indicates, although the bells and whistles of the Grammy celebration and attention were exciting, there was an element of a musician's reality that I could not forget. Regardless, we understand that it behooves Quetzal to leverage this moment, as the Grammy often validates one's past and ongoing and future work to those who are invested in these processes, as well as one's own community of listeners. Although Quetzal's music navigates both community and industry worlds, in theory we now stand to make more money per gig. This couldn't be all that bad, right?

"Imaginaries": Insurgent Pedagogies Now!

At the turn of the millennium, it was easy to recognize the imperializing nature of transnational capitalism: it crosses all borders, it colonizes and subjectifies all citizens on different terms than ever before. . . . It is also imperative not to lose sight of the methods of the oppressed that were developed under previous modes of colonization, conquest, enslavement, and domination, for these are the guides necessary for establishing effective forms of resistance under contemporary global conditions: they are key to the imagination of "postcoloniality" in its most utopian sense.

Chela Sandoval, *Methodology of the Oppressed*

I began this manuscript with my own learned perception of music as it was instilled by my father's teachings. Throughout the chapters and through a Chicana artivista feminist analysis, I have exorcised his specter as I narrated how this perception has changed over time for me and others. I have tried to articulate how music has served as a tool for national projects, and how socially constructed emotions have played a part. With an understanding that nations, through economic and social institutions, continue a colonial legacy of extracting labor from bodies, I can fathom how creative and other labor has thus been packaged and sold to build economic and social empires.[13] This arrangement has over time altered the social relations of music.

Chican@ artivistas challenged these ideas through varying methods as a way to arrive at a critical consciousness and reembodiment through community-based process. Through these multiple communal creative practices (fandango, collective songwriting), a shift in consciousness inevitably occurs. Relationality as fortified by convivencia ushers the formation and fortitude of communities by which dialogue, and thus critical consciousness, persists. In this way, Chican@ artivistas are engaging in what seems to be an effective form of resistance to alienation and individualization. As articulated by Chela Sandoval, "the methodology of the oppressed is a set of processes, procedures, and technologies for decolonizing the imagination."[14] Indeed, Chican@ artivista methods and forms of resistance fall under the guise of many postcolonial efforts, including the "social mechanisms" articulated by Sandoval and other postcolonial theorists. In the midst of community dialogues and struggles, a differential conscious allowed artivistas to see art and creative expression as an all-encompassing process, procedure, and social technique that instigates a shift into new imaginaries. These shifts continue to be felt in different ways in Eastlos communities and across California.

In the 1997 Encuentro Cultural Chicano/Indigéna por la Humanidad y contra el Neoliberalismo, both Chican@ and *indígena* participants engaged in dialogue and embodiment as a community exercise. Intersectional realities were discussed not solely through language but through performative and artistic interactions.

The *movimiento jaranero* gave way to the informal translocal dialogue *fandango sin fronteras*, which relies on embodied expression through the participatory music and dance practice of fandango. As a participant-observer in the 1997 encuentro and in *fandango sin fronteras*, both examples were a reminder to me that creative expression can be generated with and among community, and not necessarily for the goal of reaching professional musicianship or creating product, but as a way to engage in convivencia through music practice.

The practices of collective songwriting and fandango made visible how *all* art and creative expression are relational, meaning that all art and music production confer social meaning. In both examples, a value in *process* rather than *outcome* shifted my psyche. In this way, these practices proved how a community *can* be shaped and strengthened through participatory music and other creative forms of expression. The displacement of capital markets in the creation of music and dance as participatory intrinsically reorganizes a subject's mind away from capitalist music conceptions, inducing a counter-memory that moves one to ask in this moment: Where did these communal practices go? Why do we not engage in this way with each other? What keeps us from music practice with and as community? How do we get back to this way of being?

Drawing from these autobiographical ethnographic experiences, I have highlighted how these transnational and translocal methodologies have been utilized in our own trenches. I have demonstrated, both through the Entre

Mujeres project as well as through the collective songwriting method (as it was utilized in various circles), that I have adapted and implemented the experience and philosophy of Chican@ artivista praxis. Although the outcomes of these processes are never predictable or quantifiable, the impact is eventually and undoubtedly felt. As one of many Chican@ artivistas engaged in community building through music and creative expression, I can attest that these methods hold, and although there are always challenges, an emphasis and value on process renders failure obsolete.

As other theorists have noted, evaluating social movements as having "succeeded" or "failed" obscures the "merits or power of the visions themselves";[15] there have already been accounts of how the *fandango sin fronteras* movement has been "utopic" and has failed to reach social movement status. My account of Chican@ artivista methods of engaging communities and building alliances through participatory music and creative practice challenges ideas of what a "social movement" is and redirects our perceptions of how such social movements have been historically defined.

Artivistas: Where Are They Now?

After many years, and in their own ways, artivistas and participants in the 1997 encuentro have continued to build *cómo y cuando pueden*. Felicia Montes, Marisol Torres, Laura Palomares, Omar Ramirez, Jose Ramirez, Gabriel Tenorio, Cristina Gorocica, Quetzal Flores, Joe "Peps" Galarza, Yaotl Mazatl, and many others have gone on to advance their individual careers, but most importantly they continue to organize and to engage in participatory creative work as well. In this way, they have not become jaded, burnt out, or at a loss for hope. They have stayed connected, dreaming, accessible, and accountable to the community while initiating new generations of artists. Although all deserve mention, what follows are some of the most visible and salient examples.

FELICIA MONTES: *Zapartista*, Educator, and Cofounder of Mujeres de Maiz

Among the most prominent examples has been the work of the 1997 encuentro participant Felicia Montes, who has spearheaded the annual Mujeres de Maiz (MdM) multimedia art show. The first MdM took place at the Popular Resource Center in the late nineties, and the show has since become one of the most consistent and celebrated events in East LA. Women of color from all parts of the city attend, support, and participate in order to share, witness, and partake in the creative work of women of color from all racial backgrounds.[16] Montez describes the work of Mujeres de Maiz as "a spiritual artivist collective."[17] Furthermore, MdM has built a strong alliance with other communities and artists, such as the Tamil Sri Lankan American transgender-queer political-theater artist D'Lo.[18] MdM and the twenty-plus years of programming and overall impact they have had on the East LA art scene have been at the center of various academic journals and doctoral dissertations.

LAURA PALOMARES: Founder of "Anti-Malls" and Zapatista Cooperatives

The "Anti-Mall" spearheaded by the 1997 encuentro organizer Laura Palomares is another annual community-building event that has become a staple of East LA. Drawing from the idea of conscious consumerism and as a way to maintain the relationships Palomares developed with the Zapatista cooperatives, Palomares's efforts bring thousands of people together during the Christmas season. This event does more than support local artisans; it also generates an awareness and discourse around overconsumption, capitalism, money recycling, and fair trade.[19] KPFK 90.7 FM's *Uprising* host Sonali Kolhatkar says of the event, "It's at a time when everyone is out holiday shopping, and it's so much nicer when people are able to spend their hard-earned dollars in their own communities instead of giving to corporations like Walmart or Amazon or whatever. People that come to the Anti-Mall know that the vendors are chosen because of their consciousness, based on their concern for social justice . . . because of their relevance and place within community."[20]

SUYAPA PORTILLO: Community Organizer and Associate Professor

A co-organizer of the 1997 encuentro, Honduran immigrant Suyapa Portillo continues to be a social justice activist. She received her PhD in history from Cornell University and is now an associate professor for the Intercollegiate Department of Chicanx-Latinx Studies at Pitzer College. Portillo has centered her academic work on gender and labor history in the Americas, Central American immigrants and migration, Honduras and Hondurans in the United States, Central American transnational social movements, and lesbian, gay, bisexual, and transgender human rights in Central America. She continues to be an active community organizer, a dedicated professor to her students, and a thoughtful colleague.

CRISTINA GOROCICA: Poet and
Fourth-Grade Schoolteacher

Cristina Gorocica went on to be a part of the spoken-word poetry group In Lak Ech, along with other 1997 encuentro participants, including Marisol Torres, Rachel Negrete Thorson, Felicia Montes, and Liza Hita.

Gorocica also became a fourth-grade teacher and utilizes art, music, and poetry to incite critical thinking. In the spring of 2014, for example, she utilized a Quetzal composition titled "Estoy aquí" to teach in and around ideas of place, gentrification, identity, and self-love. Inspired by lived experiences in Veracruz, "Estoy aquí" was released on Quetzal's *Imaginaries* (2012). "Estoy aquí" literally means "I am here," and in this case it describes squatter culture so prevalent in the hillsides throughout Mexico. The song celebrates the dignity in these spaces and describes how inhabitants come down the hillside day after day to provide the cities with labor, flavor, and cultural intelligence.

"Estoy aquí" was part of a greater lesson plan that provided a context for and an interdisciplinary look at the Boyle Heights area. Gorocica wanted her students to understand how this place had evolved throughout history and into the present. The multiple lessons were part of a process that culminated in what Gorocica called the "Boyle Heights Historical Walk." They listened to the song, sang it, contemplated the lyrics, created drawings, and had animated discussions. They applied the lyrics to their own lives and the lives of those around them. One lesson revolved around students writing their own version of the lyrics. According to Gorocica, not only were the activities fun for the students, but they also helped stimulate discussions around identity and asset-based mapping of their communities.[21]

Gorocica invited my partner, Quetzal Flores, and me to visit with the students and to listen to their final essays and poems. The essays, drawings, and discussion we witnessed were filled with utter love for their neighborhood. Gorocica's thoughtful lesson plans inspired the students to think of their community in new ways. The most significant change was in their autoperception and sense of self-worth. As Bernice Johnson Reagon recognized, "You cannot sing a song . . . and not change your condition."[22]

By singing "Estoy aquí" and then creating their own set of new and improved lyrics, the students were able to make connections to their community and envision change that had an effect on their social and moral conditions. It was a change in subject consciousness induced by music in community, which alters the social DNA. The side effect is always hope. As Lipsitz expressed, "Running particular sounds through the body develops and cultivates a part of themselves they would not otherwise know."[23] Indeed, students quickly understood the value and importance of their own presence and its effect on community.

MARISOL TORRES: *Teatrista* and Playwright

Another In Lak Ech cofounding member, Marisol Torres, went on to receive her MFA in dramatic writing from California State University, Los Angeles, and is now a commissioned playwright. Her latest play commission was in 2019 from the Center Theatre Group in Los Angeles for her newest full-length play, titled *LA as DNA*. Torres is also a cofounder of Las Ramonas Xicana satire theater group along with Marlene Beltran Cuahtin and Jo Anna Mixpe Ley.

RACHEL NEGRETE THORSON: Poet, Painter, Crane Operator

Rachel Negrete Thorson is a mother of three boys and continues to write poetry and to paint. Negrete Thorson has expressed how art and music are central to the ways in which she has raised her sons and how they have infused the totality of her mothering experience. As a crane operator at the San Pedro loading docks, Negrete Thorson has repeatedly infused Zapatista philosophy as a member of the International Longshore and Warehouse Union (ILWU) Local 13.

TYLANA ENOMOTO: Violinist and Social Worker

After the 1997 encuentro Tylana Enomoto had some years of hiatus from the band Quetzal. She returned to play with the band in 2005 and has spent the past years conducting the collective songwriting method on the road with Quetzal and independently for various social organizations. Enomoto has been part of the last four Quetzal albums, including *Imaginaries* (2012). Enomoto earned her MSW from the University of Southern California Suzanne Dworak-Peck School of Social Work and is now a trauma therapist for the antiviolence organization Peace Over Violence (POV), where she utilizes the collective songwriting method as a tool of dialogue and healing.

QUETZAL FLORES: Musician, Producer, Arts Consultant

Quetzal Flores has been working closely with the Alliance for California Traditional Arts (ACTA) and the East LA Community Corporation in the engagement and teaching of what Flores now identifies as "cultural convening methods."

Flores has fundamentally influenced ACTA as an organization. Beginning with his tenure as a program manager for the Southern California chapter in

2013, Flores, Nayamin Martinez, Amy Kitchener, Kenya Curry, and the ACTA team curated and implemented the teaching of visual art, *son jarocho*, *teatro*, and storytelling and writing for the Arts in Corrections program in California state prisons.[24] Since its inception, ACTA's Arts in Corrections program has acquired over $2 million in funding through the California Arts Council. As a traditional arts organization, ACTA pulled from its health equity work in Boyle Heights, drawing on current and former grantees working from deep cultural heritage practices. California Arts Council funding has allowed programming to expand to sixteen men's and women's prisons statewide. Flores has rounded up many community musicians, 1997 encuentro participants, and fandango practitioners for this important work, including Omar Ramirez, Gabriel Tenorio, César Castro, and Quetzal band member Juan Perez.

In addition to the Arts in Corrections program, Flores also introduced and utilized the collective songwriting method for the California Endowment's Building Healthy Communities initiative.[25] ACTA at first failed to recognize the collective songwriting method as a viable traditional arts practice; however, after witnessing the process and the impact it had in Boyle Heights, Coachella, Merced, and Santa Ana initiative sites, collective songwriting and aspects of the artivista philosophy, experience, and teaching pedagogy have been implemented, are being documented, and will be published by ACTA in the forthcoming "SaludArte: Building Health Equity upon the Bedrock of Traditional Arts and Culture," an innovative arts organization guide.[26]

New artists in the community have been trained in the method and continue to utilize it within and beyond ACTA spaces.[27] Amy Kitchener had this to say about Quetzal Flores's artivista contribution to the organization:

> Quetzal Flores has been an influential figure in the design and development of ACTA programs since he joined the organization in 2011. He brought his skills and experience as a musician, activist, composer, producer, curator, and community organizer. He is driven to form authentic collaborations across space and time in these various roles. He practices horizontal leadership and does not take credit as the visionary artist he is—musically—but also in the way in which he creates music that is generated and shared in collaborative and community-based processes. . . . One example of his creativity is demonstrated by the Collective Songwriting methodology. . . . He has mentored many other artists in this process to maximize the collective impact. He introduced this methodology to ACTA during his tenure as Program Manager (May 2012–present), and we adopted it as a central strategy for community engagement in our arts and health equity work with the California Endowment's Building Healthy Communities–Boyle Heights.[28]

In addition to working with ACTA, Flores joined the East LA Community Corporation (ELACC) in 2016 as director of cultural vitality. As a comprehensive community-development organization, ELACC focuses on improving the "quality of life of residents" in East LA and beyond.[29] They combine services and provisions that allow residents to take leading roles in community decision-making processes. Their website states, "We see affordable housing, home ownership, and financial education as crucial steps toward a broader goal of economic stability and the well-being of the community. We believe this approach changes the system from a practice of 'planning being done to us' to 'planning being done with us.'"[30] ELACC's model is to implement four complementary components: housing development, asset and wealth building, tenant services, and community organizing.[31] Flores's charge was to infuse the organization with artivista praxis. Because most organizations compartmentalize their departments on day-to-day operations, ELACC has followed the urgings of Flores to have more interaction between departments via an engagement of process-based art and music practices. Collective songwriting and restorative justice art facilitated by Omar Ramirez are just some of many approaches their regular staff meetings might include as part of their overall organizational planning. Executive director Isela Gracian had this to say about artivista approaches in ELACC:

> Working with Artivista approaches and being in collaboration with cultural practitioners like Quetzal open a whole new dimension to the creativity of possibilities of our work. Being in an organization that contributes to eradicating social and economic challenges with programs or tactics within the same system—the day to day—can be stifling to imagining a different way of being. Having Quetzal be part of our team has accelerated our evolution, the collaboration has our juices flowing and imagination growing.[32]

Finally, in order to connect with other artists concerned with social justice activism wherever they may be, Flores cofounded Artivist Entertainment, along with the multiplatinum-selling recording artist Aloe Blacc, the Mexican Australian hip-hop MC Maya Jupiter, the percussionist and composer Alberto Lopez, and the record executive Veronica Gonzalez.[33]

OMAR RAMIREZ: Visual Artist and Educator

Omar Ramirez has been involved in ACTA efforts to teach what Ramirez has coined "restorative drawing" alongside Fabian Debora. Both have taught for a number of years in the Arts in Corrections program implemented by

ACTA. Ramirez has also been utilizing his experience and approach to art as an adjunct faculty member at California State University, Los Angeles, Scripps College, and local Los Angeles high schools. In addition, under the leadership of Ramirez's wife, Carmelita Ramirez-Sanchez, they have established the Boyle Heights Arts Conservatory, an organization that provides arts leadership, learning, and apprenticeship opportunities for local youth.

As members of Quetzal or as Chican@ artivistas, my partner and I, along with our son, Sandino, have continued to return to Veracruz and Seattle for many visits since we moved back to LA, both to visit friends as well as to build on new projects. Most recently, we returned to Seattle to engage in collective songwriting workshops with high school youth in Seattle public schools and in the King County Juvenile Detention Center.[34] Funded by the City of Seattle, Sounds Beyond Barriers was organized by a Seattle Fandango Project member, Iris Viveros, and local pianist Alex Chadsey.[35]

We have also continued to record new music projects. Our latest Quetzal album, *Puentes sonoros*, is due out in the spring of 2020 on Smithsonian Folkways. After many years and sustained relationships with musicians in Veracruz, *Puentes sonoros* is an ode to the sonic ties that continue to nourish us.

Artivista in the College Classroom

I argue for activism as an indispensable component in learning. Action promotes consciousness of one's own political practice. . . . It is usually the greatest and most difficult learning experience, particularly if it is connected to communities and issues broader than the parameters of academic life.

Joy James, "Teaching Theory and Talking Community"

In the Fall of 2013 I began a tenure-track position at Scripps Claremont College for the Intercollegiate Department of Chicana/o Latina/o Studies. In my time as an assistant professor, I developed and taught courses such as "Chican@ Music: From Genre to Experience," "Fandango as a Decolonial Tool," "Chicana Latina Gender and Popular Culture," "Collective Songwriting Theory and Knowledge Production," and "Women Who Rock: The Archive, Popular Music, and New Media." My general teaching philosophy is not only to teach important Chicana feminist content through interdisciplinary, rigorous, and challenging curricula, but equally important, to teach this via artivista community-building praxis. I believe that participatory music, dance, and creative practices in the classroom enact, allow, and intrinsically instill community and critical consciousness on many levels.

Beyond the classroom and as a resident artist for various institutions across the country, I have been able to utilize various skill sets learned in the East LA, Chiapas, and fandango trenches. From the fall of 2016 to the spring of 2019 I served as an artist in residence for ASU Gammage, the largest arts presenter in the American Southwest. With the support and encouragement of Executive Director Colleen Jennings-Roggensack, Senior Director of Programs Michael Benjamin Reed, and Campus and Community Engagement Manager Amanda Arboleda, I fulfilled the scope of their "Connecting Communities" mission. From lectures and workshops given in K–12 schools and undergraduate and graduate classrooms, to fandango workshops at Tonatierra community space and collective songwriting workshops at Perryville Women's State Prison, I have witnessed how the artivista methods have been effective modes of critical dialogue.

Returning to John Blacking, he states, "Problems in human societies begin when people learn less about love, because love is the basis of our existence as human beings. The hard task is to love, and music is a skill that prepares for this most difficult task."[36]

With an understanding that love is indeed the motivation, convivencia via cultural convening methods has brought us one step closer to experiencing love time and again. Convivencia, through music and art practices, values process and ultimately dialogue. Embedded in the specificity of a Chican@ artivista experience, my partner, Quetzal Flores, and I, along with many other artivistas, have remained committed to sharing these important practices and to seeking opportunities to develop new connections with other communities in struggle wherever we may find ourselves. At large or behind bars, in the home with our son, Sandino, in the classroom, and in community trenches—within and across US-Mexico borders—at present our goal as artivistas is to utilize music in the service of love in order to tap into our individual and collective humanity.

Now more than ever, we need to combat the anti-immigrant sentiment and brutal separation of families at the US-Mexican border, as well as the unrelenting war on black, brown, and trans bodies and on women and children. For this we need new strategies that undermine ideological and structural racism, strategies that have not been absorbed by the state—in fact, a new language and social practice adding to our social justice lexicon. Hence, the experiences I humbly offer in this book. For I firmly believe that convivencia via process-based, participatory community practices rooted in art and music can not only be used as tools of inquiry and dialogue that can help us summit to new kinds of analysis; these practices are simultaneously regenerative and strengthen our communities. These practices allow us to go beyond resistance, into actively building on the dream and tangible enactments of new worlds.

NOTES

INTRODUCTION

1. In staying true to the times I am recounting, I will use the terms Chican@ and Latin@, rather than the more recent Chicanx and Latinx; the former were understood at the time to include cis male, cis female, as well as gay, lesbian, and queer subjects, as the @ symbol resembles a *Q*.

2. See Diaz, *Flying Under the Radar*; Sauer, *Accidental Archives*.

3. Noble, "Seeing Through *¡Que Viva México!*," 173–187; Escobar, "Colonista y colonizado," 63–71.

4. Bonfil Batalla, *México Profundo*.

5. Larner, "Neoliberalism?"; Lemke, "Foucault, Governmentality, and Critique," 509.

6. Blacking, "How Musical Is Man?"; Small, "Musicking"; Turino, *Music as Social Life*; Berríos-Miranda, "Is Salsa a Musical Genre?"; McClary, *Feminine Endings*.

7. Bakare-Yusuf, "Economy of Violence"; hooks, *Ain't I a Woman*.

8. Roy, *Gendered Citizenship*, 38–77; Stoler, "Making Empire Respectable," 634–660.

9. Kabeer, *Reversed Realities*, 65.

10. Kabeer, *Reversed Realities*, 49.

11. Taylor, *Archive and the Repertoire*, 18.

12. Brady, *Extinct Lands, Temporal Geographies*.

13. Taylor, *Archive and the Repertoire*, 3.

14. Grindon, "Breath of the Possible," 21.

15. Taylor, *Archive and the Repertoire*, 2.

16. Taylor, *Archive and the Repertoire*, 2. The colloquial term *jarocho* refers to the people, music, and culture of the southern part of the state of Veracruz, Mexico. The roots of *son jarocho*, the music style of southern Veracruz, are indigenous, Spanish, and African.

17. Taylor, *Archive and the Repertoire*, 277.

CHAPTER 1. MUSIC MISUNDERSTOOD

1. As noted in Patricia Zavella's *I'm Neither Here nor There: Mexicans' Quotidian Struggles with Migration and Poverty*, the Immigration Act of 1965 allowed twenty thousand immigrants and "immediate relatives" into the United States (Zavella, *I'm Neither Here nor There*,

31). My father migrated at this time, with my grandmother's assistance. My paternal grandmother had migrated earlier to work as a domestic.

2. I have previously written about the lucrative Variedades circuit in "*Zapateado* Afro-Chicana *Fandango* Style: Self-Reflective Moments in *Zapateado*."

3. As Michelle Habell-Pallán articulates in *Loca Motion: The Travels of Chicana and Latina Popular Culture*, we were part of a long performance history in downtown LA on Broadway.

4. *Gabrielito González con el auténtico sentimiento mexicano* was the title of my brother's 1978 debut album on El Rey recordings.

5. Gordon, *Ghostly Matters*, 17.

6. Gordon, *Ghostly Matters*, 215.

7. Larner, "Neoliberalism?," 509–512.

8. Larner, "Neoliberalism?," 510.

9. Larner, "Neoliberalism?," 511.

10. Larner, "Neoliberalism?," 509.

11. Larner, "Neoliberalism?," 509.

12. Larner, "Neoliberalism?," 512.

13. Michel Foucault quoted in Lemke, "Foucault, Governmentality, and Critique," 2.

14. Michel Foucault quoted in Lemke, "Foucault, Governmentality, and Critique," 2.

15. Noble, "Seeing through *¡Que Viva México!*," 176.

16. Noble, "Seeing through *¡Que Viva México!*," 176.

17. Noble, "Seeing through *¡Que Viva México!*," 178.

18. Noble, "Seeing through *¡Que Viva México!*," 177.

19. Noble, "Seeing through *¡Que Viva México!*," 177.

20. Noble, "Seeing through *¡Que Viva México!*," 175.

21. Chávez, *Sounds of Crossing*, 45.

22. Chávez, *Sounds of Crossing*, 46.

23. I am not arguing that the *mestizo* or *mestizaje* does not exist. Rather than the biological idea of *mestizaje*, I focus on the discourse of *mestizaje* that was used by governments at different points in Mexican history. I seek to demonstrate how the term was an important tool created by the Mexican government to gather the public's imagination and thus consolidate political power in the years of the Porfiriato.

24. Bonfil Batalla, *México Profundo*, 53.

25. Bonfil Batalla, *México Profundo*, 53; my emphasis.

26. Bonfil Batalla, *México Profundo*, 53.

27. The indigenous subject was for the most part portrayed as loyal yet backward in his or her thinking.

28. Bonfil Batalla. *México Profundo*, 55.

29. Nathan Shamuyarira quoted in Turino, *Nationalists, Cosmopolitans, and Popular Music*, 172. In this pivotal text, Turino explains how emotions were an important element to consider for the National Democratic Party (NDP) in Ghana. The NDP represented a new shift in national discourse that advocated for the idea that Africans should rule themselves rather than negotiate a "partnership" with colonial power. Ironically, the NDP initiated this ideology through cultural nationalism. Publicity secretary Robert Mugabe was open about his use of emotional sentiment to win nationalist party support. Turino quotes Robert Mugabe's biographers as stating, "[Mugabe's] aim was to consciously inject emotionalism into the thinking of the nationalists. . . . To win broad based support among all Africans in Rhodesia, the struggle had to be made part of the people's daily life. He appealed to their emotions and

to their spiritual and cultural values. He encouraged them, through party publicity, to value their heritage." David Smith and Colin Simpson quoted in Turino, *Nationalists, Cosmopolitans, and Popular Music*, 171.

30. Turino, *Nationalists, Cosmopolitans, and Popular Music*, 163.

31. Kabeer, *Reversed Realities*, 16.

32. Kabeer, *Reversed Realities*, 16.

33. Rationality is a fundamental concept in liberal economic theories. It is assumed that subjects always make the most "rational" choices in economic practices. Feminist development theorists find this troublesome, as "rational" is subjective. Subjects consider or are restrained when making choices. What is rational to one subject could be irrational for the next. Thus the idea of rational choices as a universal human quality is irrelevant when considering other important subjectivities, such as gender, race, class, and sexuality.

34. Noble, "Seeing through *¡Que Viva Mexico!*," 177.

35. Bonfil Batalla, *México Profundo*; Escobar, "Colonista y colonizado"; Noble, "Seeing through *¡Que Viva Mexico!*"

36. Noble, "Seeing through *¡Que Viva México!*," 178.

37. David Brading quoted in Noble, "Seeing through *¡Que Viva México!*," 178.

CHAPTER 2. CHICAN@ ARTIVISTAS

1. Blacking, *How Musical Is Man?*, 6.

2. Blacking, *How Musical Is Man?*, 6.

3. Blacking, *How Musical Is Man?*, x.

4. Blacking, *How Musical Is Man?*, xi.

5. Blacking, *How Musical Is Man?*, xi.

6. Critiques of *How Musical Is Man?* were few yet significant, and one in particular from Charles Keil signals how Blacking fails to disclose the "ethnocentrisms" throughout his book. Indeed, Blacking's conclusion is condescending, as "Western thought and criteria remain in control" (Keil, review of *How Musical Is Man?*, 81–82). I agree with Keil's critique but cannot fault Blacking on what his project did not seek to uncover. Ultimately, Blacking's project is one that looks at Venda music culture as a subject of study and not as a way of deconstructing why Western arrangements of music conceptions are tied to capital interests. In this regard, it is loaded with the classic Western gaze.

7. Blacking, *How Musical Is Man?*, 4.

8. Pascoe, *La mona*; Cardona, "Los actores culturales"; M. Gonzalez, "*Zapateado Afro-Chicana.*"

9. Music commerce has perpetuated an economic system that requires the "musical" and the "unmusical" to construct a common sense in our conceptions of music. I am not claiming that there isn't such a thing as "musical" or "unmusical"; I merely wish to point out how this conception is tied to the general music interaction and behavior and how the conceptions revolve around commerce.

10. Self Help Graphics and Art was located on the corner of Cesar Chavez and Gage. It has since moved to a location off First Street. Started by Sister Karen Boccalero, Self Help Graphics became a space where artists could learn the art of printmaking. The space, however, also served as a site where musicians, especially from the punk scene, could have shows open to the public.

11. Habell-Pallán, "Style Council," 336–345.

12. Chavoya and Gonzalez, *Asco*.

13. Viesca, "Battle of Los Angeles," 719–739.

14. Habell-Pallán, *Loca Motion*, 6.

15. Quetzal Flores, interview, May 23, 2019, El Sereno, CA.

16. Smith, *Decolonizing Methodologies*, 6.

17. Smith, *Decolonizing Methodologies*, 3.

18. Cruz, "Epistemology of a Brown Body," 657–669.

19. Bakare-Yusuf, "Economy of Violence," 178–179.

20. Bakare-Yusuf, "Economy of Violence," 178–179.

21. Bakare-Yusuf, "Economy of Violence," 179.

22. Michael Taussig quoted in Bakare-Yusuf, "Economy of Violence," 179.

23. Bakare-Yusuf, "Economy of Violence," 179.

24. Bonfil Batalla, *México Profundo*; Taylor, *Archive and the Repertoire*.

25. Bakare-Yusuf, "Economy of Violence," 177.

26. Michael Taussig quoted in Bakare-Yusuf, "Economy of Violence," 177.

27. The black feminist scholar bell hooks has written extensively on the brutal treatment and sexual exploitation of enslaved black women. Hooks contends that due to race and sex, the black female slave received the greatest and most brutal treatment. Importantly, hooks not only reveals this history but states it has "led to a devaluation of black womanhood that permeated the psyches of all Americans and shaped the social status of all black women once slavery ended" (hooks, "Continued Devaluation," 217). Both Bakare-Yusuf and hooks uncover the material practices that continue to influence present-day knowledge and behaviors. Both scholars uncover a seldom-told history whose material trace is still being felt.

28. Bakare-Yusuf, "Economy of Violence," 182.

29. Bakare-Yusuf, "Economy of Violence," 193.

30. Bakare-Yusuf, "Economy of Violence," 193.

31. Bakare-Yusuf, "Economy of Violence," 193.

32. Bakare-Yusuf, "Economy of Violence," 175.

33. Toni Morrison quoted in Bakare-Yusuf, "Economy of Violence," 182.

34. Toni Morrison quoted in Bakare-Yusuf, "Economy of Violence," 182.

35. Kabeer, *Reversed Realities*.

36. Kabeer, *Reversed Realities*, 14.

37. Kabeer, *Reversed Realities*, 65.

38. Kabeer, *Gender Mainstreaming*, 42.

39. The social construction critique of biological determinism can be proven by showing (1) variations in one region over time, (2) variations across space (between different regions), and (3) variations in one region at the same time. The presence of gender variations in any one of these categories disproves biological determinism. Developed by Priti Ramamurthy, it is a self-reflective exercise that draws on the ways empirical research is set up to prove things change by comparing over space and time. Ramamurthy, course lecture for Women and International Economic Development, University of Washington, winter 2010.

40. Kabeer, *Gender Mainstreaming*, 43.

41. Kabeer, *Gender Mainstreaming*, 47.

42. Kabeer, *Gender Mainstreaming*, 47.

CHAPTER 3. THE POPULAR RESOURCE CENTER AND CENTRO REGENERACIÓN IN HIGHLAND PARK

1. Quetzal Flores, interview, January 6, 2012, Los Angeles, CA.

2. Quetzal Flores, interview, January 6, 2012, Los Angeles, CA.

3. Quetzal Flores, interview, January 6, 2012, Los Angeles, CA.

4. Quetzal Flores, interview, January 6, 2012, Los Angeles, CA.

5. Gonzalez Flores, "Chicano Artists and Zapatistas Walk Together"; Speed, Hernández Castillo, and Stephen, *Dissident Women*; Zavella, *I'm Neither Here nor There*.

6. Aida Salazer, interview, April 13, 2011, Los Angeles, CA.

7. Sandoval, *Methodology of the Oppressed*.

8. Sandoval, *Methodology of the Oppressed*.

9. Cruz, "Epistemology of a Brown Body," 657.

10. Sandoval, *Methodology of the Oppressed*.

11. The term *mestizo* indicates a person of mixed-race, Spanish and indigenous blood, historically tied to colonization of the Americas by the Spanish.

12. Anzaldúa, *Borderlands / La Frontera*, 10.

13. Brady, *Extinct Lands, Temporal Geographies*, 6.

14. Brady, *Extinct Lands, Temporal Geographies*, 6.

15. Brady, *Extinct Lands, Temporal Geographies*, 6.

16. Brady, *Extinct Lands, Temporal Geographies*, 6.

17. Sandoval, *Methodology of the Oppressed*, 139.

CHAPTER 4. THE BIG FRENTE ZAPATISTA

1. *In lak ech* is Nahuatl for "Tu eres mi otro yo," or "You are the other me."

2. Viesca, "Battle of Los Angeles," 720.

3. Viesca, "Battle of Los Angeles," 720.

4. Founded by Roberto Gonzalez Flores, the Eastside Café was first known as the Westside Café. These gatherings and concerts were held at Loyola Marymount University and other parts of the city. It has been renamed the Eastside Café, and its permanent space is currently in El Sereno, CA.

5. Viesca, "Battle of Los Angeles," 722.

6. Viesca, "Battle of Los Angeles," 730.

7. Wilson, *Research Is Ceremony*, 14.

8. "Cuarta Declaración de la Selva Lacandona," Comité Clandestino Revolucionario Indígena–Comandancia General del Ejército Zapatista de Liberación Nacional, January 1, 1996, http://palabra.ezln.org.mx/comunicados/1996/1996_01_01_a.htm.

9. "Cuarta Declaración de la Selva Lacandona," Comité Clandestino Revolucionario Indígena–Comandancia General del Ejército Zapatista de Liberación Nacional, January 1, 1996, http://palabra.ezln.org.mx/comunicados/1996/1996_01_01_a.htm.

10. Speed, Hernández Castillo, and Stephen, *Dissident Women*.

11. These kinds of phrases have been commonly used throughout Latin America in different struggles, protests, and other political contexts. In short, they are certainly not unique

to the Zapatistas; however, the Zapatista uprising happened concurrent to artivistas' time and youth's energies. Significantly, Zapatistas utilized the mediums of communication that were pertinent to the youth, like the internet. Zapatistas were also adamant about citing other current and past struggles, and were dedicated to bringing the memory, focus, and commonality among them all as part and parcel to their own struggle.

12. "Neza" refers to Ciudad Nezahualcóyotl, a Mexican barrio outside of Mexico City famous for its poverty and crime.

13. Eichert, Rowley, and Sandberg, *Zapatista.*

14. "Marcos Is Gay," *Green Left Weekly*, November 5, 1997, https://www.greenleft.org.au/content/marcos-gay.

15. "Marcos Is Gay," *Green Left Weekly*, November 5, 1997, https://www.greenleft.org.au/content/marcos-gay.

16. The Zapatistas held local as well as "intergalactic" meetings, or *encuentros* (encounters), to encourage dialogue for the purpose of building community.

17. L. Pérez, *Chicana Art*, 317.

18. Lowe, *Immigrant Acts*, 13.

19. The Chicano social movement of the 1960s is often referred to as El Movimiento, or "the movement."

20. L. Pérez, *Chicana Art.*

21. Quetzal Flores, interview, April 9, 2013, Los Angeles, CA.

22. Esteva, "Celebration of Zapatismo," 130.

23. Roberto Gonzalez Flores has been the most supportive of mentors and was the first person to publish on the 1997 encuentro. In his PhD dissertation he focuses on the informal learning networks between Zapatista and Chican@ communities. Gonzalez Flores, "Chicano Artists and Zapatistas Walk Together."

24. Gonzalez Flores was instrumental in forming the Westside Café, which has since been renamed the Eastside Café and is now located in El Sereno, CA.

25. The 1997 encuentro served as an example of what Gonzalez Flores refers to in his study as the "centrifugal and centripetal learning dimensions or factors" in the transnational learning networks between Chican@s and Zapatistas. Gonzalez Flores, "Chicano Artists and Zapatistas Walk Together," *In Motion Magazine*, May 9, 2009, https://inmotionmagazine.com/auto/rf_informal2.html.

26. Blackwell, "Weaving in the Spaces," 116.

27. Speed, Hernández Castillo, and Stephen, *Dissident Women*, 43.

28. In the Zapatista movement's ongoing learning and growth, the Zapatistas have taken on many new ventures since the mid-1990s. One such undertaking has been their push for mock or parallel campaigns for presidency. As members of the Congreso Nacional Indígena, or National Indigenous Congress, the Zapatistas recently advocated for the indigenous Nahua María de Jesús Patricio Martínez, a.k.a. "Marichuy," to run for president as an independent candidate; see Ruth Conniff, "Marichuy: Mexico's First Indigenous Woman Presidential Candidate," *The Progressive*, February 14, 2018, https://progressive.org/dispatches/marichuy-mexicos-first-indigenous-woman-presidential-candid-180213/.

29. The Frente Zapatista de Liberación Nacional (FZLN) established civil society dialogue committees, created actions, and informed civil society in general about the Zapatista activities.

30. The Zapatista communities have been actively recuperating the health of their

communities before and since the inception of the Zapatista uprising. Their communities, like many around the world, have suffered the loss of community members due to migration, alcoholism, poor education, health, and economic infrastructure. Oventic seemed like the right choice for the encuentro because it was Commandante Ramona's native site and we had contributed to alleviating her financial struggle due to her health issues. Quetzal Flores, interview, March 22, 2012, Los Angeles, CA.

31. Quetzal Flores, interview, March 22, 2012, Los Angeles, CA.

32. L. Pérez, *Chicana Art*, 10.

33. Flyer from Laura Palomares's personal collection.

34. Flyer from Laura Palomares's personal collection.

35. Patierno and Talreja, *Stuart Hall*.

36. The encuentro also consisted of Chican@ participants from San Diego and Long Beach in California and from parts of Texas.

37. La Neza was at that time an unincorporated squatter town with over a million immigrant dwellers from other parts of the Mexican republic who had moved to the Mexico City area seeking employment and better opportunities.

38. Quetzal Flores, interview, March 22, 2012, Los Angeles, CA.

39. "We welcome the Chicanos from Los Angeles who are here for the first Chicano-Indigenous Cultural Encounter for Humanity and against Neoliberalism!"

40. Oventic is Tzotzil Maya for "place where people meet."

41. A *porra* is a cheer.

42. "1st Cultural Encounter for Humanity and against Neoliberalism," webpage, circa October 2009, http://www.oocities.org/capitolhill/3849/culture_1.html.

43. "We have found each other" is a phrase the Zapatistas repeatedly used in their communiqués in reference to the many communities around the world who offered their support. The Big Frente Zapatista used this phrase for one of the five encuentro themes. "Nos Encontramos" was the theme of the first day.

44. The Zapatistas referred to the Spanish language as *castellano*.

45. Chusma follows a long trajectory of Chicano *teatro* specializing in the *rascuache* aesthetic. *Rascuache* is a Spanish-language term that used to hold negative connotations. At present and in the Chican@ art tradition, it signals a means to create and to perform effectively with little to no economic resources. It also implies a sense of stylish DIY know-how.

46. "Encuentro Cultural Chican@/Indigena. 1997. Oventic, Chiapas Mexico," YouTube video, uploaded by Quetzal Flores, February 19, 2016, Gonzalez_7097_08notes.docx, https://www.youtube.com/watch?v=rd3wHb2Yb3o.

47. Butler, *Bodies That Matter*, 12.

48. Sandoval, *Methodology of the Oppressed*, x.

49. Crenshaw, "Mapping the Margins," 1241–1299.

50. Crenshaw, "Mapping the Margins," 1241–1299.

51. Butler, *Bodies That Matter*.

52. Lugones, "Toward a Decolonial Feminism," 753.

53. Wilson, *Research Is Ceremony*, 76.

54. Smith, *Decolonizing Methodologies*; Wilson, *Research Is Ceremony*.

55. Smith, *Decolonizing Methodologies*, 7.

56. Wilson, *Research Is Ceremony*, 92.

57. Wilson, *Research Is Ceremony*, 77.

58. Lugones, "Toward a Decolonial Feminism," 755.

59. Sandoval, *Methodology of the Oppressed*, 9.

60. Bell hooks quoted in Sandoval, *Methodology of the Oppressed*, 110.

61. Sandoval, *Methodology of the Oppressed*, 9.

62. Sandoval, *Methodology of the Oppressed*, 140.

63. Sandoval, *Methodology of the Oppressed*, 140.

64. Sandoval, *Methodology of the Oppressed*, 140.

CHAPTER 5. FANDANGO JAROCHO AS A DECOLONIAL TOOL

1. Although we were always vigilant that our musicianship be at its best, here I mean "professionally" in the sense that we began to actively entertain a career in the formal music industry.

2. Gina Hernández and Chris González Clarke were the founders of Son del Barrio Records. Both were former active members of the Chicano movement who in later years decided to focus their energies on Chican@ music as an important political project to record and diffuse socially conscious music.

3. Vanguard Records was an appealing label to us in that they had a history of struggle within the industry themselves, yet had found a way to develop a niche. They began as a label that recorded and released blacklisted artists during the McCarthy era.

4. Steve Berlin is a member of one of the most accomplished East LA rock bands—Los Lobos.

5. The messages about women were mostly from a Chicana feminist perspective. There was an understanding that the challenges that women of color in the barrio faced were different from those of white women in privileged spaces.

6. Lipsitz, "Cruising around the Historical Bloc," 157–177.

7. I understand that the term *call-and-response* has a specific meaning in music scholarship (especially in the literature on African diaspora music); call-and-response in the *son jarocho* tradition is distinct in that the call-and-response is not always done between a single person and a chorus. Nevertheless, I utilize the term *call-and-response* because there is still a dialectic in the sense that someone "calls" a verse and another person "responds," which does not remove the *son jarocho* structure from its significant origins in both African and indigenous cultures.

8. Extensive recordings and archives now document not only the hundreds of *versos* this elder, Don Arcadio, remembered, but also the tales and descriptions of early fandangos.

9. The Instituto Veracruzano de la Cultura (IVEC) funded some of the "rescate," or rescuing, of the tradition.

10. Cardona, "Los actores culturales," 217.

11. Small, *Musicking*, 2.

12. Small defines *musicking* as follows: "To music is to take part, in any capacity, in a musical performance, whether by performing, by listening, by rehearsing or practicing, by providing material for performance (what is called composing), or by dancing" (Small, *Musicking*, 9).

13. Rodriguez, "Fandango Jarocho."

14. Libby and Cindy Harding led Los Jardin and had been playing the *son jarocho* for some time. Their father, Tim Harding, was a well-respected musician in the commercial style of the *son jarocho* and a student of Lino Chávez.

15. Gilberto Gutiérrez had spent some time in the Bay Area, with the assistance of Eugene Rodriguez; Gutierrez as well as César Castro note, however, that his prior visit to California had a different agenda and ethics around the dissemination of the fandango and *son jarocho*.

16. César Castro, interview, January 2012, Los Angeles, CA.

17. Octavio Paz quoted in Lipsitz, "Cruising around the Historical Bloc," 157.

18. Lipsitz, "Cruising around the Historical Bloc," 157.

19. García de León, introduction to *Fandango*.

20. La Virgen de la Candelaria is honored on February 2, and festivities take place before and after that date, by the Papaloapan River in an old Spanish town called Tlacotalpan. January 6 is the day to celebrate the gifts the Reyes Magos, or Three Wise Men, brought to Jesus after his birth. Children generally receive their gifts on this day.

21. I don't mean to say that there are no spectators. Rather, there is no definitive "audience." In this way, it was significantly different from how I learned to experience music as an audience member with the formal protocols of the theater. Not only can a fandango take place in any social space, but the spectator can also be a practitioner in the music, song, or dance aspects of fandango.

22. A *cajón* is a wooden box with a sound hole, used for percussion. The *marimbol*, a bass and percussion instrument, is a wooden box with a sound hole and thin strips of metal harnessed to the face. The *cajón* was more recently introduced, but archives reflect that the *marimbol* was not uncommon in fandango practice prior to the dormant period.

23. Technically, there is but one step pattern to *zapateado*, which changes in feel depending on the *son* accompanying the dance. This rhythmic phrase has been coined *café con pan*, or coffee and bread. Other than this term, there is intentionally no terminology to refer to specific steps in *zapateado*, due to the importance placed on the improvisation. This rhythmic phrase *café con pan* is merely a way to get children to grasp the mechanics of the steps.

24. I was somewhat familiar with the steps of *zapateado* from my early years of learning *folklórico*, which presents choreographed versions of *zapateado* along with other musical dance forms from Mexico.

25. Anna S. Arismendez is originally from Texas but has found a permanent home in Mexico City as a central member of Caña Dulce y Caña Brava, a female-led *son jarocho* group based in Mexico City. Arismendez is an accomplished *leona* player, singer, and *bailadora* and has recorded and toured with the group extensively.

26. Daniel Aloi, "Atkinson Forum to Explore Vibrant Mexican 'Son' Music," *Cornell Chronicle*, October 15, 2015, http://news.cornell.edu/stories/2015/10/atkinson-forum-explore-vibrant-mexican-son-music.

27. "Brava Presents the 7th Annual San Francisco Son Jarocho Festival," Brava for Women in the Arts, accessed September 25, 2019, https://www.brava.org/all-events/2019/2/6/son-jarocho-festival.

28. One such effort involved finishing a recording project by a group Andres Flores had founded while he lived in the Bay Area for a time. Andres Flores y Los Hijos de José included the Chicano musicians Federico Zuniga and Russell Rodriguez. They both led the efforts to press and sell the finished recording in order to offer sustainable funding for Andres Flores's funeral and family expenses. See Andres Flores y Los Hijos de José Facebook page,

accessed September 25, 2019, https://www.facebook.com/pg/AndresFloresyLoshijosdeJose/about/?ref=page_internal.

29. Stephen, *Transborder Lives*, xv.

30. Nina Glick Schiller quoted in Stephen, *Transborder Lives*, 19.

31. See Jarochicanos Facebook page, accessed September 6, 2019, https://www.facebook.com/Jarochicanos-270172773018467/.

32. Maya Zazhil Fernández, personal correspondence, September 5, 2019.

33. Stephen, *Transborder Lives*, 21.

34. As a former member of Mono Blanco, César Castro was invited to participate in "Fandango sin Fronteras," a collaborative production between Quetzal and Danza/Floricanto USA under the direction of Gema Sandoval. This month-long visit culminated in a performance at the John Anson Ford Theatre in the summer of 2004. Castro relocated soon after.

35. César Castro, interview, January 2012, Los Angeles, CA.

36. Cambalache includes the Chican@ East LA musicians Juan Perez (bass), Alexandro Hernandez (vocals, *requinto*, *jarana*), Chuy Sandoval (vocals, *jarana primera*), and Xochi Flores (vocals, *jarana*, *zapateado*).

37. Both Perez and Pascuzzo recorded bass for Son de Madera's album *Las orquestas del día*. Perez was also a guest artist for the group's *Son de mi tierra*, released by Smithsonian Folkways in 2009.

38. "Son de Madera: Blending Dance and Song," Smithsonian Folklife Festival blog, January 1, 2009, https://festival.si.edu/blog/2009/son-de-madera-son-jarocho-group-from-vera-cruz-mexico.

39. Ramón Gutiérrez, interview, April 2007, Xalapa, Veracuz, Mexico.

40. Octavio Rebolledo Kloques, interview, May 8, 2007, Veracruz, Mexico.

41. The name of the string, "mifren," references the phrase Hernandez would utter to the *jarochos* when he would greet them with a warm and friendly "My friend!" Although he is now fluent in Spanish, Hernandez continues to be known in all the fandango circles as "Mifren" and not by his birth name, Jacob Hernandez.

42. César Castro, personal correspondence, September 20, 2019.

43. "VI Fandango Fronterizo," YouTube video, uploaded by El Gallo Films, October 23, 2013, https://www.youtube.com/watch?v=CK-JiYZxj9w.

44. Taylor, *The Archive and the Repertoire*, xv.

45. "Fandango Fronterizo," accessed September 22, 2019, https://fandangofronterizo.blogspot.com.

46. Kodani, "Bon Odori."

47. "FandangObon - A Festival of Music, Dance and Environmental Consciousness," YouTube video, uploaded by DiscoverNikkei, January 19, 2016, https://www.youtube.com/watch?v=KK6x1A8ChgE.

48. Great Leap has had a long-standing relationship with the Aratani Theatre and director Leslie Ito.

49. "Bam butsu no tsunagari" was a collaboration between Nobuko Miyamoto, Quetzal Flores, César Castro, Rev. Masao Kodani, Elaine Fukumoto, and me. "Bam butsu no tsunagari" debuted at the first FandangObon celebration in the fall of 2014.

50. Sojin Kim, "Just Dance: Connecting Life, Death, Traditions, and Communities in L.A.," *Folklife*, August 25, 2014, https://folklife.si.edu/talkstory/2014/just-dance-connecting-life-death-traditions-and-communities-in-l-a.

51. "Sounds of California Artist Profiles: FandangObon," Smithsonian Folklife Festival, accessed June 26, 2017, http://www.festival.si.edu/2016/sounds-of-california/fandang-obon/smithsonian.

52. Alexis Ligon and Michelle Mehrtens, "Reflections on the Sounds of California," Smithsonian Folklife Festival blog, September 6, 2016, http://www.festival.si.edu/blog/2016/reflections-on-the-sounds-of-california/.

53. Arturo O'Farrill's Fandango at the Wall music project is an example of a misinterpretation of the essence of fandango and in particular the annual Fandango Fronterizo. Arturo O'Farril's full Latin jazz orchestra held a traditional performance at the border, intertweaving fandango masters from time to time. Although the executive producer Kabir Sehgal attempted to describe the essence of the project, he failed to really understand the transnational movement, the ethics, and the overall reasons for the fandango gathering. This is yet another way in which capital finds its way into the music space no matter how participatory the music space may be. See Kabir Sehgal, "Cultural Diplomacy," Fandango at the Wall, accessed September 22, 2019, http://fandangowall.com/about/.

CHAPTER 6. LOS GUARDIANES DE LA CONVIVENCIA

1. Hidalgo self-published this small poetry book in 2010 while in residence in the California Bay Area.

2. *Decima* is a ten-line stanza poetry form often used in the *son jarocho*.

3. Davis, *Blues Legacies*, 196.

4. Silvia Santos, personal correspondence, 2009.

5. Silvia Santos, interview, 2014, Xalapa, Veracruz.

6. Silvia Santos, interview, 2014, Xalapa, Veracruz.

7. Wilson, *Research Is Ceremony*, 80.

8. Johnson, *Spaces of Conflict*, xxii.

9. Latina Feminist Group, *Telling to Live*, 3.

10. Johnson, *Spaces of Conflict*, x.

11. The release of *Entre Mujeres: Women Making Music across Borders* was made possible by the community of supporters generated through a Kickstarter campaign. We managed to raise nearly $10,500 to complete the mixing, mastering, and printing of the project. "Entre Mujeres: Translocal Musical Dialogues," Kickstarter campaign, May 13, 2012 to July 3, 2012, http://www.kickstarter.com/projects/mgonzalez/entre-mujeres-translocal-musical-dialogues.

12. hooks, *Talking Back*, 26.

13. The department has since been renamed the Department of Gender, Women, and Sexuality Studies.

14. Michelle Habell-Pallán and I met at a gig in 2006 on the University of California, Santa Cruz, campus. Our children started playing together. I had been tossing about the idea of going back to school and mentioned it to her in passing. She suggested I apply to the University of Washington in Seattle. And, like how Professor Steven Loza had demystified the value of my musical experiences in my undergraduate studies at UCLA, Professor Habell-Pallán assured me that my experiences related to process and community building as a musician and a mother would contribute to feminist studies, Chicana feminist thought, and music studies in significant ways.

15. Francisco Orozco had brought Son de Madera once to perform in Washington Hall in Capitol Hill prior to our arrival. This visit, however, did not involve an elaboration or teaching of fandango. They came as a performance group.

16. Professor Dudley had previously met Quetzal Flores in Seattle during a performance at Meany Hall called "Fandango sin Fronteras," which was a collaboration between Quetzal and Danza Floricanto USA. Flores also spoke of the practice of fandango in a panel that Dudley had organized during this visit. Both through a master's thesis by Francisco Orozco and the "Fandango sin Fronteras" performance, Professor Dudley had heard of fandango, but he had never experienced fandango nor conceived of the kind of community impact it could have.

17. We taught the first *taller*, or workshop, with the instruments that were available. Since I was instructing on the *zapateado*, or percussive dance, I lent out my *jarana* and *marimbol* (*marímbula*) for the duration of the *taller*. Quetzal Flores owned three *jaranas*, and Eduardo Sierra would bring his own. Francisco Orozco owned a *jarana*, a *requinto*, and a *marimbol*. Among us we had enough instruments to teach, but we opened up the possibility for others to bring their own instruments to jam with. Participants would often bring violins, classical guitars, cellos, ukuleles, and other instruments.

18. The Simpson Center for the Humanities is one of the largest and most comprehensive humanities centers in the United States. For more information, see https://simpsoncenter. org/about.

19. Quetzal Flores, interview, January 5, 2013, Los Angeles, CA.

20. Recycling money into the community is an important artivista praxis. This philosophy can be seen in the methodologies utilized in other arenas, such as the annual "Anti-Malls" that happen all over Los Angeles, developed by the 1997 encuentro organizer Laura Palomares and her organization El Puente . . . Hacia la Esperanza. For more information, see "Anti-Mall: People b4 Profit 2008," YouTube video, uploaded by cipotapower, October 3, 2011, http://www.youtube.com/watch?v=Pv1wnly_ohs.

21. The grant language did not technically allow for the center to "purchase instruments" but rather to "rent" them. They "rented" them from Quetzal Flores, who then concretely "donated" them to Centro de la Raza.

22. The title of the speaking series comes from the expression a woman utters when she has exhausted herself physically in *zapateado* and all at once senses a near spiritual moment in the process. Translated literally, it means "leaving one's soul on the tarima." Upon having this cathartic moment in the presence of and with the help of other *bailadoras*, or female dancers, musicians, and community, this moment is especially significant in that it is the community that has contributed to one's happiness. In this sense, it is not an isolated individualistic venture for satisfaction but a community effort to reach this climactic moment.

23. A total of three panel discussions took place from 2009 to 2010.

24. "Cochinito" literally means "little pig," and we used it to refer to our "piggy bank."

25. The name Son Tequio was also used as a way to not confuse the performance aspect of the *son jarocho* with the ethics and convivencia of fandango.

26. It is difficult to transition from being a fandango teacher espousing the importance of convivencia in fandango to being a professional musician who has strict criteria as to which members are able to handle being onstage.

27. Footage of the first fandango in Seattle, Washington, can be seen at "Seattle Fandango Project - Final Night Fandango," YouTube video, uploaded by Maya Jupiter, November 10, 2009, http://www.youtube.com/watch?v=2ZuJ4DEJnKE.

28. Shannon Dudley, Miriam Bartha, and Quetzal Flores, "Seattle Fandango Project: 2009–2010 Briefing," internal document, Simpson Center for the Humanities, Seattle, Washington.

29. Thanks in part to the advocacy and efforts of Professor Shannon Dudley, Rebolloso's three children were also able to spend time in Seattle. They became part of the community and were showered with love and support from the Seattle Fandango Project.

30. Although I have interviewed and consulted with many members about the project's history, I expect that I too will be held accountable for how I represent the community. As I have stated in the opening of this book, my memory work and investigation of fandango, and in turn the Seattle Fandango Project, is one of many perspectives in a growing body of practitioners that will also have their say.

31. "Fandango Conversations: Son de Madera and Seattle Fandango Project," YouTube video, uploaded by Scott Macklin, November 16, 2010, http://www.youtube.com/watch?v=ngRE2IjcMII; "Fandango Conversations: Encuentro Fandanguero del NorthWest," YouTube video, uploaded by Scott Macklin, June 6, 2013, https://www.youtube.com/watch?v=X0ZbT0q3g5c.

32. Scott Macklin of the University of Washington approached me about presenting a talk on *fandango sin fronteras* at the independently organized TEDxSeattle. In order to exercise the ethics of fandango beyond the practice, I opened up this invitation to include other members of the Seattle Fandango Project, including Quetzal Flores, Francisco Orozco (Ethnomusicology, School of Music), Carrie Lanza (School of Social Work), Laura Rebolloso (School of Music visiting artist), Kristina Clark (community member), and Iris Viveros (community member). The TEDx presentation opened up other opportunities for us to further dialogue and explore the various liberatory aspects of fandango practice.

33. Shannon Dudley, Miriam Bartha, and Quetzal Flores, "Seattle Fandango Project: 2009–2010 Briefing," internal document, Simpson Center for the Humanities, Seattle, Washington.

34. Iris Viveros and Kristina Clark have since enrolled at the University of Washington. The Seattle campus was already familiar to them beyond the classrooms, and through the Seattle Fandango Project they had built relationships with Shannon Dudley, Michelle Habell-Pallán, and other professors, as well as with students. The experience in the project inspired them to pursue degrees concerning music and dance practice as educational, healing, and community-building tools. They are both currently positive and productive forces within their respective programs, and their community-organizing know-how continues to inspire the Seattle Fandango Project and the University of Washington.

35. Yesenia Navarrete Hunter, "Scholarship and Art as Sites of Belonging," Imagining America, September 14, 2017, https://imaginingamerica.org/2017/09/14/scholarship-and-art-as-sites-of-belonging/.

CONCLUSION. IMAGINARIES

I take part of this chapter's title from an online article (no longer available) written by Eileen Lee for the University of Washington Graduate School website, titled "The Grammy and the Graduate Student: Melding Music and Scholarship."

1. "We below and to the left" is a common phrase used by the Zapatistas before they sign off on communiqués. Poetically charged, "below and to the left" suggests where the real "left" should reside—just as the human heart does, "below and to the left" in the chest cavity.

2. Zapatistas through Subcomandante Marcos quoted in Sandoval, *Methodology of the Oppressed*, x.

3. "From the cold and more" referenced not only the Seattle weather but also the "cold" feelings of loneliness.

4. Sandoval, *Methodology of the Oppressed*, 61.

5. "Congrats to Grammy-Nominated Quetzal!," Simpson Center for the Humanities, December 6, 2012, http://depts.washington.edu/uwch/news/2012/12/congrats-grammy-nominated-quetzal.

6. Reed Johnson, "Grammys 2013: A Magical Year for Son Jarocho," *Los Angeles Times*, February 9, 2013, http://articles.latimes.com/2013/feb/09/entertainment/la-et-ms-grammys-mexican-blues-jarocho-20130210.

7. "Pre-Grammy Encounter—Forget You, We'll Stomp on Wood!," YouTube video, uploaded by Scott Macklin, February 18, 2013, http://www.youtube.com/watch?v=44HuBuga8dE.

8. "It Was a Foot Stomping Pre-Grammy Concert," Breed Street Shul, accessed April 2, 2013, https://breedstreetshul.org/it-was-a-foot-stomping-pre-grammy-concert.

9. "Felicidades to the Band Quetzal: Celebrating Their Grammy in a Unique and Dignified Manner," accessed April 3, 2013, http://www.actaonline.org/content/felicidades-band-quetzal-celebrating-their-grammy-unique-and-dignified-manner.

10. "Pre-Grammy Encounter—Forget You, We'll Stomp on Wood!," YouTube video, uploaded by Scott Macklin, February 18, 2013, http://www.youtube.com/watch?v=44HuBuga8dE.

11. Lencho was nominated for two Grammys and won one Grammy with Los Texmaniacs from Texas.

12. "See you later, cockroach!" Lorenzo Martinez, cell phone message, February 12, 2013.

13. Bakare-Yusuf, "Economy of Violence," 171–183.

14. Sandoval, *Methodology of the Oppressed*, 68.

15. Kelley, *Freedom Dreams*, vii.

16. "Mujeres de Maiz 2009 Multi-Media Live Art Show Part 1," YouTube video, uploaded by cinematikaDcorazon, February 28, 2010, http://www.youtube.com/watch?v=Gibes8bYYuU; "Mujeres de Maiz 2009 Multi-Media Live Art Show Part 2," YouTube video, uploaded by cinematikaDcorazon, February 28, 2010, http://www.youtube.com/watch?v=-uBb0j3lWAA.

17. Mujeres de Maiz interviewed by Sonali Kolhotkar in KPFK 90.7 studios, YouTube video, accessed May 3, 2013, http://www.youtube.com/watch?v=ulCGBvraQBU.

18. Mujeres de Maiz interviewed by Sonali Kolhotkar in KPFK 90.7 studios, YouTube video, accessed May 3, 2013, http://www.youtube.com/watch?v=ulCGBvraQBU.

19. "Anti-Mall People b4 Profit," YouTube video, uploaded by cipotapower, October 4, 2011, http://www.youtube.com/watch?v=-YBTAg0UhK8.

20. "Anti-Mall People b4 Profit," YouTube video, uploaded by cipotapower, October 4, 2011, http://www.youtube.com/watch?v=-YBTAg0UhK8.

21. A discussion of asset mapping for East LA youth is timely and necessary, for East Los Angeles is currently plagued by abandonment and poverty, which often instigates violence, but also makes it coveted for its prime real estate. Much of East LA, Boyle Heights in particular, is sprinkled with remnants of historic architecture, which makes this troubled area

an investor and "house flipper" magnet. Second Street Elementary students know how gentrification is changing the energy of their neighborhood, as new and trendy businesses are quickly springing up and changing familiar spaces into unwelcoming ones.

22. Bernice Johnson Reagon quoted in Lipsitz, "Education for Liberation," 266.

23. Lipsitz, "Education for Liberation," 266.

24. "ACTA's Arts in Corrections Program: Long Version," YouTube video, uploaded by Alliance for California Traditional Arts, March 22, 2015, https://www.youtube.com/watch?v=yAgpZd-dqmE&t=242s; "ACTA's Arts Program at California Correctional Institution Offers a Pathway towards Rehabilitation," YouTube video, uploaded by Alliance for California Traditional Arts, February 17, 2018, https://www.youtube.com/watch?v=bhhjSOkLvEE&t=72s.

25. "Collective Songwriting in Boyle Heights," YouTube video, uploaded by Alliance for California Traditional Arts, May 16, 2016, https://www.youtube.com/watch?v=F8GJgObsL6U&t=3s.

26. George Lipsitz and Alliance for California Traditional Arts, "SaludArte: Building Health Equity Upon the Bedrock of Traditional Arts and Culture," forthcoming.

27. Flores and I have mentored a new generation of artists in the collective songwriting method, including members of Cuicani and Vanessa "La Neza" Calderon and her group La Victoria.

28. Amy Kitchener, personal correspondence, July 27, 2019.

29. East LA Community Corporation website, accessed December 7, 2016, http://www.elacc.org.

30. East LA Community Corporation website, accessed December 7, 2016, http://www.elacc.org.

31. East LA Community Corporation website, accessed December 7, 2016, http://www.elacc.org.

32. Isela Gracian, personal correspondence, July, 18, 2019.

33. Artivist Entertainment website, accessed September 22, 2019, http://artivistentertainment.com.

34. "King County Juvenile Detention—Sounds Beyond Barriers," YouTube video, uploaded by Scott Macklin, September 14, 2015, https://www.youtube.com/watch?v=s3kOzhGJshc.

35. The Seattle Fandango Project member Alex Cody Chadsey authored a grant for the City of Seattle Office of Arts and Culture. After witnessing a collective songwriting workshop given by Quetzal Flores and me while on tour in a continuation high school in Houston, Texas, Chadsey had been so moved by the experience, he decided to try and find funding for us to engage in this process with Seattle youth. "Sounds Beyond Barriers," YouTube video, uploaded by Scott Macklin, March 27, 2013, http://www.youtube.com/watch?v=YeqXThGRvXM.

36. Blacking, *How Musical Is Man?*, 103.

DISCOGRAPHY

Andres Flores y Los Hijos de José. *El Camino*. San Jose, CA: Round Whirled Records, 2018.

Cambalache. *Constelación de sonidos*. Independent, 2017.

———. *Una historia de fandango*. Independent, 2013.

Chuchumbé. *Chuchumbé*. Santa Cruz, CA: Chuchumbé Productions, 2000.

Conjunto Jarocho Medellín de Lino Chavez. *Veracruz*. Serie México Musical. Mexico: RCA Camden, 1981.

———. *Veracruz Hermoso*. Mexico: RCA Camden, 1961.

Entre Mujeres: Women Making Music across Borders. Independent, 2012.

Grupo Mono Blanco. *Sones jarochos: Volumen V*. Mexico: Ediciones Pentagrama, 1997.

———. *¡Fandango! Sones Jarochos from Veracruz*. Washington, DC: Smithsonian Folkways, 2018.

Grupo Mono Blanco y Stone Lips. *El mundo se va a acabar*. Urtext, 1997.

La Negra Graciana. *Sones jarochos con el Trio Silva*. Mexico City: Corasón, 1994.

Los Alvarados. *El Movimiento Chicano!* Infal Records, 1970.

Ozomatli. *Don't Mess with the Dragon*. Beverly Hills, CA: Concord Records, 2007.

Quetzal. *Die Cowboy Die*. Quetzalmusic.org, 2006.

———. *Imaginaries*. Washington, DC: Smithsonian Folkways, 2011.

———. *Puentes sonoros*. Washington, DC: Smithsonian Folkways, 2020.

———. *Quetzal*. San Francisco, CA: Son del Barrio Music, 1998.

———. "Si me quieres escribir" and "Viva la Quince Brigada." On *Spain in My Heart: Songs of the Spanish Civil War*. West Chester, PA: Appleseed Recordings, 2003.

———. *Sing the Real*. Santa Monica, CA: Vanguard Records, 2002.

———. *Worksongs*. Santa Monica, CA: Vanguard Records, 2003.

Rolas de Aztlán: Songs of the Chicano Movement. Washington, DC: Smithsonian Folkways, 2005.

Son de Madera. *Caribe mar sincopado*. Mexico: Fonarte Latino, 2014.

———. *Las orquestas del día*. Irvine, CA: Moondo Records, 2006.

———. *Son de Madera*. Mexico: Urtext, 1997.

———. *Son de mi tierra*. Washington, DC: Smithsonian Folkways, 2009.

Sones jarochos. Cuauhtémoc, Mexico City: Ediciones Pentagrama, 2007.

Valens, Ritchie. *The Complete Ritchie Valens*. London: Jasmine Records, 2010.

BIBLIOGRAPHY

Alexander, M. Jacqui, and Chandra Talpade Mohanty, eds. *Feminist Genealogies, Colonial Legacies, Democratic Futures.* New York: Routledge, 1997.

Anderson, Benedict. *Imagined Communities: Reflections on the Origin and Spread of Nationalism.* Rev. ed. London: Verso, 1991.

Anzaldúa, Gloria. *Borderlands / La Frontera: The New Mestiza.* San Francisco: Spinsters / Aunt Lute, 1987.

Bag, Alice. *Violence Girl: East L.A. Rage to Hollywood Stage; A Chicana Punk Story.* New York: Feral House, 2011.

Bakare-Yusuf, Bibi. "The Economy of Violence: Black Bodies and the Unspeakable Terror." In *Gender and Catastrophe*, edited by Ronit Lentin, 171–183. London: Zed Books, 1997.

———. "Scattered Limbs, Scattered Stories: The Silence of Biafra." *African Identities* 10, no. 3 (2012): 243–248.

Berríos-Miranda, Marisol. "Is Salsa a Musical Genre?" In *Situating Salsa: Global Markets and Local Meanings in Latin Popular Music*, edited by Lise Waxer, 23–50. New York: Routledge, 2002.

Berríos-Miranda, Marisol, Shannon Dudley, and Michelle Habell-Pallán. *American Sabor: Latinos and Latinas in US Popular Music.* Seattle: University of Washington Press, 2018.

Blacking, John. *How Musical Is Man?* Seattle: University of Washington Press, 1973.

Blackwell, Maylei. "Weaving in the Spaces: Indigenous Women's Organizing and the Politics of Scale in Mexico." In *Dissident Women: Gender and Cultural Politics in Chiapas*, edited by Shannon Speed, R. Aída Hernández Castillo, and Lynn M. Stephen, 115–154. Austin: University of Texas Press, 2006.

Bonfil Batalla, Guillermo. *México Profundo: Reclaiming a Civilization.* Austin: University of Texas Press, 1996.

Brady, Mary. *Extinct Lands, Temporal Geographies: Chicana Literature and the Urgency of Space.* Durham, NC: Duke University Press, 2002.

Braojos, Ricardo, dir. *Fandango: Searching for the White Monkey.* San Pablo, CA: Los Cenzontles Mexican Arts Center, 2006.

Broyles-González, Yolanda. *Lydia Mendoza's Life in Music / La Historia de Lydia Mendoza: Norteño Tejano Legacies.* New York: Oxford University Press, 2001.

Butler, Judith. *Bodies That Matter: On the Discursive Limits of "Sex."* New York: Routledge, 1993.

Cantú, Norma E., and Olga Nájera-Ramírez, eds. *Chicana Traditions: Continuity and Change.* Urbana: University of Illinois Press, 2002.

Cardona, Ishtar. "Los actores culturales entre la tentación comunitaria y el mercado global: El resurgimiento del son jarocho." *Politica y Cultura*, no. 26 (January 2006): 213–232.

Casillas, Dolores. "Sounds of Belonging: A Cultural History of Spanish-Language Radio in the United States, 1922–2004." PhD diss., University of Michigan, 2006. Microfilm.

Chávez, Alex E. *Sounds of Crossing: Music, Migration, and the Aural Poetics of Huapango Arribeño*. Durham, NC: Duke University Press, 2017.

Chavoya, C. Ondine, and Rita Gonzalez, eds. *Asco: Elite of the Obscure; A Retrospective, 1972–1987*. Berlin: Hatje Cantz, 2011.

Clark, Rebecca, Sara Diaz, and Martha Gonzalez. "Intersectionality in Context: Three Cases for the Specificity of Intersectionality from the Perspective of Feminists in the Americas." In *Intersectionality und Kritik: Neue Perspektiven für alte Fragen*, edited by Vera Kallenberg, Jennifer Meyer, and Johanna M Müller, 75–102. Wiesbaden, Germany: Springer VS, 2013.

Connor, Walker. *Ethnonationalism: The Quest for Understanding*. Princeton, NJ: Princeton University Press, 1994.

Cott, Nancy F. *The Grounding of Modern Feminism*. New Haven, CT: Yale University Press, 1987.

Crenshaw, Kimberlé. "Mapping the Margins: Intersectionality, Identity Politics, and Violence against Women of Color." *Stanford Law Review* 43, no. 6 (July 1991): 1241–1299.

Cruz, Cindy. "Toward an Epistemology of a Brown Body." *International Journal of Qualitative Studies in Education* 14, no. 5 (2001): 657–669.

Cusick, Suzanne G. "On Musical Performances of Gender and Sex." In *Audible Traces: Gender, Identity, and Music*, edited by Elaine Barkin and Lydia Hamessley, 25–48. Zurich: Carciofoli, 1999.

Daniel, Yvonne. *Dancing Wisdom: Embodied Knowledge in Haitian Vodou, Cuban Yoruba, and Bahian Candomblé*. Urbana: University of Illinois Press, 2005.

Davis, Angela Y. *Blues Legacies and Black Feminism: Gertrude "Ma" Rainey, Bessie Smith, and Billie Holiday*. New York: Pantheon Books, 1998.

Delgado Bernal, Dolores, C. Alejandra Elenes, Francisca E. Godinez, and Sofia Villenas, eds. *Chicana/Latina Education in Everyday Life: Feminista Perspectives on Pedagogy and Epistemology*. Albany: State University of New York Press, 2006.

Dempster, Alec. *Loteria Jarocha: Linoleum Prints*. Erin, Ontario: Porcupine's Quill, 2013.

Denzin, Norman K., Yvonna S. Lincoln, and Linda Tuhiwai Smith, eds. *Handbook of Critical and Indigenous Methodologies*. Los Angeles: Sage, 2008.

Diaz, Ella Maria. *Flying Under the Radar with the Royal Chicano Air Force: Mapping a Chicano/a Art History*. Austin: University of Texas Press, 2017.

Diaz, Sanchez, and Alexandro Hernandez. "The Son Jarocho as Afro-Mexican Resistance Music." *Journal of Pan African Studies*, Vol. 6, no. 1 (July 2013).

Dudley, Shannon. *Music from Behind the Bridge: Steelband Spirit and Politics in Trinidad and Tobago*. New York: Oxford University Press, 2008.

Eichert, Benjamin, Rick Rowley, and Staale Sandberg, dirs. *Zapatista*. Big Noise Films, 1999.

"Encuentro Cultural Chican@/Indigena. 1997. Oventic, Chiapas Mexico." YouTube video, uploaded by Quetzal Flores, February 19, 2016. https://www.youtube.com/watch?v=rd3wHb2Yb3o.

Engels, Friedrich. "The Origin of the Family, Private Property, and the State." In *The Marx-Engels Reader*, edited by Robert C. Tucker, 734–759. Originally published 1844. New York: W. W. Norton, 1978.

"Entre Mujeres-Laura Rebolloso y Martha Gonzalez-Xalapa Veracruz." YouTube video, uploaded by Quetzal Flores, February 4, 2009. http://www.youtube.com/watch?v=NH imfF6_1cs&feature=youtube_gdata.

Escobar, Juan Pablo Silva. "Colonista y colonizado: La Época de Oro del cine mexicano." *Revista Austral de Ciencias Sociales*, no. 15: (2008): 63–71.

Esteva, Gustavo. "Celebration of Zapatismo." *Humboldt Journal of Social Relations* 29, no. 1 (2005): 127–167.

———. *Grassroots Post-Modernism: Remaking the Soil of Cultures*. New York: Zed Books, 1998.

"EZLN - Our Word Is Our Weapon." YouTube video, uploaded by thedecoy1981, 2006. http:// www.youtube.com/watch?v=WxRDwA9SXbw.

"FandangObon - A Festival of Music, Dance and Environmental Consciousness." YouTube video, uploaded by DiscoverNikkei, January 19, 2016. https://www.youtube.com/ watch?v=KK6x1A8ChgE.

"Fandango Conversations: Encuentro Fandanguero del NorthWest." YouTube video, uploaded by Scott Macklin, June 6, 2013. https://www.youtube.com/watch?v=X0ZbT0q3g5c.

"Fandango Conversations: Son de Madera and Seattle Fandango Project." YouTube video, uploaded by Scott Macklin, November 16, 2010. http://www.youtube.com/ watch?v=ngRE2IjcMII.

Feldman, Heidi Carolyn. *Black Rhythms of Peru: Reviving African Musical Heritage in the Black Pacific*. Middletown, CT: Wesleyan University Press, 2006.

Figueroa Hernandéz, Rafael. *Son jarocho: Guía histórico-musical*. Self-published, CreateSpace, 2012.

Freire, Paulo. *Pedagogy of the Oppressed*. 30th anniversary ed. New York: Continuum, 2000.

García, Alma, ed. *Chicana Feminist Thought: The Basic Historical Writings*. New York: Routledge, 1997.

Garcia, Laura E., Sandra M. Gutierrez, and Felicitas Nuñez, eds. *Teatro Chicana: A Collective Memoir and Selected Plays*. Austin: University of Texas Press, 2008.

García de León, Antonio. "El Caribe Afroandaluz: Permanencias de una civilización popular." Mexico: Consejo Nacional para la Cultura y las Artes / Instituto Veracruzano de la Cultura, 1992.

———. *Fandango: El ritual del mundo jarocho a través de los siglos*. Mexico: Consejo Nacional para la cultural y las Artes / Instituto Veracruzano de la Cultura, 2006.

González, Anita. *Afro-Mexico: Dancing between Myth and Reality*. Austin: University of Texas Press, 2010.

———. *Jarocho's Soul: Cultural Identity and Afro-Mexican Dance*. Lanham, MD: University Press of America, 2004.

Gonzalez, Martha. "Caminos y Canciones en Los Angeles, CA." In The Tide Was Always High: The Music of Latin America in Los Angeles, edited by Josh Kun. Berkeley: University of California Press, 2017.

———. "Chican@ Artivistas at the Intersection of Hope and Imagination." Journal of the Society for the Study of Gloria Anzaldúa Conference, El Mundo Zurdo. University of Texas at Austin, July 2014.

———. "Creating a Mexican-Afro-Cuban-American Beat." Zócalo Public Square, December 5, 2014, http://www.zocalopublicsquare.org/2014/12/05/creating-a-mexican-afro-cuban-american-beat/chronicles/who-we-were/.

———. "Mixing in the Kitchen: Entre Mujeres Feminine Translocal Composition." In Performing Motherhood: Artistic, Activist, and Everyday Enactments, edited by Amber

E. Kinser, Kryn Freehling-Burton, and Terri Hawkes. Ontario, Canada: Demeter Press, 2014.

———. "'Sobreviviendo': Immigration Stories and Testimonio in Song." Center for Latino Research at DePaul University, 2015.

———. "Sonic (Trans) Migration of Son Jarocho Zapateado: Rhythmic Intention, Metamorphosis, and Manifestation in Fandango and Performance." In *Cornbread and Cuchifritos: Ethnic Identity Politics, Transnationalization, and Transculturation in American Urban Popular Music*, edited by Wilfried Raussert and Michelle Habell-Pallán, 59–71. Tempe, AZ: Bilingual Press, 2011.

———. "*Zapateado* Afro-Chicana *Fandango* Style: Self-Reflective Moments in *Zapateado*." In *Dancing across Borders: Danzas y Bailes Mexicanos*, edited by Olga Nájera-Ramírez, Norma E. Cantú, and Brenda M. Romero, 359–378. Urbana: University of Illinois Press, 2009.

Gonzalez Flores, Roberto. "Chicano Artists and Zapatistas Walk Together, Asking, Listening, Learning: The Role of Transnational Informal Learning Networks in the Creation of a Better World." PhD diss., University of Southern California, 2007.

Gopinath, Gayatri. *Impossible Desires: Queer Diasporas and South Asian Public Cultures*. Durham, NC: Duke University Press, 2005.

Gordon, Avery F. *Ghostly Matters: Haunting and the Sociological Imagination*. Minneapolis: University of Minnesota Press, 1997.

Habell-Pallán, Michelle. *Loca Motion: The Travels of Chicana and Latina Popular Culture*. New York: New York University Press, 2005.

———. "The Style Council: Asco, Music, and 'Punk Chola' Aesthetics, 1980–84." In *Asco: Elite of the Obscure; A Retrospective, 1972–1987*, edited by C. Ondine Chavoya and Rita Gonzalez, 336–345. Berlin: Hatje Cantz, 2011.

Hernandez-Leon, Rubeno. "How did son jarocho become a music for the immigrant rights movement?" *Journal of Ethnic and Racial Studies*, November 8, 2018.

Herrera, Claudia, ed. *The African Presence in México: From Yanga to the Present*. Chicago, IL: Mexican Fine Arts Center Museum, 2006.

Hesse-Biber, Sharlene, and Michelle L. Yaiser, eds. *Feminist Perspectives on Social Research*. New York: Oxford University Press, 2004.

Hidalgo, Patricio. *Piedras y flores*. Self-published, Los Guardianes del Fandango Jarocho, 2010.

Hong, Grace. "'The Future of Our Worlds': Black Feminism and the Politics of Knowledge in the University under Globalization." *Meridians* 8, no. 2 (2008): 95–115.

hooks, bell. *Ain't I a Woman: Black Women and Feminism*. Boston, MA: South End Press, 1981.

———. "Continued Devaluation of Black Womanhood." In *Feminism and Sexuality: A Reader*, edited by Stevi Jackson and Sue Scott, 216–223. New York: Columbia University Press, 1996.

———. *Talking Back: Thinking Feminist, Thinking Black*. Boston, MA: South End Press, 1989.

Huber, Lindsay Pérez. "Disrupting Apartheid of Knowledge: *Testimonio* as Methodology in Latina/o Critical Race Research in Education." *International Journal of Qualitative Studies in Education*, no. 6 (2009): 639–654.

"IV Fandango Fronterizo / Border Fandango." YouTube video, uploaded by El Colego de la Frontera Norte - El Colef, October 19, 2011. http://www.youtube.com/watch?v=0sq68NJczvc.

James, Joy. "Teaching Theory and Talking Community." In *Academic Repression: Reflections from the Academic Industrial Complex*, edited by Anthony J. Nocella II, Steven Best, and Peter McLaren, 37–46. Oakland, CA: AK Press, 2010.

Johnson, Gaye Theresa. *Spaces of Conflict, Sounds of Solidarity: Music, Race, and Spatial Entitlement in Los Angeles*. Berkeley: University of California Press, 2013.

Kabeer, Naila. *Gender Mainstreaming in Poverty Eradication and the Millennium Development Goals: A Handbook for Policy-Makers and Other Stakeholders*. Ottawa, Ontario: Canadian International Development Agency, 2003.

———. *Reversed Realities: Gender Hierarchies in Development Thought*. London: Verso, 1994.

Kallenberg, Vera, Jennifer Meyer, and Johanna M. Müller, eds. *Intersectionality und Kritik: Neue Perspektiven für alte Fragen*. Wiesbaden, Germany: Springer VS, 2013.

Keil, Charles. Review of *How Musical Is Man?*, by John Blacking. *Contemporary Sociology* 5, no. 1 (1976): 81–82.

Kelley, Robin D. G. *Freedom Dreams: The Black Radical Imagination*. Boston, MA: Beacon Press, 2003.

Kodani, Masao. "Bon Odori: The Death Gathering of Joy." In *Joy, Remembrance, Death: Obon Music for North America*. Los Angeles, CA: Southern District Dharma School Teachers League, 2016.

Larner, Wendy. "Neoliberalism?" *Environment and Planning D: Society and Space* 21, no. 5 (October 2003): 509–512.

Latina Feminist Group. *Telling to Live: Latina Feminist Testimonios*. Durham, NC: Duke University Press, 2001.

Lemke, Thomas. "Foucault, Governmentality, and Critique." *Rethinking Marxism* 14, no. 3 (September 2002): 49–64.

Lentin, Ronit, ed. *Gender and Catastrophe*. London: Zed Books, 1997.

Lipsitz, George. "Cruising around the Historical Bloc: Postmodernism and Popular Music in East Los Angeles." *Cultural Critique*, no. 5 (1986): 157–177.

———. "Education for Liberation, Not Mainstream Socialization: The Improvisation Pedagogy of Students at the Center in New Orleans." In *Improvisation and Music Education: Beyond the Classroom*, edited by Ajay Heble and Mark Laver, 266–280. New York: Routledge, 2016.

Lorde, Audre. *Sister Outsider: Essays and Speeches*. Trumansburg, NY: Crossing Press, 1984.

"Los Super Seven 'La Morena.'" YouTube video, uploaded by vmsuicide, August 29, 2007. http://www.youtube.com/watch?v=MVxzPDq5U0I.

Lowe, Lisa. *Immigrant Acts: On Asian American Cultural Politics*. Durham, NC: Duke University Press, 1996.

Loza, Steven. *Barrio Rhythm: Mexican American Music in Los Angeles*. Urbana: University of Illinois Press, 1993.

Lugones, María. "Purity, Impurity, and Separation." *Signs* 19, no. 2 (Winter 1994): 458–459.

———. "Structure/Antistructure and Agency under Oppression." *Journal of Philosophy* 87, no. 10 (October 1990): 500–509.

———. "Toward a Decolonial Feminism." *Hypatia* 25, no. 4 (Fall 2010): 742–759.

Marx, Karl, and Friedrich Engels. *The Marx-Engels Reader*. Edited by Robert C. Tucker. 2nd ed. New York: W. W. Norton, 1978.

McClary, Susan. *Feminine Endings: Music, Gender, and Sexuality*. Minneapolis: University of Minnesota Press, 1991.

Mohanty, Chandra Talpade. "Cartographies of Struggle." In *Third World Women and the Politics of Feminism*, edited by Chandra Talpade Mohanty, Ann Russo, and Lourdes Torres, 1–49. Bloomington: Indiana University Press, 1991.

———. *Feminism without Borders: Decolonizing Theory, Practicing Solidarity*. Durham, NC: Duke University Press, 2003.

Molina, Ruben. *Chicano Soul: Recordings and History of an American Culture*. La Puente, CA: Mictlan, 2007.

Monsiváis, Carlos. *EZLN: Documentos y comunicados 5; La marcha del color de la tierra*. Mexico City: Ediciones Era, 1994.

Mora, Sergio de la. *Cinemachismo: Masculinities and Sexuality in Mexican Film*. Austin: University of Texas Press, 2006.

Moraga, Cherríe, and Gloria Anzaldúa, eds. *This Bridge Called My Back: Writings by Radical Women of Color*. 2nd ed. New York: Kitchen Table / Women of Color Press, 1983.

Muñoz, José Esteban. *Disidentifications: Queers of Color and the Performance of Politics*. Minneapolis: University of Minnesota Press, 1999.

Nájera-Ramírez, Olga, Norma E. Cantú, and Brenda M. Romero, eds. *Dancing across Borders: Danzas y Bailes Mexicanos*. Urbana: University of Illinois Press, 2009.

Narvaez, Rafael F. "Embodiment, Collective Memory and Time." *Body and Society* 12, no. 3 (September 2006): 51–73.

Noble, Andrea. "Seeing through *¡Que Viva México!* Eisenstein's Travels in Mexico." *Journal of Iberian and Latin American Studies* 12, nos. 2–3 (2006): 173–187.

Oseguera Rueda, Rubí del Carmen. *Biografía de una mujer veracruzana*. Mexico City: DEMAC, 1998.

Paredes, Américo, and Richard Bauman, eds. *Toward New Perspectives in Folklore*. Austin: University of Texas Press, 1972.

Partnoy, Alicia. "On Being Shorter: How Our Testimonial Texts Defy the Academy." In *Women Writing Resistance: Essays on Latin America and the Caribbean*, edited by Jennifer Browdy de Hernandez, 173–192. Cambridge, MA: South End Press, 2003.

Pascoe, Juan. *La mona*. 2nd ed. Xalapa, Mexico: Universidad Veracruzana, 2003.

Patierno, Mary, and Sanjay Talreja, dirs. *Stuart Hall: Representation and the Media*. Northampton, MA: Media Education Foundation, 2002.

Pérez, Emma. *The Decolonial Imaginary: Writing Chicanas into History*. Bloomington: Indiana University Press, 1999.

Pérez, Laura E. *Chicana Art: The Politics of Spiritual and Aesthetic Altarities*. Durham, NC: Duke University Press, 2007.

Phillips, Erica E. "Las Cafeteras Defy Tradition." *LA Weekly*, December 29, 2011. http://www.laweekly.com/las-cafeteras-defy-tradition/.

Pratt, Mary Louise. *Imperial Eyes: Travel Writing and Transculturation*. London: Routledge, 2010.

"Pre-Grammy Encounter—Forget You, We'll Stomp on Wood!" YouTube video, uploaded by Scott Macklin, February 18, 2013. http://www.youtube.com/watch?v=44HuBuga8dE.

"Quetzal." YouTube video, uploaded by University of California Television (UCTV), January 31, 2008. http://www.youtube.com/watch?v=3rD_zayv-l8

"Quetzal - Grito de alegria." YouTube video, uploaded by kingpinronin, January 25, 2008. http://www.youtube.com/watch?v=PgVv31Dh3RA.

"Quetzal - Jarocho elegua." YouTube video, uploaded by kingpinronin, January 25, 2008. http://www.youtube.com/watch?v=pbXcNC4kSwg.

"Quetzal - Live at the El Rey Theatre." YouTube video, uploaded by quetzalofficial, September 21, 2006. http://www.youtube.com/watch?v=acWysObgvyc.

"Quetzal - Planta de los pies." YouTube video, uploaded by quetzalofficial, September 18, 2006. http://www.youtube.com/watch?v=g5xAWYUG92g.

"Quetzal y Son de Madera @ JAT-Decide." YouTube video, uploaded by Quetzal Flores, February 4, 2009. http://www.youtube.com/watch?v=j4uCVZU7MR8.

Ramamurthy, Priti. Course lecture for Women and International Economic Development, University of Washington, winter 2010.

Rappaport, Joanne. *Intercultural Utopias: Public Intellectuals, Cultural Experimentation, and Ethnic Pluralism in Colombia*. Durham, NC: Duke University Press, 2005.

Raussert, Wilfried, and Michelle Habell-Pallán, eds. *Cornbread and Cuchifritos: Ethnic Identity Politics, Transnationalization, and Transculturation in American Urban Popular Music*. Tempe, AZ: Bilingual Press, 2011.

Rebolledo Kloques, Octavio. *El marimbol: Orígenes y presencia en México y en el mundo*. Xalapa, Mexico: Universidad Veracruzana, 2005.

Reyes, David, and Tom Waldman. *Land of a Thousand Dances: Chicano Rock 'n' Roll from Southern California*. Albuquerque: University of New Mexico Press, 1998.

Rice, Timothy. *May It Fill Your Soul: Experiencing Bulgarian Music*. Chicago: University of Chicago Press, 1994.

Rodriguez, Luis Carlos. "Fandango Jarocho: A Cultural Jam Session." *LatinoLA*, September 6, 2002. http://latinola.com/story.php?story=454.

Roy, Anupama. *Gendered Citizenship: Historical and Conceptual Explorations*. New Delhi, India: Orient Longman, 2005.

Said, Edward W. *Orientalism*. New York: Pantheon Books, 1978.

Saldívar-Hull, Sonia. *Feminism on the Border: Chicana Gender Politics and Literature*. Berkeley: University of California Press, 2000.

Sandoval, Chela. *Methodology of the Oppressed*. Minneapolis: University of Minnesota Press, 2000.

Sangtin Writers, and Richa Nagar. *Playing with Fire: Feminist Thought and Activism through Seven Lives in India*. Minneapolis: University of Minnesota Press, 2006.

Sauer, Stephanie. *The Accidental Archives of the Royal Chicano Air Force*. Austin: University of Texas Press, 2016.

"Seattle Fandango Project - Final Night Fandango." YouTube video, uploaded by Maya Jupiter, November 10, 2009. http://www.youtube.com/watch?v=2ZuJ4DEJnKE.

Sen, Gita, and Caren Grown. *Development, Crises, and Alternative Visions: Third World Women's Perspectives*. New York: Monthly Review Press, 1987.

Shukaitis, Stevphen, and David Graeber, eds. *Constituent Imagination: Militant Investigations, Collective Theorization*. Oakland, CA: AK Press, 2007.

Small, Christopher. *Musicking: The Meanings of Performing and Listening*. Middletown, CT: Wesleyan University Press, 1998.

Smith, Linda Tuhiwai. *Decolonizing Methodologies: Research and Indigenous Peoples*. London: Zed Books, 1999.

Song, Min Hyoung. *Strange Future: Pessimism and the 1992 Los Angeles Riots*. Durham, NC: Duke University Press, 2005.

Speed, Shannon, R. Aída Hernández Castillo, and Lynn M. Stephen, eds. *Dissident Women: Gender and Cultural Politics in Chiapas*. Austin: University of Texas Press, 2006.

Stephen, Lynn. *Transborder Lives: Indigenous Oaxacans in Mexico, California, and Oregon*. Durham, NC: Duke University Press, 2007.

Stoler, Ann L. "Making Empire Respectable: The Politics of Race and Sexuality in the Making of 20th-Century Colonial Cultures." *American Ethnologist* 16, no. 4 (November 1989): 634–660.

"Susana Baca, La Madera y La Mujer at Mujeres de Maiz." YouTube video, uploaded by SolArt, March 8, 2010. http://www.youtube.com/watch?v=iOPDFanB4tk.

Swarr, Amanda Lock, and Richa Nagar, eds. *Critical Transnational Feminist Praxis*. Albany: State University of New York Press, 2010.

Taylor, Diana. *The Archive and the Repertoire: Performing Cultural Memory in the Americas*. Durham, NC: Duke University Press, 2003.

"TedxSeattle - Martha Gonzalez - 04/16/10." YouTube video, uploaded by Tedx Talks, April 26, 2010. http://www.youtube.com/watch?v=qPR4GXlUy-M.

Torres, Edén E. *Chicana without Apology = Chicana sin Vergüenza: The New Chicana Cultural Studies*. New York: Routledge, 2003.

Trinh, T. Minh-ha. *Woman, Native, Other: Writing Postcoloniality and Feminism*. Bloomington: Indiana University Press, 1989.

Tucker, Sherrie. *Swing Shift: "All-Girl" Bands of the 1940s*. Durham, NC: Duke University Press, 2000.

Turino, Thomas. *Moving Away from Silence: Music of the Peruvian Altiplano and the Experience of Urban Migration*. Chicago: University of Chicago Press, 1993.

———. *Music as Social Life: The Politics of Participation*. Chicago: University of Chicago Press, 2008.

———. *Nationalists, Cosmopolitans, and Popular Music in Zimbabwe*. Chicago: University of Chicago Press, 2000.

"VI Fandango Fronterizo." YouTube video, uploaded by El Gallo Films, October 23, 2013. https://www.youtube.com/watch?v=CK-JiYZxj9w.

Viesca, Victor Hugo. "The Battle of Los Angeles: The Cultural Politics of Chicana/o Music in the Greater Eastside." *American Quarterly* 56, no. 3 (September 2004): 719–739.

Waxer, Lise, ed. *Situating Salsa: Global Markets and Local Meanings in Latin Popular Music*. New York: Routledge, 2002.

Wilkman, Jon, dir. *Chicano Rock! The Sounds of East Los Angeles*. PBS Home Video, 2009.

Wilson, Shawn. *Research Is Ceremony: Indigenous Research Methods*. Black Point, Nova Scotia: Fernwood, 2008.

Zavella, Patricia. *I'm Neither Here nor There: Mexicans' Quotidian Struggles with Migration and Poverty*. Durham, NC: Duke University Press, 2011.

INDEX